EXPLORING WOMEN ACROSS THE WORLD

EXPLORING WOMEN ACROSS THE WORLD

Sumanlata

AKANSHA PUBLISHING HOUSE
NEW DELHI • GUWAHATI • VISAKHAPATNAM

AKANSHA PUBLISHING HOUSE
4649-B/21, Ansari Road
Darya Ganj, New Delhi - 110 002
Ph.: 23263193 / 9811582579 / 09435116718
Fax: 011-23263193
Email: ektabooks@yahoo.com
www.akanshapublishinghouse.com

Exploring Women Across The World

First Published 2010
ISBN 978-81-8370-236-2

PRINTED IN INDIA

Published by Akansha Publishing House, New Delhi and Printed
Harmain Offset Press

Contents

Preface

> "To stand up for the freedom of others is one of the marks of those who are free, just as to fail to do so is one of the marks of those who are ready to be enslaved."
>
> —*Alan Paton*

As an established fact, women constitute about a half of the total human population on this earth. Amidst plenty of others, she plays important role for reproduction of human species. But she is considered weaker sex and discriminated on various accounts in almost all societies with varying degree and magnitude all across the world.

Naturally, to make the issues of emancipation of woman and equality of sexes primary, one needs a culture in which conjugality is central to man-woman relationship. One seeks emancipation from and equality with one's husband and peers, not with one's father or son. If the conjugal relationship itself remains relatively peripheral, the issues of emancipation and equality must remain so too. According to others, these women are exceptions which prove nothing. To psychologists, who, as you know, are used to thinking in strange ways, there is always a continuity between the commonplace and the exceptional. As is already Moreso, in India, competition, aggression, power, activism, and intrusiveness are not so clearly associated with masculinity.

In fact, in mythology and folklore, from which norms

often come for traditionally undefined social situations, many of these qualities are as frequently associated with women. That is why in some areas of life, disjunctive with the traditional life style and not having clearly defined or well-developed norms, women do not start with as much handicap as in many other societies.

And the first task that faces her to to devise means of de-emphasising some aspects of her role in family and society and emphasising others. So that the completeness of her identity comes nearer to realisation without a total break with its cultural definition and without becoming disjunctive with its psycho-biological distinctiveness.

In the West, that may mean defying the limits of conjugality and giving a new dignity to the maternal role of woman; in India, it may involve transcending the partial identity imposed by motherhood and winning a new respect for conjugality. Partial identities always extract a price from those who live with them, either as victims or as beneficiaries. Indian women have paid terribly for our intensitivity, but they have also extracted a heavy toll from a society which has not yet learnt to live with all aspects of womanhood.

The present endeavour is to portray the real picture of women across the world. Various issues like their role, status and problem of discrimination are elaborately dealt with taking instances from different countries—horizontally and vertically—of the globe. The vital information is organized under the following main topics—Introduction; Women in the United States of America; Women in Mexico; Women in the Palestine; Women in Bangladesh; Women in Thailand; Cuban Women and Society; Women in Nigeria: Issues & Challenges; Women in China; Women in the West; Women in Vietnam; Appendix; and Bibliograpby etc.

It is hoped that the contents will enrich the knowledge of researchers, teachers, policy planners and social activists in the field of women and gender studies.

In fact, this work is the outcome of the analysis and synthesis of succinct information derived from various authoritative sources—both primary and secondary, e.g. book articles, research reports, documents, magazines and websites. We are deeply beholden to all those whose works/ findings are utilized here by way of citation or other.

I am thankful to my seniors, colleagues, friends and family members for their wholehearted support, guidance, assistance and inspiration. I express my gratitude to Ace Books India for evincing keen interest in this project and materializing it superbly in the present shape.

Definitely, will feel amply rewarded if this could serve the purpose of all those for whom it is meant.

—Sumanlata

1

Introduction

> "If all men were on an equality, the consequence would be that all must perish; for who would till the ground? who would sow it? who would plant? who would press wine?."
>
> —*From the Latin*

At the level of values, human progress can be seen as an expanding awareness of the subtler and more institutionalised forms of inequity and the suffering born of it. Person-to-person aggression and personal sadism have been punished since almost the dawn of civilisation. For its survival, every society had to do that. But, as Bertrand Russell was fond of pointing out, social ethics always lag behind private ethics. So slavery, racialism, colonial exploitation and genocide were not only permitted, but often encouraged.

Of course, some controls were maintained. The sacred texts everywhere did try to define social rights and social wrongs. They also prescribed limits to group violence. But the observance of such limits was not informed with an understanding of the less obvious forms of ill-treatment of man by man and of the social institutions and psychological defences which supported them. It was many centuries of civilisational growth before, some like Owen, Marx and

Kropotkin formulated ambitious explanations of intra-species aggression in terms of social groupings, till then seen as "naturally" different.

Today, the idea of a continuum between the exploiters and the exploited, between the aggressors and their victims, is commom place. It was not so only a century ago. There were still other and subtler forms of inequity. It was Sigmund Freud who pointed out the inequities associated with biological strata like age and sex. Though Friederich Engels had noted earlier the vulnerability of women in general and western women in particular, in some ways he had merely extended the formal model of class analysis to the condition of woman. Freud had less faith in human nature and was even less willing to grant that economic institutions were the only means of oppression which nature and human intellegene could devise. He traced the root of inequity to a more fundamental stratificatory system, "designed" to derive its strength from man's evolutionary experience, namely psycho-biological growth. As a pioneer, he understandably directed attenditon to the biological stratum which was most vulnerable at the time, namely, children. For the first time in human history, Freud systematically analysed how we have, over the centuries, exploited our children, using them to express our sadistic and narcisistic impulses. He also showed how we have built enormous defences to deny to ourselves our cruelty and exploitation. There were times when infanticide and torture of children were widespread in the world.

Yet some of the most sensitive and humane leaders of thought of the age never protested. In fact, torturers of children included man like Milton and Beethoven. Child labour was acceptable till about fifty years back in reputedly the most civilised parts of the world. Sexual exploitation of children was not uncommon; among those who indulged in it were some of the greatest Greek philosophers. Now it would be rash to conclude that the man was a vicious hypocrite. He was no more a hypocrite than the defenders of the democracy of Greek city states, which rested on the slavery of the masses. They just did not have a large enough span of moral awareness.

Human morality had not acquired that much depth at that point in history. Gregory Zilboorg's deservedly famous paper suggests something very similar for the man-woman relationship. Here too oppression results from attempts to deny one's deepest anxieties which are projected to an exploitative relationship institutionalised over centuries. The most socially valued attributes of the male, Zilboorg argues, are a result of natural selection imposed upon him by the female's original power to instinctively sense, which mate was biologically fitter. It was this primal dominance which arouses in man insecurity and jealously, and hostility towards woman. He has a phylogenetic awareness that his primordial role is "highly specialised as no more than a temporary and ephemeral appendage to life," as a "parasite" fertiliser. We can only add that till now he has had no civilisational awareness that he has been trying to work through this basic hostility by limiting the full possibilities of woman an by sheer oppression.

It is an indicator of how far man has succeeded in these efforts that in many societies the evolutionary and biological primacy of woman has given way to an institutionally entrenched jealousy of man in her. It is this complex psychosocial phenomenon which Freud analysed at length. There is enough data from some of the major western societies to support him. He merely missed the historical tragedy that is involved in this reversal of roles.

All this is by way of a long digression. The moral of the story is this. The present awareness of the constricted role of woman in Indian society and in public affairs is part of an ongoing process of civilisation change and must be so analysed. This demands that we must identify the structure of defences, individual as well as cultural, which has given meaning to the role of woman in Indian society and which has been challenged in recent times by new waves of social consciousness. Only then can we hope to isolate and control the long-term processes of social and psychological changes in this sphere.

Everybody knows about the different survival rates of boys and girls in India. But only scattered individuals and groups feel passionately about it, in spite of the fact that the size of the vulnerable sector of young girls in India is larger than that of the landless labourers. Even fewer persons are sensitive to the fact that this indirect female infanticide—or, to use Johan Galtung's term, structural violence towards woman—is mainly a function of maternal neglect, a weird expression of woman's hostility towards womanhood and also, symbolically, towards her own self.

This classic instance of the psychological defence of turning against self, by identifying with the aggressive male, draws attention to the way in which some social institutions have made woman herself a participant in her self-repudiation and intra-aggression. The oppressive reality for woman, one might suggest, is now only partially outside her. A part of that reality has been introjected through a long historical process of social learning. And the learning has been thorough. It has been said that man's cruelty towards man is exceeded only by man's cruelty towards woman. But even man's cruelty towards woman is no match to the cruelty of woman towards woman.

An agricultural society has its own distinctive symbiotic relationship with nature. Since the times of neolithic agriculture, this distinctiveness has lain in the central roles of woman in society and culture. It was she who was primarily involved in "gentling and nurturing and breeding"; it was her "capacity for tenderness and love" which gave the earliest agricultural settlements of man their touch of "security, receptivity, enclosure, nurture"; and it was she opened up the full possibilities of civilisational growth. However, a number of studies have shown that such a society tends to emphasise the feminine principle in nature, to see nature as a mother who is irascible and unpredictable, and propitiable only through a wide variety of rites and rituals. Particularly in societies where nature continues to be the dominant partner in the man-nature dyad, important themes in folklores and religious texts are often the fecundity and bounty of nature as well as her frequent denial of sustenance of men who have only poor means of controlling the fickle mother and are totally dependent upon her for survival. This is indeed true of India.

Though the Brahmanic traditional attempted to limit the dominance of woman in society, the pre-Aryan dominance of woman was retained in many areas of life, particularly in the symbolic system. this undeniably is a motherful culture in which femininity is inextricably linked with *prakriti* or nature and *prakriti* with *leela* or activity. Similarly, the concept of *adi shakti*, primal or original power, is entirely feminine in India. It is the male principle in the godhead, *purusha,* which is reliable but passive, weak, distant and secondary. That is why the deities that preside over those critical sectors of life which one cannot control—such as success of crops and occurrence of famines (food), protection against cholera and small pox (personal survival), and child birth and child health (perpetuation of race)—are all feminine, motherly figures. All the more cruel rituals, which are mentioned as indicators of Indian medievalism, have centred round the femine goddesses: *sati*, child sacrifices at *sagar sangam*; infanticide for longevity of dams, bunds and buildings; human sacrifices of various forms. The *thugs*, including the large number of Muslims among them, considered themselves devotees of Kali. For that matter, most of the marginal groups, such as thieves and dacoits, have sought meaning as social beings by being devotees of one black goddess or another, that is, at another level, by identifying—and identifying with—an aggressive, treacherous, annihilating mother. In other words, the ultimate authority in the Indian mind has always been feminine.

It is pertinent to note that is a congruence between this structure of authority and the traditional family and socialisation systems. Studies of child-rearing done in the more orthodox sectors of Indian society have repeatedly shown that in the critical years of life the mother is the only true and close authority to which the child is exposed. In his relationship with others, the Indian child is mainly categorised by a wide spectrum of pre-defined roles and role-specific behaviour. There is distance and fragmentation of self in these interpersonal relationships. It is only with respect to his mother that he is his whole self and recognisable as an individual. Associated with this in the son is a deep feeling of ambivalence towards a controlling yet discontinuous mother. He often sees her as a treaherous betrayer, mainly because of her intermittent presence and nurture which are in turn due to the exigenicies of her familial role, social obligations, mores and taboos. The Indian's phantasy life is to a great extent organised around this image of an angry, incorporative, flickle mother, against whom his anger is directed and from whom, through a process of projection, counter-aggression is feared.

His model of male indentification, too, is the father who is more a mother's son than a woman's husband and, therefore, swayed by the same phantasies and fears. For the Indian mother, on the other hand, the son is the major medium of self-expression. It is her motherhood that the traditional family values and respects; her wifehood and daughterhood are devalued and debased. The woman's self-respect in the traditional system is protected not through her father or husband, but through her son. Also, it is through the son—and for that matter, on the son—that she traditionally exercises her authority. Here, thus, is a case of psycho-ecological balance. What the nature and economy emphasises, the family and the cultural system underscores.

No wonder all major social reforms and attempts at social change after the beginning of British rule have centred around woman and femininity. It is by protesting against or defying the traditional concepts of woman and womanhood that all India modernisers have made their point. On the other hand, all forms of conservatism and protests against western and modern encroachments on the Indian society have taken shelter in and exploited the symbol of motherhood. Thus, the mother-son relationship is the basic nexus and the ultimate paradigm of human social relationships in India.

To an extent, this is true of all cultures, but only in a few cultures have the loneliness and self-abnegation of woman as a social being found such elaborate justification in her symbolic status as a mother. Since motherhood is a comprensatory mechanism, the society has the scope to manipulate the control a woman by forcing her to take on her motherly identity whenever cornered and a man by forcing him to take on the son's role whenever in crisis. The culture tends to "push" all critical public relations to fit or exploit that symbolic paradigm. Yet, simultaneously, the Indian society inculcates in women a certain self-doubt and in men a certain ambivalence towards womanhood.

This ambivalence is very different from the ambivalence which the western man feels towards woman or the universal fear which Zilboorg, Bettelheim, and Salzman diagnose. In this society, except for small sectors in which martial values predominate, the man's fear is not that he will lapse into womanliness and thus lose his masculinity or potency. In fact, potency here is not generally something you strive for, protect or protest in the external world.

The masculine fear here is that a man may run afoul of the cosmic feminine principle, that woman will betray, aggress or at least fail to protect. There are two major corollaries of such an uncertainty about the cosmic feminine principle. The first of these can be stated in the form of a dialectic, but is perhaps a matter of the various planes at which the Indian man lives his psychological life. At one plane, he is continually afraid that he may become too autonomous of the maternal principle of authority, too defiant as a son of the power of cosmic motherhood, and too close to open anger towards his mother.

On the other, he is constantly anxious that he will be incorporated by an all-encompassing, powerful mother, lose his autonomy and individuality altogether, and be reduced to the "safe" but totally ineffective role of the father.

Secondly, bisexuality in India has always been an indicator of saintliness and of yogic accomplishments.

Perhaps it is an indicator of having successfully coped with or transcended one's deepest conflicts about femininity and masculinity. Perhaps it has something to do with the traditional concept of *ardhanarishwara*, associated with the god who combined godly grandeur with yogic asceticism, namely Shiva. However, it be, one who is closer to godliness is expected to show a little less concern with the wordly division between the sexes and a little more ability to transcend the barriers imposed by one's own sexual identity. He is expected to subscribe to values which are unbound by the society's prevalent sexual identities. In India, unlike in many western societies, the softer forms of creativity and the more intuitive and introspective styles of intellectual and social functioning are not strongly identified with femininity. Nor is masculinity that closely linked to certain forceful, potency-driven, "hard" and hardheaded modes of intrusive behaviour. Sex-role-specific qualities here are differently distributed. In fact, the concept of potency in Indian high culture has always had a private, introversive quality about it. The Brahman's concept of ritual and intellectual potency has nothing in common with the manifest extroversive concept of potency in the modern West.

Brahmanic potency is "derivable," in the same way as in medieval Europe's monasterial orders, from displaced sexual potency through abstinence and denial of one's sexual self. This has another aspect. In the twilight zones in which creative minds dwell, there is always a certain stress upon the ability to turn inwards and live in one's own inner world; the ability to accept intuition, tenderness and *caritas* as values; a certain sensitivity to one's natural environment and to the "latent" communications among men and the capacity to use media of self-expression which mobilise feelings, imageries and phantasies. in the West, this has invariably meant becoming more feminine. That is why psychological studies of creative men in the West frequently show that one of the best predictors of creativity in men is the extent of their psychological femininity. It is in the western content that Berdyaev has argued that the figure of Christ is androgynous, and that "all creators must be so if they are to conceive and bear greatly and whole."

Understandably too, there are elements of pathos and loneliness associated with such a search for bisexuality in societies where, even at the level of symbols, males dominate. The Indian, apparently, is not more creative only when he is more feminine or, to put it less obtusely, when he can better accept his feminine self. His creativity also consists in his being able to identify the cosmic femine principle with his own internal concept of authority and, then, in defying this authority and simultaneously making large-scale symbolic separations for this defiance. This is a major ingredient of the relationship between womanliness and creativity in India.

The isomorphism between one's inner controls and the society's concept of authority sharpens one's sensitivity to the basic symbolic system of the culture and makes one more rooted in the culture's style of self-expression. One the other hand, this defiance of one's final and most intimate authority gives an edge to one's defiance of the shared concept of authority outside. And, you do not have to be a psychologist to recognise that this defiance is one of the basic bricks of creative effort. There is another aspect of this linkage between creativity and womanliness in India. Public defiance rationalises one's more guilt provoking private defiance. If the public defiance of authority is linked to the cause of woman, either as an exercise in reform geared to her good or as a purely intellectual exercised in understanding her problems, the structure of rationalisation becomes stronger and more usable.

It binds the moral anxiety triggered by one's defiance of one's internal authority and, at another level, atones for that defiance. This astonement—through working for the cause of woman or, in its intellecualised version, through understanding woman—has been perhaps the single most important theme in the history of social creativity in India. Some years back someone pointed out to me how formidable and powerful the women in *Mahabharata* were and how the story revolves round them.

When one looks at the styles of creative self-expression during the last two hundred years, a period characterised by a fast tempo of social change and a breakdown of many aspects of the older life style, one cannot but marvel at the crucial role that woman as a symbol and womanliness as an aspect of Indian identity have played.

This dynamism is clearer in some parts of the country than in others, which only means that some communities have a greater capacity than others to superbly dramatise the psychological problems of the society at large. For instance, in Bengal this role has been heavily and dramatically underscored. Perhaps the region's tribal base, unsure Brahmanisation, deep symbiotic links between means of livelihood and cultural products, and strong feudal traditions have something to do with this.

At least from Rammohun Roy through Iswarchandra Vidyasagar, from Bankim Chandra Chatterji through Sarat Chandra Chatterji to Satyajit Ray, from Vivekananda to Aurobindo—womanhood as a symbol and womanliness as a subject of study have been the centre pieces of creative consciousness in different sectors of Bengali life. Whether it is Bengal or the country as a whole, certain closely related modes of symbolic adaptation have dominated India's distinctive style of entry into the modern world. What came, as if in a flux, in the British period was an entire authority system which involved the invalidation at many levels of the traditional equation between femininity and power, the old concept of propitiation through rituals and magic, and the primal mythical personification of nature as an inviolate cosmic mother. Some like Rammohun Roy and Iswarchandra Vidyasagar tried to redraw the traditional definition of womanly identity, trying to introduce into it new elements drawn from reinterpreted traditions and to endogenise certain western themes. their own deeper ambivalence towards woman found in these efforts a personal adaptive device. Some with mass appeal like Sarat Chandra Chatterji and Goverdhanram Tripathi among writers, and Vidyasagar and Gandhi among reformers tried to legitimise woman's wifely role in particular and public role in general by stressing in them aspects of her motherliness. Some others like Ramkrishna Paramhansa and Aurobindo found in motherhood the supreme concept of a new godhead, rooted in tradition on the one hand, and capable of balancing the over-emphasis on masculinity in the Semetic religions on the other other. In act, their appeal to many westerners was this concept of a godhead which could be counter-poised against the patriarchal orientations dominating the western view of man and nature.

Still others like Bankim Chandra Chatterji and Vivekananda linked this traditional image of sacred motherhood to the modern concept of motherland, hoping thereby to give a new sanctity to the concept of nation in an essentially apolitical society. Even Gandhi tried to give a new dignity of women by making a new equation between womanliness and political potency, denying in the process the western association between maleness and control over public affairs and statecraft, rejecting the martial tradition in India, which like martial traditions in most societies, debased womanhood, and abrogating the colonial identity which equated femininity with passivity, weakness, dependence, subjugation and absence of masculinity.

To conclude, the redefinition of womanhood in India during modern times has meant the redefinition of the concept of man and of public functioning. In this on going process, the emancipation of woman and her equality with man have been important but not the main issues. They may today lead to vicious debates in small groups of already-privileged woman in the modern sector, but for the majority in the hinterlands these themes have never been relevant dimensions for social analysis and intervention.

Naturally, to make the issues of emancipation of woman and equality of sexes primary, one needs a culture in which conjugality is central to man-woman relationship. One seeks emancipation from and equality with one's husband and peers, not with one's father or son. If the conjugal relationship itself remains relatively peripheral, the issues of emancipation and equality must remain so too. According to others, these women are exceptions which prove nothing. To psychologists, who, as you know, are used to thinking in strange ways, there is always a continuity between the commonplace and the exceptional. As is already said that, in India, competition, aggression, power, activism, and intrusiveness are not so clearly associated with masculinity.

In fact, in mythology and folklore, from which norms often come for traditionally undefined social situations, many of these qualities are as frequently associated with women. That is why in some areas of life, disjunctive with the traditional life style and not having clearly defined or well-developed norms, women do not start with as much handicap as in many other societies.

Obvious examples of such areas are politics and public affairs and some of the scientific and religious activities. In such sectors, public success does not seem to detract from private womanliness. In other words, the Indian woman can, in such instances, more easily integrate within her feminine identity the participation in what by western standards are manly activities, but in India, are either not defined in terms of sex roles or are tinged with trans-or bisexual connotations. In these areas Indian women do not have to fight the same battle that their western sisters have had to fight, though some of them do pretend to give battle to existing norms in these areas, too. That of course, is shadow-boxing. And we are not concerned here with those for whom the search for freedom and dignity as women has become a search for a new neurotic stablility, a stability which they hope would defend them as successfully against self-awareness as the now-crumbling defences were once doing. For the more sensitive woman, the challenge is nothing less than redefinition of herself.

And the first task that faces her to to devise means of de-emphasising some aspects of her role in family and society and emphasising others. So that the completeness of her identity comes nearer to realisation without a total break with its cultural definition and without becoming disjunctive with its psycho-biological distinctiveness.

In the West, that may mean defying the limits of conjugality and giving a new dignity to the maternal role of woman; in India, it may involve transcending the partial identity imposed by motherhood and winning a new respect for conjugality. Partial identities always extract a price from those who live with them, either as victims or as beneficiaries. Indian women have paid terribly for our intensitivity, but they have also extracted a heavy toll from a society which has not yet learnt to live with all aspects of womanhood.

In that respect theirs is not, what Rollo May would call, a case of "authentic innocence" but that of "pseudo innocence." This innocence leads one to participate in a structurally violent system because of the unawareness of one's power to intervene in the real world and because of the indirect psychosocial benefits of being a victim. But then, ultimately, this is no different from ancient wisdom.

In the present work, we have tried to portray women across the world. Vital information is furnished of select countries all over the world representing East and West.

NOTES

1. Erik Erikson "Race and the Wider Identity," in *Identity, Youth and Crisis* (New York, 1968), pp. 295-320.
2. Friederich Engels, *The Origin of the Family, Private Property, and the State* (New York, 1942).
3. L. DeMause, *The Evolution of Childhood* (New York, 1975).
4. Masculine and Feminine, Some Biological and Cultural Aspects," *Psychiatry,* 1944 (7), pp. 257-296.
5. Leon Salzman, "Feminine Psychology Revisited, Circa 1970," *American Journal of Psychoanalysis,* 1971 (31) pp. 123-133.
6. Erik H. Erikson, "Inner and Outer Space: Reflections on Womanhood." *Daedalus,* 1964 (93), pp. 582-606.
7. Karl Menninger, *Love Against Hate* (New York, 1942), Chapter 4.
8. Lewis Mumford, *The City in History* (London, 1961),
9. Smoker, Barbara, Women and the Patriarchal God, *The Secularist* (33), May-June 1975, pp, 67-68.

10. Heinrich Zimmer, *Philosophies of India* (New York, 1956).
11. M.S. Gore, *Urbanisation and Family Change,* (Bombay, 1968),
12. Sudhir Kakar, "Aggression in Indian Society: An analysis of Folk Tales," *Indian Journal of Psychology,* 1974, (49), pp. 119-126,
13. G. Morris Carstairs, *The Twice Born* (Bloomington, 1957); Philip Spratt, *hindu Culture and Personality,* (Bombay, 1966).
14. N. Berdyaev, *The Meaning of the Creative Act* (translated by D.A. Laurie), (New York, 1954).
15. Frank Baron, "The Psychology of Cereativity," in Frank Barrown et al, *new Frontiers in Psychology* II, (New York, 1965), (40);
16. D.W. Mackinnon, "The Personality Correlates of Creativity: A Study of American Architects," in P.E. Vernon (ed.), *Creativity,* (Penguin, 1970), pp. 289-311,
17. Binay Ghosh, *Vidya Sagar O Bengali Samaj* (Calcutta, 1958), Vols. I-III; Indra Mitra, *Karuna Sagar Vidyasagar* (Calcutta, 1969).

2

Women in the United States of America

> "Undertake something that is difficult; it will do you good. Unless you try to do something beyond what you have already mastered, you will never grow."
>
> —*Ronald E. Osborn*

United States of America, which is considered as a Super Power of the present day world has had a long history of making what the US is now.

Here in this chapter we intend to portray the picture of US women. First we have furnished some vital statistics of US women. This follows the status of women in historical perspective. At the end of the chapter some facts about violence and crime against women are depicted.

US Women: Facts and Figures

1. Of the 121 million women age 16 years and over in the U.S., 72 million, or 59.5 percent, were labor force participants—working or looking for work.
2. Women comprised 46.5 percent of the total U.S. labor force and are projected to account for 47 percent of the labor force in 2016.

3. Women are projected to account for 49 percent of the increase in total labor force growth between 2006 and 2016.
4. 68 million women were employed in the U.S.—75 percent of employed women worked on full-time jobs, while 25 percent worked on a part-time basis.
5. The largest percentage of employed women (39 percent) worked in management, professional, and related occupations; 33 percent worked in sales and office occupations; 21 percent in service occupations; 6 percent in production, transportation, and material moving occupations; and 1 percent in natural resources, construction, and maintenance occupations.
6. The largest percentage of employed Asian and white women (46 and 41 percent, respectively) worked in management, professional, and related occupations. For both black and Hispanic women, it was sales and office occupations—32 and 33 percent, respectively.
7. The 10 most prevalent occupations for employed women in 2008 were—
    1. Secretaries and administrative assistants, 3,168,000
    2. Registered nurses, 2,548,000
    3. Elementary and middle school teachers, 2,403,000
    4. Cashiers, 2,287,000
    5. Retail salespersons, 1,783,000
    6. Nursing, psychiatric, and home health aides, 1,675,000

7. First-line supervisors/managers of retail sales workers, 1,505,000
8. Waiters and waitresses, 1,471,000
9. Receptionists and information clerks, 1,323,000
10. Bookkeeping, accounting, and auditing clerks, 1,311,0

8. The unemployment rate for women was 5.4 percent and for men it was 6.1 percent in 2008. For Asian women, it was 3.7 percent; white women, 4.9 percent; Hispanic women, 7.7 percent; and black women, 8.9 percent.
9. The median weekly earnings of women who were full-time wage and salary workers was $638, or 80 percent of men's $798. When comparing the median weekly earnings of persons aged 16 to 24, young women earned 91 percent of what young men earned ($420 and $461, respectively).
10. The ten occupations with the highest median weekly earnings among women who were full-time wage and salary workers were—
    1. Pharmacists, $1,647
    2. Chief executives, $1,603
    3. Lawyers, $1,509
    4. Computer software engineers, $1,351
    5. Computer and information systems managers, $1,260
    6. Physicians and surgeons, $1,230
    7. Management analysts, $1,139
    8. Human resource managers, $1,137
    9. Speech-language pathologists, $1.124

10. Computer scientists and systems analysts, $1,082
11. Women accounted for 51 percent of all workers in the high-paying management, professional, and related occupations. They outnumbered men in such occupations as public relations managers; financial managers; human resource managers; education administrators; medical and health services managers; accountants and auditors; budget analysts; biological scientists; preschool, kindergarten, elementary, middle, and secondary school teachers; physical therapists; writers and authors; and registered nurses.

12. Of persons aged 25 years and older, 29 percent of women and 30 percent of men had attained a bachelor's degree or higher; 31 percent of women and men had completed only high school, no college.
13. The higher a person's educational attainment, the more likely they will be a labor force participant (working or looking for work) and the less likely to be unemployed.
14. For women age 25 and over with less than a high school diploma, 33 percent were labor force participants; high school diploma, no college, 53 percent; some college, but no degree, 63 percent; associate degree, 72 percent; and bachelor's degree or higher, 73 percent.
15. For women age 25 and over with less than a high school diploma, their unemployment rate was 9.4 percent; high school diploma, no college, 5.3 percent; some college, but no degree, 5.1 percent; associate

degree, 3.7 percent; and bachelor's degree or higher, 2.7 percent.

[Source: U.S. Department of Labor, Bureau of Labor Statistics, *Employment and Earnings, 2008 Annual Averages and the Monthly Labor Review*, November 2007.]

In the history of social science in the United States, the late nineteenth century marked the rise of professionalism, of a search for a scientific method that would shift the study of man from speculation to empiricism, and of an effort to define man in his natural state without the aid of traditional moral judgments or value-laden preconceptions. Until 1885, remarked Albion W. Small (1916:726), "benevolent amateurishness" characterised American attempts to deal scientifically with human experience. But the appearance of the first generation of professionally trained social scientists marked "a revolution in the analysis of social problems" (O'Neill 1966: 291). The attempt to ground the study of human experience in a scientific method led the practitioners of the new sciences to examine other disciplines for materials that might be applicable to the study of man and his institutions. One major source for many scientists was the cluster of ideas that comprised evolutionary theory. As used by the students of human experience, evolutionism was applied not only to that biological phenomenon, the species *Homo sapiens,* but also to human social institutions, such as government and the family.

This chapter will survey the literature of twenty American scientific periodicals between 1885 and 1900 for the application of evolutionist thought to a social problem that was of great concern in the rapidly changing society of late nineteenth century America: the place of the woman. Although the primary emphasis here is on the impact of one set of ideas upon another, certain social phenomena of the time were unquestionably influential in shaping social scientific perspectives on the American woman.

The growth of industrial capitalism and its demands for a large labour force meant at best that a woman did not need to marry unless she so chose, at worst that many whose husbands had inadequate incomes had to work in order to survive. In either case, there were increasingly large numbers of women whose lives were no longer confined to the home.

In the words of Falkner (1897:112-113): "As women's labours are eliminated from the household, the greater the proportion of women workers whose labour is removed from the quasi-patriarchal form of the family and made to harmonise with the conditions of modern industry." The great changes wrought by geographic mobility and rapid urbanisation also exacerbated the fears of many traditionalists that the American family was being destroyed. Further, many believed that a declining birthrate among native Americans (which was caused, according to two rival notions of the day, either by the increasing independence of women or by their decreasing health), combined with the influx of immigrants from strange and un-American lands in southern and eastern Europe and the Orient, would result in a mongrel race.

In 1889, British scholar Grant Allen stated in an article considered pertinent enough to Americans to be reprinted in *Popular Science Monthly* (1889:173) "To the end of all time, it is mathematically demonstrable that most women must become the mothers of at least four children, or else the race must cease to exist." Eighteen years later, this belief still retained its potency: in 1907, Theodore Roosevelt was exhorting American women to marry and produce their share of four for the good of America.

Further, the feminist push for the vote, for an adequate education, for justice in the areas of property laws, divorce, the right to a job and to control over their own earnings, all sent great shock waves through the value Systems of many Americans. American scientists, of course, were no exception. Many of their arguments about these issues, both pro and con, were phrased in the language of what the laws of evolution "proved" about the natural capacities of the woman. These capacities usually were less than (or at least different from) those of the man. One gentleman, writing in the *American Journal of Sociology,* granted that the category "human beings" must include "women, children, slaves, foreigners" (Crafts 1896:507); while he was somewhat more revealing in his assumption of feminine inferiority than were many others, his attitude was not atypical. In any case, whether she was considered man's inferior, his equal, or his superior, "the new woman" (a common catch-phrase of the 1890's) was the object of much concern — and not a little moralising—by the scientists of human experience.

Notably, in 1895, psychologist G.T.W. Patrick evaluated the evidence from "modern anthropological studies" that bore upon the four leading theories of women's "peculiarities." Patrick's paper deserves some attention, because it included essentially all the major bioevolutionist speculations about human sex differences as they were understood by late nineteenth century American scientists.

The four theories as listed by Patrick (1895:210) were:

1. Woman is a "stunted or inferior man and represents arrested development."

2. Woman is a grown-up child, belonging to "the child type."
3. Woman is indeed a "child type," but this is "in truth the race type and represents greater perfection" than man, "whose natural characteristic is senility."
4. Throughout the animal world, the female is physically superior in size and vitality, "and more truly represents the essential qualities of the species

Patrick examined the physical and psychological evidence for each of these theories in some detail. The data bearing upon psychological differences between male and female are particularly interesting, because remnants of yesterday's science can still be found in today's folk wisdom. Briefly the female's perception is "decidedly quicker," although "less accurate"; she is more subjective (thus a poorer critic and rarely an impartial judge); her mind is better adapted to the "concrete and individual" than to the formation of abstract concepts; her memory is superior; she is better at "quick associative reasoning," but lacks "logical feeling" and is "less disturbed by inconsistency.... Analysis is relatively distasteful to them [women], and they less readily comprehend the relation of the part to the whole." Their thought is "less methodical and less deep."

Notably, woman is more patient and more intuitive; she excels in tact, reaches her mental maturity earlier, and is very good at routine work but cannot endure protracted overwork. She is less original ("woman's thought pursues old rather than new lines"), more conservative (she "acts as society's balance-wheel"), more emotional, but less prone to strong passions and "appetites," more religious, and more moral. She is fearful and timid. Her 'greatest virtue is altruism; her greatest vice, untruthfulness (Patrick 1895: 215-218).

He concluded that all four theories were in part confirmed, except in their implications of feminine inferiority. Yet the female is truly different from the male and ought to be treated accordingly. May not woman be "too sacred to be jostled roughly in the struggle for existence"? Does she therefore not deserve from man "a reverent exemption from some of the duties for which his restless and active nature adapts him"? (Patrick 1895: 225).

Romanes' list of feminine virtues and defects overlapped considerably with Patrick's. He presented the female as inferior to the male except in the more altruistic emotions (she is "mentally and physically the weaker vessel" (1887:385]), while denying that she is inferior (her "type of human nature" is at least equal to the male's), and made a rather patronising bow to her (she is "the sweetest efflorescence of evolution" [1887:397]).

Despite Patrick's and Romane's peculiar disclaimer of feminine inferiority, the argument about which sex was higher on the phylogenetic scale consumed much scientific energy and was spread across many pages in late nineteenth century scientific periodicals. To answer the question, debaters from the sciences of human experience borrowed heavily from biological sources. We shall look at five such biological concepts and some uses to which they were put in determination the relative evolutionary positions of male and female. They are: (1) environmental determination of sex, (2) variation, (3) physical sturdiness and vitality, (4) the evolution of the maternal instinct, and (5) inheritance through the male. Among the plethora of theories attempting to solve the riddle of what caused an organism to be male or female, there were those stating that environmental stimuli such as temperature and nutrition were the causative factors. When such a theory of external determination of sex was cast in an evolutionist mold, it could be used to contrast the female unfavourably with the male.

For example, W. K. Brooks (1885:325) stated that a "favourable environment" (defined as one conducive to a high birthrate) causes "an excess of female births, and an unfavourable environment an excess of male births." Brooks' materials indicate how primitive the early collection of demographic data must have been: wild animals, Hottentots, and residents of rural areas, barren regions, and cold climates have a high rate of male birth, while either more fortunate counterparts—domesticated animals, Boers, and residents of towns, fertile regions, and warm climates — have a high rate of female

Why does this law of nature hold? Because

> the female is the conservative factor in reproduction, and new variations are caused by the influence of the male. While the environment remains favourable, no change is needed, but as the conditions of life become unfavourable, variation becomes necessary to restore the adjustment (Brooks 1885: 328).

Thomas (1897:31) believed that human males tend to be catabolic; females, anabolic. Or, put another way, "femaleness is an expression of the tendency to store nutriment" (1897:34). Not only are there basic metabolic differences between male and female but metabolic factors also determine which sex an organism will be. The female is the result of a surplus of nutrition or of outbreeding: both, factors increase metabolism, and increased metabolism produces females. Thomas used demographic techniques to prove his point. Two of many interesting examples are data from furriers ("furriers testify that rich regions yield more furs from females and poor regions more from males"

[1897:32]) and statistics about Jews ("among the Jews, who frequently marry cousins, the per cent of male births is very high" [1897:37]). Thomas drew heavily upon these biochemical differences between the sexes in discussing the evolution of human society and the female's place. By placing her nearer to the plant, and thus lower on the evolutionary scale, Thomas limited her roles in human society to "natural" expressions of her anabolic nature, as all social structure and function stem from this "fundamental contrast in the metabolism of the sexes" (1897:59).

The human female's roles all focus on maintaining the human community, and the chief means of so doing is through reproduction and care of the young. While it would be going too far to say that theories of environmental determination of sex had to lead to a conclusion that the male is higher than the female on the phylogenetic scale, it is clear that Brooks' and Thomas' theories did exactly that. Similarly, both Brooks and Thomas spoke of variation in a manner that was weighted in favour of the male. This orientation was not peculiar to these men: assumptions of the superiority of variation *per se,* and the superior variation of the male were common to late nineteenth century discussions of male-female differences. Variation was considered important because it was presumably the mechanism of adaptation to the environment.

Thomas' second use of the term can be traced to Haeckel's evolutionary interpretation of von Baer's biogenetic law. Its application to male-female differences, by Thomas and others, hinged on the idea that the female is closer to the child in evolutionary development. As Thomas put it, the woman is "intermediate in development between the child and the man" (1897: 40). The woman has "infantile somatic characters" (i.e. a greater proportion of fat to muscle) and, as befits one not advanced to the developmental plane of the male, "a greater tendency to atavism" 1897: 34, 40).

Thomas' third use of the term is closely tied to the second; it is that males vary more from each other, or from some norm. If this has mixed blessings for the male in one sense (there are more males than females at the extremes of genius and idiocy), its implications for the superiority of the white civilised male are nonetheless very clear: "Morphological differences are less in low than in high races, and the less civilised the race the less is the physical difference of the sexes" (1897: 43,41). All three meanings of Variation implied that progress comes through the male. Because an evolutionist by definition valued change, in the sense of adaptation to the environment, the sex that varied more, in whatever sense of the word, was the progressive sex.

However, there were dissenters from these perspectives on variability. Patrick noted that Which sex one thought to be superior depended upon one's evaluation of the importance of variation (1895: 224). Anthropologist Daniel G. Brinton. (1894) pointed out that Havelock Ellis believed that the female's lesser variability makes her the source of evolutionary development. Ellis' reasoning was that the female is closer to the child, and that this is to her advantage. Man, on the other hand, quickly deteriorates from age three onward; to an extent, his growth is a plunge downward to degeneration and senility. "Hence, the true tendency of the progressive evolution of the race is to become child-like—to become feminine."

Eliza Burt Gamble agreed with the common view that the male shows greater variability in secondary sexual characters but disagreed that this advances the species

(Patrick 1894a). On the contrary, "ornaments" such as "colors, wattles, beard" are produced at the cost of deterioration. It is the female who is at the highest stage of development in all orders of life. Ellis and Gamble, then, accepted the notion that the female is the less variable sex but found this to be to her advantage in the evolutionary. Pearson and Alice Lee (1897) found that the civilised female is more variable than the male, and that this greater variability is caused by the decrease in the struggle for existence. Because the lessened struggle affects woman more than it does man, she therefore has the greater tendency toward variation. Several writers commented on the greater physical sturdiness of the female but drew opposing conclusions about its meaning for her place on the evolutionary scale.

Thomas felt that her hardiness was yet further evidence of her backwardness. He noted that "lower forms" can regenerate a lost organ. While the human female is not capable of such a feat, nonetheless "the lower human races, the lower classes of society, women and children" all have a better tolerance for surgery than does the physiologically more sensitive male of the higher races and classes (Thomas 1897: 50).

However, Gamble and A. Mosso (1892), both of whom believed the female is higher up the scale than is the male (Mosso cited as evidence the female's pelvic structure and her absence of body hair), stated that her greater physical hardiness (males die earlier and are more prone to disease) combined with the "fact" that more favourable conditions are needed to produce the female are proof of her superiority.

The evolution of the maternal instinct was a subject of great interest to late nineteenth century scientists. As might be expected, W. I. Thomas had a great deal to say about it. First of all, natural selection provided the human female with the "altruistic sentiments" that make her wish to care for her newborn.

Among the "lower animal forms," the "physiological waste" involved in spawning a thousand eggs is nature's way of ensuring the survival of one, in the absence of any natural feeling of mother love.

> But a higher type of development involves a closer association between the parent and offspring, and this is secured through natural selection by a modified structure in the female, culminating among the mammals in the intra-uterine development of the young and the disposition in the female to care for the young after bringing tnem forth. The expansion of the abdominal zone in the female in connection with this modification of her reproductive system is the physical basis of the altruistic sentiments. Feeling is a physiological change, and its seat is not the encephalon, but the viscera.... The superior physiological irritability of woman, whether we call it sensibility, feeling, emotionality or affectability, is due to the fact of the larger development of her abdominal zone, and the activity of the physiological changes located there in connection with the process of reproduction (Thomas 1897: 60-61).

The first social unit in human society was thus the mother-child bond. However, the maternal instinct was not limited to this dyad, but expanded to all society. "Both social feeling and social organisation are thus primarily feminine in origin—functions of the anabolism of woman.

G. Stanley Hall's discussions of motherhood (1891) focused, not upon its evolutionary origins, but upon its importance in ensuring that the child would pass through the proper stages of mental development. Thus, motherhood is the woman's most important function. The mother "soon comes to stand in the very place of God" to the infant. At this stage of development, the less the child's rudimentary religious sentiments are cultivated toward the mother, "the more feebly they will be later felt toward God. This, too, adds greatly to the sacredness and the responsibilities of motherhood" (1991 :199).

Further, "the mother must not lose her influence over the child before adolescence, when the maternal influences and hometies should be at their strongest and best" (1891 :200). A sacred trust indeed—and with only a passing mention of the importance of the father at this stage, Hall's psychology implicitly supported the conventional division of labour between the sexes: the mother in the home with the children, the father out in the world, earning their living.

The evolution of the maternal instinct as an argument for a sex-based division of labour had a central place in the thinking of George J. Romanes and Edward D. Cope. Romanes believed that the maternal instincts are "perhaps the strongest of all influences in the determination of [her] character." They are inherited and cumulative, and derive from the long infancy and childhood of human children (Romanes 1887:392). For Cope (1888), the existence of the maternal instinct was terribly important, because it was an effective weapon to be wielded against advocates of woman suffrage (which was, of course, a major issue in 1888). Within the family, he argued, the sexes have different functions based upon their "best emotions." These exalted feelings are the maternal instinct of the female and the masterful behavior of the male.

These emotions and their correlative, the sex-based division of labour, evolved as follows: When the mode of reproduction changed from non-sexual to sexual, the male was freed from the "disabilities" of maternity to take a more active part in the struggle for existence. However, the female has continued to inherit the maternal "disability" (a curiously 'pejorative description of her "best" emotion) that keeps her from being active in the world.

Thus, the biological imperative has decreed that the home is woman's proper sphere, while political activity must be the prerogative of the man. In support of this belief, Cope drew upon two common arguments based upon woman's innate limitations: woman is neither rational (therefore, she cannot be just) nor physically capable of enforcing any law she might enact. In addition, he added a more singular argument against the subversion of "the natural evolution of humanity" that would result from granting women the vote—one based upon use inheritance. In effect, the vote would make woman's "feminine virtues" disappear altogether after a few generations, because "as in all evolution, disuse ultimately ends in atrophy" (1888:728).

Gazing bleakly into the future, Cope predicted that the home would disappear, for women "would produce a race of moral barbarians, which would perish ultimately through intestine strife" (1888: 728). The Darwinian principle of inheritance through the male could be used as another "proof" of woman's inferiority. This theory stated that inheritable characters were transmitted more fully to the male offspring; hence, over time, man gradually became superior to woman.

Sometimes, however, elements of the Anglo-Saxon racism which was so prominent in the late nineteenth century complicated scientific discourse on the subject, so that some females proved to be biologically superior to some males. For example, Cope believed that the female of a "higher race" is superior to the male of a "lower race" because she has inherited (from her father, of course) "the general progress of the race (1888:722).

Because Cope believed that inherited characters are much more influential than are acquired ones, the male of the species, particularly the male of the penultimate races, not only must be the source of race progress, but also is the parent through which such progress is transmitted. The idea of the male's role in inheritance received a wild twist in a pair of articles appearing in *Science* ("The persistency of family traits": Williams 1892). The first article stated that the first male to impregnate a female indelibly stamps the characteristics of all future offspring. Moreover, "the influence of the male as determining the character of the offspring increases with each successive pregnancy of the female by the same male."

Both social and biological scientists, as we have seen, applied evolutionist thought to "the woman question" in a manner that, instead of casting new light upon old prejudices, all too often perpetuated them with the aid of scientific "proofs." There were those, however, who disputed the validity of such judgments. In the words of one dissident, "the real tendencies of women can not be known until they are free to choose, any more than those of a tied-up dog can be" (Tanner 1896). One factor that would help women to become "free to choose" was education. The question of educating women was hotly debated in the late nineteenth century, and those on either side of the issue turned to biological and social science for definitive answers. For those scientists who worked within an evolutionist framework, science had to answer two questions: first, what kind of education did woman's natural capacities permit her to receive; and second, aside from the question of capacity, would the continued development of the race be served by educating her for anything outside her family duties? All too frequently the answers to these questions reinforced each other, as science and conventional social values became hopelessly entangled. Bioevolutionist theory unquestionably provided important support for those who wished to maintain the traditional American practice of educating the female (if at all) in subjects that would be useful to her in her role as wife and mother. To take the principle of variation as an example, it was only a short step from the "fact" that the female is underrepresented among geniuses (Thomas 1897: 43; Patrick 1895: 216) to a belief that if she attempts to compete intellectually with men, she is wasting her time and fighting nature's dictates.

It was also easy to move from the belief that "the female is the conservative factor in reproduction" (Brooks 1885:328) to the idea that she is of conservative and unoriginal mind. ("Her tendency is toward reproduction, while man's is toward production" [Patrick 1895: 216].) There were, of course, opponents of such beliefs. One observer commented that "the prevalent theory of the essentially conservative nature of woman intelligence seems to me a fiction of the male intelligence, maintained in order to keep this inconvenient radicalism of woman in check" (J.D. 1894).

Many social scientists believed that evidence from biological science showed the female's chief abilities to be reproduction and child care (the latter because of her natural "altruism," developed over eons by the long infancy of human children); showed her to be less variable, less logical and rational, more emotional and instinctual, and more prone to break down physically from mental overwork than was the more highly developed male. These beliefs; of course, had great implications for the question of what subjects she could be expected to learn.

And behind all the debate over her "natural" capacities loomed the twin specters of the decline of the traditional family (with its traditional helpmeet and mother) and of "race suicide," caused by the apparently declining birthrate in the educated classes. If it could be demonstrated that the female brain was anatomically inferior to that of the male, this would be powerful evidence to be used against those women who demanded the right to an equal education. There would be actual proof of British physician Withers-Moore's dictum (transplanted to a leading American periodical) that "Bacon's mother (intellectual as she was) could not have produced the *Novum Organum,* but she, perhaps she alone, could and did produce Bacon" (Linton 1886).

In his initial article, Hammond claimed that with "nations low in the scale of progress" (1887a:731), male and female brain size is very similar. However, the evolution of higher civilisation brings with it an increasing difference in favour of the male brain, with the crucial factor being the relative amount of gray matter. Therefore, "the larger the brain the greater the mental power of the individual" (1887a: 730-731).

Gardener promptly supplied evidence from "twenty leading brain anatomists, microscopists, and physicians of New York" (1887: 266) to refute Hammond's statements. Hammond immediately counterattacked with HIS set of authorities, and threw a sneak punch against the presumptuous lady anthropologist and her "defective logical power, which appears, for the present at least, to be a characteristic of most female minds" (1887b: 555). Often scientists refused to say that women's minds were inferior to men's—merely that they were Different.

This was a variant of the "separate but equal" doctrine that in this same period in American history was being applied by whites to Negroes. As this "difference" was applied to the education of women, however, it condemned them to be kept ignorant of many subjects that were suited only to the masculine mentality. And the lack of such study (principally in science and mathematics), in addition to the disparagement of women's attempts to educate themselves sufficiently to broaden the narrow confines of their socially defined role, worked as a self-fulfilling prophecy to perpetuate the ideas of the female's limited "natural" mental capacity. Hammond, for example, believed that it was "the height of absurdity" to let girls study boys' subjects: "The effort to cram mathematics, for example, into the female mind almost always results in failure." He had "seen many cases of girls whose nervous systems have been woefully disturbed in the endeavor to master algebra, geometry, spherical trigonometry, and other mathematical branches of knowledge that could not by any possibility be of use to them" (1887a: 722). And even if they knew their studies well, it "would not enhance their loveliness or render them any happier" (1887a: 722). (It seems a virtual certainty that no scientist ever evaluated the appropriateness of a course of study for males on the grounds of whether or not it would make them handsomer or happier.)

Romanes, as noted above, denied the inferiority of the "feminine type of human nature," At the same time, however, he insisted upon her "marked inferiority of intellectual power," particularly her lack of originality (1887: 383). He believed that this handicap would never be overcome, for one could not suppose that "any exception to the general laws of evolution can have been made in her favour" (1887:394). Romanes did not oppose the education of woman, provided that the curriculum neither trained her for "any professional or otherwise foolish rivalry with men" nor encouraged "intellectual specialisation" (1887:400). Its purpose was solely to enhance her natural skills as wife and mother.

The idea that the better-educated woman would be a better mother motivated much of the effort devoted to female education throughout the nineteenth century in America. It was within this context that Cope urged that a woman be given as much education as a man (consistent with maintaining her health), because women are "the mothers of the human race" (1888: 724). Cope sought to quiet the fears of those who worried about the pernicious effects of education upon the home: "For the normal woman, the home-life is both the easiest and the happiest" (1888: 725). In short, no true woman would want to leave her sphere. To force her to do so (as a victory for the pro-suffrage forces would presumably do) would "check the development of woman as such" (1888: 725).

Patrick's survey of the scientific evidence bearing upon sex-linked differences in intellectual capacity indicates what the woman seeking an education in 1895 must have been up against. She was believed to be "particularly adapted" to vocal music, the stage, learning languages, writing novels, and teaching. She was, however, "less adapted" to science, discovery, and invention; she could not compare to men in logic (she lacks "logical feeling" and is "less disturbed by inconsistency"), nor in arts, sciences, and philosophy (her thought is "less methodical and less deep"). She might well outperform man in college, because she would reach her mental maturity earlier, but he would excel afterward, when it really mattered.

Within the bioevolutionist perspective, then, scientific opinion about the natural capacities of woman shaped the concepts of these same scientists about what nature had decreed woman could (and should) learn. By and large, most opinion severely limited her options. However, enough differences of opinion existed to occasionally touch off spirited debates. Two Italian scholars had opposing ideas on the subject that were sufficiently interesting to the psychologist-editors of the *Pedagogical Review* to warrant their summary and transmission to the American scientific community (Chamberlain 1892). "Professor Sergi of Rome" announced that woman's smaller brain and inferior intellect ("Where is the female Titian, Wagner, Goethe, Shakespeare? Where the lady Darwin or Edison?") were a "blessing to humanity," for "'if woman were equal to man in intellectual power, it would introduce into the social struggle a new and violent competition'" (Chamberlain 1892: 478). Sergi believed that woman should be educated to develop her twin abilities of "equilibirum and practicality," and not to compete with men. ("Useful to her would be knowledge of social facts and happenings, the constitution of the family, regulation of the state and the like," and "such facts of scientific character as might be of use in the household.")

A. Mosso, who felt the female was phylogenetically superior to the male, emphatically denied Sergi's conclusions. If the female is inferior to the male, stated Mosso, the reasons are social, for man has enslaved her, and male supremacy has created and maintained the division of labour. She is entirely able to compete intellectually with men (Mosso 1892: 232). If the question of woman's natural capacity for education aroused much debate among evolutionists, so too did the issue of whether such education might be harmful to the development of the race. In the late nineteenth century, when America was being (as it seemed to some) overrun by immigrants, "the good of the race" required American women to bear children in numbers sufficient to keep the superior native stock from being eliminated.

Would educating the female reduce the number of children she would otherwise have? Would it make those offspring she did manage to produce sickly and feeble? Many Americans were obsessed by such fears; for scientific authority they had the famous Herbert Spencer. Spencer postulated that because the "cost of reproduction" is much greater for the female than for the male, she must maintain good health in order to be able to reproduce. Education has a pernicious effect upon her reproductive capacity, because "absolute or relative infertility is generally produced in women by mental labour carried to excess,"

Thus, "the deficiency of reproductive power" among upper-class girls.

> may be reasonably attributed to the overtaxing of their brains — an overtaxing which produces a serious reaction on the physique. This diminution of reproductive power is not shown only by the greater frequency of absolute sterility; nor is it shown only in the earlier cessation of childbearing; but it is also shown in the very frequent inability of such women to suckle their infants. In its full sense, the reproductive power means the power to bear a well-developed infant, and to supply that infant with the natural food for the natural period. Most of the flat-chested girls who survive their high-pressure education are incompetent to do this (Spencer 1896:11, 485-486).

American scientific periodicals provided space for those who considered the issue of whether or not the female's reproductive capacities were drained by mental work and the implications this had for her education. The *Popular Science Monthly* in particular devoted a relatively large amount of space to the matter. The same Withers-Moore who extolled Mrs. Bacon's reproductive capacities warned that the woman who overstudies draws upon her "capital stock or vital force and energy" and is left "quite inadequate for maternity." Because of her selfishness, "the human race will have lost those who should have been her sons" (Linton 1886:173).

Lucy M. Hall, a physician at Vassar, undertook to correct Withers-Moore. While Dr. Hall agreed that "in America the small and rapidly diminishing numbers in the family is a matter of grave national import" (1887: 612), one of her studies showed that "the largest families of the present generation belong to the most highly educated of the women" (1887: 614). The two major reasons why women have small families are, first, physical disability (stemming from a multiplicity of causes, which range from the obviously physical, such as tight corsets and lack of exercise, to more nearly psychogenic factors, such as "pampered idleness" and a turning in upon themselves because they have nothing else to do); second, a disinclination to bear children. In either case, higher education has no pernicious effect upon reproduction—indeed, just the opposite is true. Mosso agreed with Hall. If a woman goes to college, she will not become unfeminine: 562 women who received degrees from Cambridge and Oxford had more children than did other women who were not so educated. Among those with ideas on the subject was John Dewey, and his views were decidedly not in sympathy with those of Hall and Mosso Dewey

(1886) examined a study by the Massachusetts Labour Bureau of the health college alumnae. The general conclusion of the study had been that "the pursuit of collegiate education is not in itself harmful" (Dewey 1886:609).

Dewey, however, disagreed. He noted (1886:610) that

> the most important fact regarding the higher education of woman is, that we are educating wives and mothers. Few probably will regret this, but those few must still admit the fact in a society constituted like ours.

Given this undeniable truth, Dewey pointed to the implications of certain data: (I) of female graduates, 74 per cent were single and only 26 per cent were married, although the average years since graduation numbered more than six; (2) of married graduates, 37 percent had no children, although the average length of marriage was 6.2 years; (3) the 109 graduates who had borne children had produced only 205, of these, 12 per cent had died; (4) among all married couples, there were 1.2 children per five years of marriage. Dewey left these figures "to speak for themselves." Given his emphasis upon educating women for the wife-mother role, the message seems clear indeed.

Grant Allen, who calculated that the survival of the race depended upon each woman producing a minimum of four offspring, cited "Darwinian principles" (the community must increase to ensure "national health and vigor" [1889: 170)) and Francis Galton ("a certain amount of overpopulation is necessary for survival of the fittest" [1889: 172, note]) to demonstrate that women must not "shirk their natural duties" (1889:171). If woman was to be little more than a brooder hen, this necessity shaped the nature of the education she should receive. Clearly, she was not to be trained to leave the home, for each defection would mean that "a heavier task must be laid upon the remainder" of her sex (1889: 171). But the problem was not simply that the educated woman might choose not to become a breeder; if she were given "false education" (i.e. admitted to the curricula formerly reserved for men), she would become "unsexed." She would become "a dulled and spiritless epicene automaton .... Both in England and America, the women of the cultivated classes are becoming unfit to be wives or mothers." Even if she married, she would be "ill adapted to bear the strain of maternity." If there were children, these could only be "feeble and futile descendants".

There was, then, considerable argument about whether education did or did not drain the "vital force" of women. Both supporters and opponents of this theory, in citing contrary sets of data concerning the number of children produced by educated women, accepted (at least implicitly) the idea that woman's major function was to produce large numbers of healthy children for the good of the race, and that education was helpful to the extent that it did not interfere with this function.

In a reply to Grant Allen, Alice B. Tweedy (1890) remained within the ground rules of the discussion, but she shifted its focus. Although she denied that college education affects the health of female students or the production of healthy children, she said that the decline in the number of marriages was, in one sense, fortunate, because educated women were no longer forced to marry, "in defiance of natural selection" (1890:752). If the right to choose a husband (even on bioevolutionist grounds) were important, then some women need not marry. The "natural selection" argument had been shifted from Allen's emphasis on overproduction of offspring so that the fittest of these might survive and advance the race, to Tweedy's emphasis on a kind of natural selection that was based, paradoxically, upon the female's freedom of choice. If the good of the race was important, so too was the good of the individual.

Still another evolutionist perspective appeared in an unsigned "Review of: *The family,* by Charles F. and Carrie Thwing" (1887). The reviewer's feeling was that the growing social and legal independence of women was helping to curb the growth of population, which was reaching its limits. If some women could achieve self-support, the reviewer went on, then they would not need to marry.

Remaining single, they would not contribute to the birthrate. And so,

> evolution seems to be creating motives and an environment that will modify the effects of the most powerful of human instincts, and just at a time that will prevent the pressure from being too abruptly imposed upon civilisation.

Although the question of education was not raised explicitly here, it was nevertheless present. Economic independence was not likely to come to the uneducated woman, and both those who would let her achieve autonomy and those who would tie her to her traditional sex roles were well aware of that.

Virtually all of the evolutionists examined thus far focused upon the female's "natural" physical and mental traits in a manner that reflected their belief that her most important functions must take place within the family unit, subordinate to the husband. Or as Romanes put it quoting an unnamed authority on the subject: "'The position of man is to stand, of woman to lean'".

Many social scientists believed that just as the

evolutionary process bad led woman upward to her place within the walls of the patriarchal Victorian home, so had the family institution itself evolved from its prehistoric origins to its status as the keystone of Western civilisation. Thus theories of the origin and evolution of the family had great import for "the woman question."

It is remarkable that late nineteenth century students of the family accepted a set of common assumptions: first, that all races, societies, and institutions go through the same stages of cultural evolution, although the "higher" races attain heights of civilisation never reached by less gifted peoples, second, that the study of animal societies and primitive tribes gives valid evidence of civilised man's social institutions as they were at "lower" stages; third, that the study of cultural artifacts, such as myths, ancient ruins, and "survivals," provides further knowledge of the origins of human institutions; and fourth, that the family in some form was the original social institution from which all other human institutions followed.

As one social scientist proclaimed, "Here was the first social tie on earth, the beginning of the state" (Mason 1889: 10). Although it was commonly accepted that the family was the first social unit, there was wide disagreement about its original form. Was it patriarchal or matriarchal? Promiscuous or monogamous?

Social scientists argued the issues in their periodicals. Those who believed that the family was originally patriarchal cited the theories of Aristotle and Maine; those who felt that it was promiscuous and matriarchal (the two forms were often linked by theorists) drew upon the work of Morgan and McLennan; and those who insisted that it was monogamous had the considerable authority of Westermarck behind them. The majority of social scientists who commented upon the matriarchal-patriarchal dispute in the periodicals sampled agreed that the family had originally been matriarchal in structure. One who disagreed was Adolpho Posada, who surveyed the late nineteenth century "researches, opinions, and speculations" concerning the prehistoric family and then came out in favour of the theory of patriarchal origin. Three bits of linguistic evidence were offered in support: (1) the radicals "pa" and "ma" appear in many languages to denote father and mother; (2) "pa" is easier to pronounce, and therefore it is an older sound than "ma"; and (3) "pa" is a harsher sound than "ma," and therefore it must be associated with male authority.

E. B. Tylor (1896) believed that the original unit had been patriarchal, that it had shifted to an exogamous maternal system at a later stage of development when tribes decided to bring in more men in order to strengthen themselves, and that still later it had "reverted" back to the lower paternal form. This occurred for two reasons dictated by nature: (1) because reversion itself is natural, and (2) because the man's superior strength makes him the natural head of the family.

One who opted for matrilineality and female dominance ("mother-right") in the original form of marriage was O. T. Mason (1889). However, although this form obviously did not persist, Mason did not deal directly with the implications of a sex-based shift in power. Instead, he merely noted that evolutionary theory tells us that the human species could not have survived, much less have been the "most favoured" (because it has made the most progress), if one half had persecuted the other. W.J. McGee (1896) developed a theory that three "culture grades" of "marital regulations and observances" preceded the era of Old Testament history, with its patriarchal and polygynous marital customs. In the first stage, marriage is "a collective institution for the benefit of the group" (1896:379), a "single great family of women" with "warlike spouses.' Marriage is monogamous at this most primitive level, partly because it is the wish of the ' reigning women, partly because man's desire for marriage is "feeble." In this stage the man is a suitor "not so much from personal inclination as from tribal incentive" (1896:338). Monogamy itself at this early stage is "perhaps a heritage from bestial ancestry," which hardly gives it the high valuation it had when it emerged as the model of Christian marriage. W.I. Thomas accepted a matriarchal theory of early social organisation, not because paternity was uncertain (as McLennan and Morgan had said), but because the mother-child bond was "the closest in nature.'

This closeness derived from the maternal instinct and from constant contact. Thus, physiology and propinquity made the mother-child dyad the first social unit, to be followed later by a maternal system of organisation. "The primitive respect shown mothers" is a "survival" from the maternal stage. However, Thomas disagreed with those (such as Bachofen) who equated the maternal system of descent with political power. Thus, he took up the question that Mason had ignored:

> While it is natural that the children and the group should grow up about the mother it is not conceivable that woman should definitely or long control the activities of society, especially on their motor side. In view of his superior power of making movements and applying force, the male must inevitably assume control. There has never been a moment in the history of society when the law of might, tempered by sexual affinity, did not prevail.

Notably, even in the lower prematernal and maternal

stages of social organisation, the male was "the carrier of the social will" (Thomas 1898: 761-763). Solotaroff (1898) stated that "social sentiment" was the original social tie that preceded any form of family organisation, although he agreed with Thomas that the first family unit may well have been mother and child He did not, however, invoke the "closeness" of this bond, citing instead the temporary nature of sexual unions, which was caused by the earliest humans having a definite mating season and by the sexual fickleness of the male.

Fortunately, the evolutionary mechanism proved immensely helpful, as "natural selection worked in favour of those offspring only which were nourished by the secretions of the mother, and thus Nature herself dispensed with paternal care" (1898:234, note). Thorstein Veblen (1899), alone among the social scientists sampled, spoke of the original family as "the household of the unattached woman." This form was characterised by "an absence of coercion or control in the relation between the sexes" and by a fairly enduring monogamous relationship terminable by the choice of either partner. As we shall see, this stage of family organisation disappeared with the evolution of society from savagery to barbarism.

In fact, the preceding perspectives on the original form of the family are instructive not only as relics from early social science, but also for their assumptions about the place of the primitive female. In the absence of fact, these scientists drew conclusions that were based in large measure upon their own culture-specific values. Thus, it is hardly surprising to learn that the original male had "natural" authority; that he was the natural head of the family; that the female had a greater sense of social responsibility and a weaker sex impulse; and that motherhood conferred upon woman an exalted status that placed her somewhere near the angels. Although the long and arduous process of evolution had supposedly culminated in a male and female that were very different from the original savage pair, the prehistoric couple who sprang from the pens of these scientists would have fit without too much difficulty into late nineteenth century civilised society.

Regardless of the position taken on the question of the original family, it was generally agreed that at some "stage of development" the male became dominant, by reason of his greater strength, his stronger sex drive, his insistence upon exogamous marriage, or some similar reason relating to his greater sexuality or aggressiveness.

Tylor cpted for the male's superior strength; John R. Commons, Veblen, Thomas, and Solotaroff agreed that strength was a key factor, combined with the male's greater sexual aggressiveness and desire for variety, which led to a restless search for wives from outside the tribe. W. J. McGee stressed the sexual factors. Whatever reasons were given for man's takeover, it was agreed that the evolutionary process had so determined the outcome that there had been no alternative.

John R. Commons also commented on the female's essential helplessness, so that the need for food, clothing, and shelter "bind wife and children to the fate and service of the bread-winner" (1899: 8). He believed that self-consciousness, man's distinctive psychic characteristic, had emerged in the evolutionary process at the exogamous stage of family development — that is, at the time when men began to desire more than one wife. Commons' reasoning on this point is rather interesting. Following McLennan, he stated that exogamous mating arose because the custom of female infanticide produced a shortage of women. Murder would seem to have been a direct way of expressing the feeling of one sex that the other was undesirable. But then, following Westermarck, Commons listed among reasons for the desire for plural wives some that would indicate that the female was highly desirable, in a limited sort of way: "freedom from periodical continence, attraction for female youth and beauty, taste for variety, desire for offspring, wealth, and authority" (1899: 12). At any rate, with the rise of the institutions of polygyny and slavery, the patriarchate came into existence.

As noted earlier, Thomas equated the male's authority with his superior physical strength and motor skills, which came from his anabolic qualities. As man's motor skills and "militaristic" nature led him to expand his tribe's territory, women and slaves (some of the slaves obviously must have been male, but none had the good fortune to belong to "the progressive races" who "managed the space problem best") became unfree because "neither class showed a superior fitness on the motor side." At the end of the nineteenth century, however, woman were once again becoming free because violence, according to Thomas's hopeful reading of the trend in civilised society, was no longer the major means of dominance (1898: 776).

In McGee's three-stage theory of the beginnings of marriage, the shift from a matrilineal to a patrilineal system came in the third stage, although there were warning signs in stage two: at this point monogamy persisted chiefly through "inertia," and upper-status males had already begun to take female captives. In the third stage, the male became the suitor, polygyny and wife capture became the norm, and the power of divorce (and punishment for adultery) passed from the female to the male. The motivation for mating shifted from the collective good to individual initiative. "At least in the higher stages, complete subordination or even partial enslavement of women" existed. And the whole process was guided by nature's own hand, for "the course of development was shaped at each stage by the survival of the fittest among the groups" (McGee 1996: 383).

Veblen marked the transition from an egalitarian marital relationship to male dominance at the barbarian stage of culture, when the formerly peaceable male became predatory and began seizing women as trophies. Might became right, for "men who are trained in predatory ways of life and modes of thinking come by habituation to apprehend this form of the relationship between the sexes as good and beautiful" (Veblen 1899: 507).

In most of these speculations upon the origin of male dominance, it was explicitly stated that the female was not only the subordinate partner, but also the male's personal property. Remember, for example, Commons' statement that the emergence of self-consciousness — that characteristic which marks man off from the mere animals—made possible the development of polygyny and slavery. At that point, when the male began his "individual appropriation" of women, the right to own private property that had been taken by force was commonly acknowledged for the first time. At that historic point Commons (1899: 12-14) marked "the true beginning of the human family."

Veblen's description of "ownership-marriage" (1899: 508) based upon actual (and later, ceremonial) wife capture and Thomas' discussion of women and slaves as "unfree classes" were further indicators that social scientists saw early marriage as a coercive property relationship. Further, both men felt that the owner-owned relationship still survived in the marriage institution of their own day. Thomas

(1898:770-771) attributed the woman's "socially constrained position in history" and her "hindrances" to the barbarous custom of wife purchase, which treated her as property to be bought and sold, And Veblen called the male-headed household a predatory institution which, for the female, is a condition of servitude. However, both Veblen and Thomas saw indications that the late nineteenth century woman might be regaining some measure of equality within the family. Thomas thought that the devaluation of violence would emancipate her, while Veblen saw the rise of the modern peaceful industrial society, which was incompatible with the old customs of status and ownership, as the liberating factor.

Thomas (1899b) viewed the status of women as property from a slightly different angle in "Sex in Primitive Morality." Here he spelled out the implications of moral codes, which he believed were originally developed by the dominant male sex, imposed upon women, and maintained by physical force. With the rise of the patriarchal family system, men dictated child marriage for females, insisted on suicide for widows, assumed the right of killing or mutilating an adulterous wife and her lover, hired out their wives as prostitutes, and developed other similar practices which assumed the owned status of the female. Woman accepted this male-imposed morality and has been a "faithful follower" ever since. However, Thomas expressed the hope that eventually the relatively more "feminine" behaviors (such as the Sermon on the Mount, non-resistance, asceticism, and chivalry) would become more prevalent as women became more independent, and developed "forms of activity appropriate to their nature" (1899b: 784-787). Although Thomas did not mention the fact, all these "feminine" behaviors are usually associated with males.

It is not far from an assumption that there are distinctive masculine and feminine behaviors to the belief in a sex-linked division of labour based upon these behaviors. In addition to the bioevolutionist arguments for such a division (essentially, that the woman's peculiar psychic capacities and instincts dictate her presence in the home), there were certain biocultural arguments predicated upon the evolution of the family and its functions.

Edward T. Devine (1894) remarked that woman's economic function (consumption) had been unjustly ignored by those who concentrated on man's economic function (production). Chivalrously he set out to rectify this neglect. First, Devine stated that "harmonious groups" advance the social progress of the race" by being victorious over "the older and cruder groups." And they win because they "yield greater pleasure."

Although it may not be immediately apparent, the thesis is based- entirely upon the traditional division of labour, for the home is a harmonious blending of many parts, and the "mother's love for the family and the home she has made them" is "the very keystone in this arch of enjoyment that we call home." Devine insisted that this pretty picture was "not a sentimental but a purely economic view of woman's work," for "the power to confer pleasure is an economic concept" (1894: 327-48).

Just as Devine glorified the Victorian woman's role, so too did Mason and Thomas insist upon the unique beauty of primitive woman's domestic functions. Devine's domesticated female consumed what her man produced; similarly, the "share" of Mason's modern AND prehistoric woman was to "gather up and conserve the spoils" that her mate had won in his strenuous war on nature and on his fellow-man" (1889: 4).

Mason's early woman was extremely busy and creative: she was the first cutler, butcher, currier, pack animal, gardener, farmer, tanner, tailor, etc. As the first "toy-maker, milliner, modiste, hatter, upholsterer, and wall decker," she created "at a single pass half a dozen modern industries ; it was "her role of industrialism" that was to "transform the face of the earth" (1889: 6).

If she no longer controls these industries, it is because man has "co-operated" with woman's arts to develop them into modern industry, now that "militancy no longer demands all man's waking moments" (1889: 8). Fortunately, she still has her role as mother, because human offspring are so slow to mature, and "if there should ever come a time when this office may be delegated to irresponsible and paid assistants, the best that woman ever did for this world will be canceled" (1889:9). Thomas' list of the jobs of primitive woman was very similar to Mason's, but it was couched in his animal-vegetable theory of sex differences. Hence, the labours of animal-like man required "strength, violence, speed," and "craft and foresight" (1899a:474). In short, he hunted and fished. The natural labours of plantlike woman required "slow, unspasmodic, routine, stationary" skills.

She (1) was interested in shelter for herself and her children; (2) cultivated plants (being plantlike, this was only natural); (3) prepared food; (4) wove baskets and made pottery to hold the food; and (5) developed Spinning, weaving, and dyeing, which was "to be expected" of one so close to the vegetable.

Thomas, too, had the male eventually taking over the female's industries with his superior organising capacities and the inventive and technological skills developed in making weapons. At that point a surplus of food was at least possible, thanks to the male, and the conditions for culture came into existence at last. Eventually the men withdrew their ladies from labour, because of their "desire to preserve the beauty of women, and their desire to withdraw them from association with other men" (1899a:476).

Notably, Veblen, as usual, looked on the darker side. At the barbarian stage, when men became predatory and enslaved women, the division of labour also was changed to reflect the seizure of power. Men assigned themselves the "honorific employments" (particularly associated with hunting and fighting); women were assigned the "humiliating employments" (those associated with peace keeping). This has carried over to the present, he noted — for women's work is still considered inferior to men's (1899:507). However, he expected the situation. to change, as Western civilisation evolved into peaceable industrialism and the patriarchal household disappeared. Although Veblen welcomed the changing social structure that he hoped would liberate the female, many other social scientists of his time decidedly did not. It is ironic that a number of the arguments used to keep the female in her traditional place were phrased in the language of evolutionism, for evolution presupposed change.

Yet an increasing number of American women of the latter nineteenth century were not intimidated by the flood of "scientific" arguments against their greater participation in American life.

> As a general thing, when the importance of individuality has been insisted on, the individuality in view is that of man. It is he who has been exhorted to assert himself; to be true to his Opinions, to live his own life; the exhortation has not been to any great extent

> addressed to his wife or his sisters. Enough for them if they can be so fortunate as to minister not unworthily to some grand male individuality. Women, however, though not particularly invited to the lecture, have been listening to it, and—what people do not always do with lectures or sermons—are applying it to themselves.

In the preceding pages we have portrayed the views of diferent scholrs about the women in the United States. It is remarkable that in addition to above academics analysis, women in the US have better states in all spheres of life. But it cannot be said an ideal position.

In the following section we are presenting some facts about violence and crime against women in the context of present days advanced US society.

Facts about Violence Against Women in the United States

Despite the fact that advocacy groups like NOW have worked for two decades to halt the epidemic of gender-based violence and sexual assault, the numbers are still shocking. It is time to renew our national pledge, from the President and Congress on down to City Councils all across the nation to END violence against women and men, girls and boys. This effort must also be carried on in workplaces, schools, churches, locker rooms, the military, and in courtrooms, law enforcement, entertainment and the media.

Murder

In 2005, 1,181 women were murdered by an intimate partner. That's an average of three women every day. Of all the women murdered in the U.S., about one-third were killed by an intimate partner.

Domestic Violence (Intimate Partner Violence or Battering)

Domestic violence can be defined as a pattern of abusive behavior in any relationship that is used by one partner to gain or maintain power and control over an intimate partner. According to the National Center for Injury Prevention and Control, women experience about 4.8 million intimate partner-related physical assaults and rapes every year. Less than 20 percent of battered women sought medical treatment following an injury.

Sexual Violence

According to the National Crime Victimization Survey, which includes crimes that were *not* reported to the police, 232,960 women in the U.S. were raped or sexually assaulted in 2006. That's more than 600 women every day. Other estimates, such as those generated by the FBI, are much lower because they rely on data from law enforcement agencies. A significant number of crimes are never even reported for reasons that include the victim's feeling that nothing can/will be done and the personal nature of the incident.

The Targets

Young women, low-income women and some minorities are disproportionately victims of domestic violence and rape. Women ages 20-24 are at greatest risk of nonfatal domestic violence, and women age 24 and under suffer from the highest rates of rape. The Justice Department estimates that one in five women will experience rape or attempted rape during their college years, and that less than five percent of these rapes will be reported. Income is also a factor: the poorer the household, the higher the rate of domestic violence — with women in the lowest income category experiencing more than six times the rate of nonfatal intimate partner violence as compared to women in the highest income category. When we consider race, we see that African-American women face higher rates of domestic violence than white women, and American-Indian women are victimized at a rate more than double that of women of other races.

Impact on Health and Social Services

According to the Family Violence Prevention Fund, "growing up in a violent home may be a terrifying and traumatic experience that can affect every aspect of a child's life, growth and development. . . . children who have been exposed to family violence suffer symptoms of post-traumatic stress disorder, such as bed-wetting or nightmares, and were at greater risk than their peers of having allergies, asthma, gastrointestinal problems, headaches and flu." In addition, women who experience physcial abuse as children are at a greater risk of victimization as adults, and men have a far greater (more than double) likelihood of perpetrating abuse.

Impact on Health and Social Services

The Centers for Disease Control estimates that the cost of domestic violence in 2003 was more than over $8.3 billion. This cost includes medical care, mental health services, and lost productivity.

Legislation

In 1994, the National Organization for Women, the NOW Legal Defense and Education Fund (now called Legal Momentum), the Feminist Majority and other organizations finally secured passage of the Violence Against Women Act, which provided a record-breaking $1.6 billion to address issues of violence against women. However it took nearly an additional year to force the Newt Gingrich-led Congress to release the funding. An analysis estimated that in the first six years after VAWA was passed, nearly $14.8 billion was saved in net averted social costs. VAWA was reauthorized in 2005, with nearly $4 billion in funding over five years.

Violence between Same-sex Couples

According to the National Coalition of Anti-Violence Programs, "domestic violence affecting LGBT individuals continues to be grossly underreported . . . there is a lack of awareness and denial about the existence of this type of violence and its impact, both by LGBT people and non-LGBT people alike."

Myths regarding gender roles perpetuate the silence surrounding these abusive relationships; for example, the belief that there aren't abusive lesbian relationships because women don't abuse each other. Shelters are often unequipped to handle the needs of lesbians (as a women-only shelter isn't much defense against a female abuser), and transgendered individuals. Statistics regarding domestic violence against LGBT people are unavailable at the national level, but as regional studies demonstrate, domestic violence is as much as a problem within LGBT communities as it is among heterosexual ones.

REFERENCES

Bureau of Justice Statistics (table 2, page 15), *Criminal Victimization in the United States, 2006 Statistical Tables.*

Bureau of Justice Statistics (table 4, page 17) *Criminal Victimization in the United States, 2006 Statistical Tables* (PDF).

Bureau of Justice Statistics, *Intimate Homicide Victims by Gender.*

Bureau of Justice Statistics, *Intimate Partner Violence in the U.S.: Victims.*

Bureau of Justice Statistics, *There has been a decline in homicide of intimates, especially male victims.*

Bureau of Justice Statistics, *Victim Characteristics: Age.*

Bureau of Justice Statistics, *Victim Characteristics: Race.*

CDC, *Understanding Intimate Partner Violence* (PDF).

Deptartment of Justice, *About Domestic Violence.*

Family Violence Prevention Fund, *The Facts on Children and Domestic Violence.*

National Coalition Against Domestic Violence (NCADV), *Domestic Violence Facts* (PDF).

National Coalition of Anti-Violence Programs (NCAVP), *Lesbian, Gay, Bisexual, and Transgender Domestic Violence In the United States in 2007* (PDF).

National Institute of Justice (pages 6-7), *Sexual Assault on Campus: What Colleges an Universitie Are Doing About It* (PDF).

NCADV, *Comparison of VAWA 1994, VAWA 2000 and VAWA 2005 Reauthorization Bill* (PDF).

NCAVP, *Lesbian, Gay, Bisexual, and Transgender Domestic Violence In the United States in 2007* (PDF).

NOW, *The Violence Against Women Act: Celebrating 10 Years of Prevention.*

University of North Carolina, *Analyses of Violence Against Women Act suggest legislation saved U.S. $14.8 billion.*

US Census Bureau (page 12), *National Crime Victimization Survey* (PDF).

3

Women in Mexico

Before disucssing women in Mexico, we would like to reproduce some vital facts about women of Mexico.

Vital Facts

Life expectancy: females as a % of males, 2007	107
Adult literacy rate: females as a % of males, 2000–2007	96
Enrolment and attendance ratios: females as a % of males, Net primary school 2000–2007, enrolled	99
Enrolment and attendance ratios: females as a % of males, Net primary school 2000–2007, attending	100
Enrolment and attendance ratios: females as a % of males, Net secondary school 2000–2007, enrolled	99
Enrolment and attendance ratios: females as a % of males, Net secondary school 2000–2007, attending	—
Contraceptive prevalence (%), 2000–2007	71
Antenatal care coverage (%), At least once, 2000–2007	86
Antenatal care coverage (%), At least four times, 2000–2007	—
Delivery care coverage (%), Skilled attendant at birth, 2000–2007	93
Delivery care coverage (%), Institutional delivery, 2000–2007	86
Maternal mortality ratio, 2000–2007 reported	62
Maternal mortality ratio, 2005, adjusted	60
Maternal mortality ratio, 2005, Lifetime risk of maternal death. 1 in:	

Mexico is a multicultural country so to talk about Mexican women as a whole is quite a complicated task. Any generalisation could lead to a misunderstanding of the whole, which is the sum of a wide variety of parts. This whole is a mosaic with pieces that differ because of ethnic characteristics, social classes, geographical regions, the degree of socioeconomic-political integration into an urban society, and many other factors. This paper seeks to describe several representative bits of the mosaic as the Mexican women express and experience it. Generalities about Mexican women are totally misleading. Often they are made by those who believe that a study of a village in the State of Morelos, such as Tepoztlan, is a model for all rural areas, but this is a distorted view of the typical rural Mexican.

Nor do the studies about *colonias* surrounding Mexico City provide adequate material about the urban Mexican. Even worse is the assumption that the impaired image of the Mexican living in the northern border states is applicable to the whole.

Octavio Paz in his book *The Labyrinth of Solitude,* says: "The history of Mexico is the history of man seeking his parentage, his origins... He wants to go back beyond the catastrophe he suffered... to return to the center of that life from which he was separated one day... (1961). Perhaps this is why some Indian communities have not been assimilated into the "national culture."

The national culture consists of a group of individual cultures which are related and interacting in a geographic area and which coexist under a centralised power, such as the Aztecs and Mayas who have become completely acculturated and who have almost disappeared. But the marginal cultures exist almost without any contact or' relation to the rest of the country, as in the case of the Lacandones and Seris peoples. There are also "indiocolonial" groups who have changed their language and dress but who have conserved their Indian institutions; and the rural mestizo communities, which are very conservative and far from being industrialised, In Mexico it is still possible to step back into prehistory and find people who live by hunting and gathering wild seeds and fruits.

There are still 53 living indigenous languages which have, surprisingly, survived, besides the dozens of cultures which show a great internal vitality, and which are still determining Mexican history and appear to be far from final liquidation. This panorama has made Mexico a "paradise" for the anthropologist, as well as for adventurers who often hide behind fellowships and degrees and whose writings lack seriousness and scientific exactness. We know of anthropological and/or sociological studies where generalisations are made on the basis of observations of one person or very small groups, whose values and lifestyles are often misunderstood. They are written by foreigners who have spent some months touring around without the slightest change in their own cultural habits and who after a short stay have thought they penetrated the core of Mexican culture. They have not taken into consideration the fact that the persons they considered as objects of study and who know they are being studied protect themselves in various ways.

On a visit to a small village of Mazahua Indians, some mestizos, and a few foreigners, it was noteworthy that no one invited the visitors into their homes, a Mexican sign of welcome. Instead they inquired with some mistrust "Have you come to study us?" Later it was discovered that their fear and their rejection of the idea of being objects of research were related to their frequent exposure to visitors representing foundations, universities, and/or linguistic institutes. It is true that to be scientific one has to observe, analyse, and systematise, but a contribution to science loses its significance and honesty if it is used to gain personal prestige, or to obtain money from the publication of books, corporation fellowships, university degrees, etc.

The only acceptable reason for making people an object of study even temporarily would be to make available the information for the benefit of those being studied so that it could be used to help them reach a better human status. This is particularly the case with women. Some of the differences among Mexicans are closely related to the geographical variants throughout the country: jungle and desert, mountain and plateau, and an extensive seacoast. The corresponding climates, which are not always pleasantly tropical, often make survival difficult and do not provide the best conditions for food production.

The 50 million inhabitants of Mexico live in a number of different ways. Economic development is unequal so that many people live in big, modern cities that compete with those of any part of the world, while others still live in the pretechnological era, in small villages scattered throughout miles of empty lands. Mexico is a complex of cultures. There is a large indigenous population; approximately 50 per cent of the total population are peasants; and a significant percentage is completely urban. Among the Indian groups, the Taharahumaral Indian in the north has a different culture from the Tzeltal in the south, or the Otomi in the central part. This is also true of the peasants and the urban populations living in different geographical areas. One has to be aware of this complexity in order to recognise the limitations of our knowledge about the realities of Mexico as given in statistics and figures. Nor can we forget that people are in process, not static, and are therefore changeable.

Most important to understand the social status of the Mexican women are historical events which have left very deep impressions. At the time of the violent invasion of the Spanish conquerors, Indian communities were organised in many different ethnic groups under the imperialist rule of the Central Aztec kingdom. This was a very important fact, for it permitted cultural relationships and communication between the groups, and at the same time it enabled the Spanish to make use of the tensions created by the internal conflicts between the Aztec Empire and its tributary subjugated neighbors.

It was so important that several authors think that Mexicans were conquered by themselves, since Cortes and his small number of troops could only have won with the help and alliances of dissident groups (Kirkpatrick 1958: 55-56, 70). Also Cortes used his mistress, Malintzin, an Indian woman, as an official translator, ambassador, and counsellor, because of her brilliant mind and wide knowledge of the Mexican reality of the time. In spite of all her good qualities, Mexicans consider Malintzin a traitor: her name is used as an insult. Was she voluntarily helping the conqueror; was she given to him as a present; was she sold to him, as is still the custom of some Indian groups, to be used as a guide, informant, translator, as well as sexual object? She never was his official wife; for that role a lady was brought from Europe.

No doubt, the conqueror was imitated, and many women were taken in the same way or simply violated. This was a very bitter experience that created anxiety and left a strong impact on a society where virginity and chastity were noble virtues for both man and woman. This historical fact, in the opinion of many authors, is one of the factors contributing to the degradation of the feminine image and to the fact that women have been considered intrinsically as traitors and unworthy of confidence (Ramirez 1970:48-51).

It is pertinent to note that judging by the social participation and the importance of Indian women at that time, it would seem that they were still in a matrilineal society or at least in a transitional stage, in contrast with the culture of the conquerors where the patriarchy was fully established. Many aspects of the life of Indian women help to support this theory. The new wife was taken by her mother or an older female family member to her husband's home where she was received and fed by her mother-in-law and welcomed by the female relatives of the boy who could send her back if they disapproved of her.

Women had many religious and social duties related to the delivery and reception of newborn babies. Most important, women developed plant cultivation and animal domestication. Some studies of matrilineal societies have shown that the important thing was to know "who the mother was" in terms of inheritance and group identification. Women had some economic power and their participation in government, justice, and war-making were very important.

The most important virtues for women were strength, decency and honesty, religious devotion and piety, knowledge and skill in handicrafts, chastity (important for both boys and girls), and modesty (Hellbom 1967:247). From the time of the Conquest to the present the dominant cultural patterns, both in rural and urban areas, have been patriarchal and male—oriented. The human dignity of women has seriously deteriorated because of the *macho* violations which have converted Mexican women into concubines and servants.

Notably, an important time in our history was 1910, when the people's insurrection disrupted all social structures and opened up new possibilities for women. Their active participation was recorded in a number of songs and stories, but at the same time the most famous women soldiers also had to be very special lovers or the love objects of every one.

La Adelita, Juana Gallo, La Valentian, and many anonymous women, such as la Jesusa Palancares, (Poniatowska 1971:69) fought side by side with men. La Valentain, recently interviewed at the age of 79, lives alone and forgotten. She remembers how at 16, she decided to fight and went to the battlefront dressed as a man. After five months of service her sex was discovered and she was discharged because she was a woman (Leyzaola 1973:36-37). This moment of history has been exploited in many ways by the Mexican movies and other mass media.' For example, in the 1940's they created a different feminine image, no longer the very sad and suffering prostitute or the cabaret girl but the domineering female, the cold loye-priestess who lends her body but never gives it.

The myth was incarnated in Maria Felix, the female model who knows she is used as an erotic object, but whose weapon is her cold beauty. When the myth was enacted she was presented as the central figure of a folklorised Revolution in the role of a *guerillera* soldier or as a general, a woman who lived with the soldiers in the battlefields. From silk and velvet dresses she changed to campaign boots, rifles, and bullet belts. Her language was crude and she insolently entered into every field traditionally reserved for men. However, she eventually surrendered herself to love, and then went back to "normalcy," to her traditional feminine role. Later, to continue as a movie star, this woman had to forget her "womanhood" and take on male characteristics, even outside her films.

After the Revolution ended, around 1917, education for women became possible as a result of industrialisation. The machine began to take economic activity out of the home and into the factory, replacing the labor power of women and children especially in the textile industries. Though many women are leaving the home to work in factories, the traditional reaction is that they should only work when there is a real economic need, e.g. with widows or some divorcees.

In Mexican society it is now axiomatic that it is men who are to work outside of the home. At the beginning of the Industrial Revolution most men and women worked together cultivating the land, making handicrafts and sharing some of the domestic tasks. However, this was not seen as sufficient justification for women to accompany the men into industry.

The Indigenous Rural Women: Luis Gonzalez, a Mexican anthropologist with the National Center for Indigenous Pastoral Care, lists four criteria for distinguishing the differences among rural women: somatic or physical; psychological; linguistic; and cultural (lifestyles, relationships, social organisation, traditions). According to the 1970 national census, which used only the linguistic criteria, there were 29 different indigenous groups in Mexico making up a total of 3,100,000 people. Using the four criteria listed above, there were at this time about sixty different groups totalling between 10 and 15 million people.

The Mestizo Rural Woman. The mixing of races increased throughout the seventeenth Century and then began to decrease. This resulted in a great variety of mestizo groups, depending on the degree of Iberian influence in an area and on the groups making up the mixtures. In addition, the Africans, brought in at a later period, also played their part in the racial mixture in some areas, and we cannot overlook the Anglo-Saxon influence in some parts of the country.

There are distinct cultural differences not only between indigenous groups, but also between groups of mestizos. The strongest prehispanic cultures in Mexico were concentrated in the central and southern regions, where the Spanish Conquest began. Its influence in the north came later and was of a lesser degree. Furthermore, in the north the indigenous groups were still nomads or semi-nomads and were also influenced by the Anglo-Saxon culture.

Social classes adopt different customs not only in the urban and rural settings, but from region to region. In some areas social classes are still determined by wealth, as for example, in Monterrey. In other areas, classes are determined by an "aristocratic lineage," as, for example, in Puebla.

As a result of the Agrarian Reform, a new class appeared, the *ejidatarios,* the landowners who are the beneficiaries of the land reform. In many cases they have become the oppressors of the landless, the day laborer who works the land while the new owner rests or gets drunk. The wife of the new landowner is on a different level from the wife of the laborer, as in the *ejidos,* the former public lands, of Paso del Rio, Colima.

It is important here to reproduce the findings of an empirical study.

From January to October, 1971, a team made up of a social science graduate, two social workers, a teacher, and a secretary carried out a socio-religious survey in the *ejido* area of Paso del Rio, Colima. The rural men and women in Paso del Rio were interviewed on the question of work inside and outside of the home as part of research on the family which included man-woman relations, parent-child relations, extra-familial relations of the sexes, etc. ("Estudio socio-religioso de Paso del Rio" 1971:129-210). This 'is a community made up of four sub-communities: The collective *ejido* de Cofradia Juarez; the individual *ejido* of Periquillo; Rincon de Lopez, an *ejido* in process of integration; and a community made up of small landowners, small merchants, employees, and laborers. The team defined communities as "groups conditioned by the norms and customs of a traditional society...."

A traditional society is generally accepted as one which is structured on generalised Western sociocultural presuppositions (Diaz Guerrero, 1970, of the Autonomous National University of Mexico), which supports the image of man as strong, domineering, conquering, and of woman as dependent, conformist, routinised, timid. It is a society in which to be a man is synonymous with being privileged, while to be a woman means to have a series of limitations which can only be overcome with the help of a man.

The team found that the women of Paso del Rio, especially those of Cofradia Juarez and Periquillo, were not happy with their social status at the time of the study.

Women and Work Outside the Home

The questionnaire included two questions to detect the attitudes of both men and women with respect to the activities of women inside the home and gainful employment outside the home. Contrary to what might be expected, in Rincon de Lopez, the group that we would expect to be the most traditional because it was the most isolated, the work of the women was accepted by a larger percentage than in Periquillo and Cofradia Juarez.

In Periquillo 68.4 per cent of the men were opposed to women working; in Cofradia Juarez, 64 per cent; and in Rincon de Lopez, only 30,7 per cent. As far as the women were concerned, the larger percentage of those who still thought that "women's place is in the home" were in Periquillo, with 16.7 per cent; while in Cofradia Juarez it was 11.9 per cent, and in Estacion, only 4.2 per cent. However in Rincon de Lopez 100 per cent of the women were in favor of women working. Favorable opinions about women working do not necessarily indicate ideas favoring some degree of liberation. The reason given most often by both men and women for accepting the work of women outside the home is the need for financial help in the home. Women's work becomes the answer to a need. If the need did not exist she would not have to work, according to the male response of 4 per cent in Cofradia Juarez, of 7.17 per cent in Rincon de Lopez, and of 5.9 per cent of Estacion. These men were willing to accept the work of woman only if she were single, or a widow, or if her husband were ill.

Only 10.5 per cent, 15.4 per cent and 5.9 per cent of the men in Periquillo, Rincon de Lopez, and Estacion would leave some initiative to women in the decision to work so that they could buy some personal things for themselves. The idea that women might dispose of their own money is still unacceptable to the great majority of the population: 16.7 per cent and 14.3 per cent of the women in Periquillo and Rincon de Lopez gave this same response. Of the 88.1 per cent of the women of Cofradia Juarez who agreed that women should work outside the home, 42% gave an interesting reason: "So that the woman would be valued for her own self" Woman wants to be valued for what she is, she wants to occupy the place in the home and in society which rightfully belongs to her, she wants to move from being an *object* to being a *subject*. This desire to be valued for her own self would indicate that at the present this is not the case. One of the reasons given by men for women not working was: "She is not capable." If she is not considered capable, can she be given a place in the family, in society?

A small percentage of men admit that "every human being should work." This response was also given by 2.4. per cent of the women in Cofradia Juarez. In Rincon de Lopez a response was given that did not appear in the other communities — the conceding of a right: "Women have the right to earn money." This response was given by 15.4 per cent of the men, but curiously by no woman.

In Estacion, possibly because of the influence from the city of Tecoman, a response was made which it would be difficult to conceive of in Periquillo and Cofradia Juarez, and perhaps a bit easier to understand in Rincon de Lopez, "Woman has the right to progress." This reply was given by 25 per cent of the women but only 5.9 per cent of the men.

Reasons for Not Working Outside the Home

All the women who do not accept the idea of women working give as their only reason: "Women should be in the home." Among the men, the majority gave this reason and the reason that "Women are not capable of working."

Four per cent of the men of Cofradia Juarez said that "Woman was born for the kitchen." Of the men of Pariquillo 10.5 per cent and of Rincon de Lopez 15.4 per cent do not accept the idea of women working because "It is not decent" for a woman to work. They want her to go out of the home "clean": these are the exact words used. Why should work defile a woman while it ennobles a man?

Because, according to the traditional family stereotypes, woman must be submissive and dependent because she is inferior to man. Man must protect her because she is weak and cannot defend herself. The women of Paso del Rio, at least a good percentage of them, did not accept this role. They wanted not only to have more, but to be more.

According to a large percentage of the population, women should be in the home. But what should she do in it? Much has been said about men and women sharing in the various activities of the family. How was this viewed in Paso del Rio? The family is considered "the socialising group." The advancement of its members with a view to their integration in the society depends largely on the family. The internal organisation of the family may have different characteristics according to the concept it has of the roles of men and women and 'children.

The traditional family is characterised by a complete separation of the work which the man and the woman do in the bosom of the family, while in the modern family there tends to be a sharing of the work by all. A question was included in the study to see if the man collaborated in the domestic duties of the home or if he held them in contempt, considering them as woman's work." In Cofradia Juarez the larger percentage of the men listed household tasks as "woman's work," but 40.5 per cent of the women wanted the men to help take care of the children at least.

It was here that there was the largest number of children per family. Among the most conservative women on this point were those of Rincon de Lopez. This was contrary to what was expected, since 100 per cent of them accepted the fact that women may work outside the home. Household tasks, according to traditional standards, are predominantly woman's responsibility. The fact that a group of men at least accepted the idea of sharing in this work is a sign of some lessening of the contempt in which women are held. The tensions which are provoked by the traditional thinking about women and the present social evolution demand that women have a new consciousness of their status and that society assume responsibility for giving them their rightful place.

It is obvious from the studies that the education of rural women must be revised, and the cooperation of all will he necessary if they are to be stimulated to assume their responsibilities with a new sense of involvement.

A much greater preparation is needed than that which sufficed in a traditional society, for example, in the concept of motherhood, which has been one of the most important factors in creating a distorted concept of the meaning of being a woman. If the rural woman in particular is not prepared for greater social cooperation she runs the risk of being enslaved rather than liberated, by a consumer society in which human values count for little.

Coming to the urben context the main urban centers are Monterrey and Chihuahua in the north; Guadalajara and Morelia on the Pacific coast; Jalapa, Veracruz, and Merida on the Gulf coast; Puebla, San Luis, and Toluca in the Central part; and the macropolis, Mexico City. Several problems related to our underdevelopment are easily seen in population concentration. This is a result of the growing rural migration to urban centers that are thought of as a paradise of possibilities and a magic panacea for every social, economic, and political problem. Of course the reality is quite different. This internal migration is making cities into typical underdeveloped centers. Angela Alessio Robles (Alessi Robles), an engineer working for the urban planning office of the Mexico City government wrote that our urbanisation process shows exactly the opposite effects to those in industrialised countries:

1. Accelerated population growth due to rural migration creates marginal groups, similar to the prehistoric nomads, which become sort of "modern urban hunters."
2. The migration rate is' so high that instead of increased urbanisation, what actually results is a "ruralisation of the big city."
3. "Housing and living space are minimal and lead to promiscuity and other social problems. According to the last census, due to the influence of the consumer society, meager economic resources are invested in buying superfluous apparatus and clothes rather than in housing improvement or family savings.
4. Health and sanitary agencies are insufficient to prevent growing pollution and conditions for widespread epidemics.

How does this kind of utbanisation, or city ruralisation, affect women? In the first place internal migration creates transitional "rural-urban" groups in the multiplying misery belts around cities. It makes Mexican suburbia the poorest and most marginated areas.

Here the women are servants, factory workers, and very often prostitutes. Birth rates have been more or less constant during the last 40 years, but there is a decrease in the number of young women and an increase in older women. On the other hand, although the natural rural growth has been greater than the natural urban growth, internal migration has contributed to an unnatural urban growth, three to four times greater than the rural growth. This migration consists mainly of young people, of whom a majority are women.

Migration affects the labor market, and although Mexico is not a fully industrialised country, it is suffering all the illnesses of one and has a disproportionately large working force.

Further study *(Perfil de Mexico en 1980* [1972] of the Autonomous University of Mexico) of social research analysed the occupational margination by sex in the working population from 21 to 60 years of age as seen in the showing Table.

The women are mostly employed in services and their salaries are always lower than men's, very often for the same kind of work, and sometimes for harder work. This makes women the most marginal of the marginal. Recent studies show that in migrant groups only 27 per cent of the men, but 64 per cent of the women are marginals. They belong to a "culture of silence, a situation in which one is not allowed to express an opinion, creating auto-repression. They are modern slaves who are given the hardest jobs that nobody else will do. They are fatalists ("everything we suffer is God's will"), personally insecure, with inferiority complexes and submissive attitudes. All of this prevents them from making decisions even about their own bodies and lives.

Almost 70 per cent of Mexican women are living this way.

Occupation by Sexes

Marginal Occupational groups are (1) street vendors; (2) non-qualified workers in service; (3) unskilled factory workers; (4) unskilled construction workers; (5) agricultural workers.

Group		*1*	*2*	*3*	*4*	*5*
Per cent men		59.8	28.2	78.3	100	94.2
Per cent women		40.2	71.8	21.7	0.0	5.8
Monthly income (in Mexican pesos)						
	Men	1251.00	1012.00	1109.00	810.00	
	Women	907.00	446.00	881.00		

In her contribution to the book, *Women that Speak Out,* Guadalupe Zentina comments about her studies on married women's work (1971:165):

Out of a group of working women she found that the motivation for working for 62 per cent was economic, and for some 29 per cent it was also economic, and for some 29 per cent it was also economic but related to a "better" education for children. Only 2 per cent saw work as a means of increasing their personal growth. There is also a correlation between work motivation and education: 13.8 per cent of the group had no formal schooling, 32.8 per cent had finished elementary school, and duly 5.1 per cent had attended universities. Since it is assumed that married women should not work, it follows they will become economically unproductive and dependent. Only special circumstances are they allowed to work. In 1968; 20 per cent of the married women were employed, mainly' in services. Traditionally the role of the woman has been related almost exclusively to her role as a mother.

Maternity functions are still considered most important, so most of her productive life is dedicated to child birth and care. Thus factories, banks, and other employing agencies are reluctant to hire married women. The resulting economic dependence creates extreme subordination, psychologically and socially.

Several studies in Mexico City by a team of IMES and a group of social workers in 1970 showed that 23 per cent of the men accepted the fact that their wives could work in the following occupations 40 per cent, as a dressmaker; 31.4 per cent, as a servant; 8.5 per cent as a factory worker; 6 per cent, as a nurse. The acceptance of dressmaking had to do with the fact that the wife would not have to go out and could still take 'care of everything at home (Instituto Mexicano de Estudios Sociales 1969). One of the cultural taboos against women working is the belief that manhood is proved by the ability to earn the money to meet the family needs. If the man is not able to earn a sufficient income or if he is unwilling to give her all he makes, the wife must adapt or make "magic economics" with any 'amount she receives, even if it means a miserable survival.

A study in Monterrey showed that 87 per cent of the women workers were single; 3.6 per cent, single mothers; 3.6 per cent, widows or divorced, and only 2.3 per cent were married (Estudio Socio-religioso de Ntra. Sra. de Lourdes, 1970). Most of these working women are part of the migrant population and suffer very severe culture shock in the cities, especially when they come from Indian groups.

Indian women are accustomed to working with their husbands in agricultural tasks. However, in non-rural areas women are excluded from sharing the work of their husbands, especially in developed areas using machines. When women are rejected as workers, they are confined at home with their dependent children and the tedious slavery of housework.

This means that it is easier for them to be reached by consumer advertising through radio and television. It is painful to see how the mass media reinforce and perpetuate old cultural patterns which limit women's participation in collective production and life. In a consumer society women have a most important role but only as consumers who want all the items which the producers advertise.

As per 1970 census, out of 15 million working women (12 to 60 years old) twelve and a half million are housemaids. Young girls learn their duties through a rather had "training"; without previous preparation they are expected to learn the use of electrical aparatus when they come from place where there is no electricity. They are poorly paid and badly exploited. There is no time limit on their work in the evening they must be ready to begin again at six in the morning. They must take care of the children and do the cooking and all the work in the house. If after some time, the girl isn't able to do everything, she may be sent away without notice. This causes a tremendous trauma for most of them.

They find themselves in the hostile environment of the big cities without knowing how to deal with it. Many of these girls end up in prostitution either because of ignorance and naivete' or because they aren't able to make a living any other way. The general attitude towards women, the cultural shock experienced by girls coming to the cities, their lack of preparation for technical activities, and general unemployment, very often result in their being pushed into prostitution, which is frequently entered as the last reçourse for survival.

A study made in 1970 in one of the Mexican border cities, which are some of the most important prostitution markets, shows that 90 per cent of a group of five thousand women came from rural areas or small cities. They are exploited mainly by American men who cross the border any time they wish. This situation is repeated in Ciudad Juirez, Tijuana, Reynosa, Matamoros, and other places.

Middle-class women are slightly better off, but in 1970 they made up only about 9.5 per cent of the total population and their numbers seem to he decreasing. Women are expected to leave their jobs when they get married so they can devote all their time to the house and children. All of this means a great change in their economic possibilities and personal development. This is true with slight variations for every social group from the popular sector to the highest classes.

They are always economically, psychologically and emotionally dependent. The traditional image of the woman in urban areas is that of the mother, a woman with as many children as possible, loving and self-denying, ready to give everything without getting anything but the recognition of being a good wife and, above all, model as a mother.

For millennia woman has been enslaved, exploited, or at least marginated and subordinated by man. Man has appropriated for himself the ruler's scepter, the center of the world, and the prerogative of giving it form, organising it, orienting it. Woman has had to accept the masculine patterns of thought and action, in the family, in education, and in recreation as well as in politics, in the economy, and even in religion.

Women have had to live by masculine standards in abnegation and fidelity, the qualities which man has "generously" assigned to woman as the exclusive privilege of being feminine. In order to maintain the many forms of slavery or exploitation, of subordination or margination, man has invented for woman a series of qualities, all of which are a counterbalance for his faults and vices.

Woman must be self-denying so that man can be irrational; chaste and faithful, to make up for his degeneracy and infidelity; tender and gentle, so that he can behave like a beast. Man has also created the myth of the weaker sex without which the other myth, the myth of the stronger sex which implies "supremacy, would not be possible.

But woman no longer moves only in the closed circle of her family. Her home is no longer the four walls of a house. It is the street culture, public life. Woman should conscientiously contribute to the development of her country, but this 'will require a new mentality, a change for which woman herself is not prepared. A woman economist, former Director of the School of Economics at the Autonomous University of Mexico recently wrote:

> "Neither biology nor tradition can impose procreation on women as their only possible destiny. Today women combine these essential functions with economic, political, and social tasks of their choice which permit the development of their potentialities as human beings and their contribution through a full giving of themselves." (Navarrete 1969:35, 104).

To conclude, it is worth mentioning that fulfillment of woman does not come only with her participation in the decision-making process at all levels, although that is essential. It does not have to do so much with *having more* as with *being more*. The fulfillment of woman will come when she is free, when women and men are equal, and when they make effective use of their freedom for the whole of society in Mexico.

REFERENCES

Benitez, Fernando, 1972, *Los Indios de Mexico.* Editorial Era.

De La Colina, Jose, 1973, "Aventuras y tribulaciones del cine mexicano." *Revista de Revistas,* July 25, Mexico.

Diaz Guarrero, Rogelio, 1970, *Estudios de psicologia del mexicano* (reprinted edition). Editorial Trillas.

Elu De Lenero, Ma. Del Carmen, 1969, *Hacia donde va la mujer mexicana.* Instituto Mexicano de Estudios Sociales.

Estudio socio-religioso de Ntra. Sra. de Lourdes 1970, Unpublished private study, Monterrey, Nuevo Leon, Mexico. *Estudio Socio-religioso de Paso del Rio* 1971, Unpublished private study. Colima, Mexico.

Hellbom, Anna Britta, 1967, *La participacion cultural de las mujeres indias y mestizas en el Mexico precortesiano y postrevolucionario.* Stockolm: The Ethnolographical Museum.

Instituto Mexicano De Estudios Sociales, 1969, "Extudio sociografico de la colonia Cailos, Cd. Mexico." Unpublished mimeograph.

Kirk Patrick, F.A., 1958, *Los conquistadores espanoles* (sixth edition). Espasa Calpe, Argentina.

Leyzaola, Margarita, 1973, "Valentina, Valentina...." *Revista de Revistas.* July 18, Mexico.

Navarrete, Ifigenia, 1969, *La mujer y los derechos sociales.* Mexico: Ediciones Oasis.

Parroquia Aguilas, 1970, "Estudio sociografico." Mexico: Instituto Mexicano de Estudios Sociales. Unpublished manuscript.

Paz, Octavio, 1961, *The Labyrinth of Solitude.* New York: Grove Press.

Perfil de Mexico en 1980, 1972, Volumes two and three. Mexico: Editorial Siglo XXI.

Poniatowska, Elena, 1971, *Hasta no verte Jesus mio* (seventh edition). Mexico: Editorial Era.

Pozas, Ricardo, Isabel H. Pozas, 1971, *Los indios en las clases sociales de Mexico.* Mexico: Editorial Siglo XXI.

Ramirez, Santiago, 1970, *El mexicano, psicologia de sus motivaciones* (sixth edition). Mexico: Editorial pax..

Ramos, Samuel, 1962, *Profile of man and culture in Mexico.* University of Texas Press.

Rojas Avendane, Mario, 1973, "Los mercados de sirvientas en la region de los Tuxtlas, Ver." July 22, Mexico: Excelsior.

4

Women in the Palestine

Palestine is a disturbed society which has been suffering the pangs of turmoil and trouble since Israel's occupation of the area. Women have been the worst sufferers of war and turmoil.

Here in this chapter, we have made an attempt to reproduce the situation of women in the occupied Arab Territories.

Basic Facts on Women

Life expectancy: females as a % of males, 2007	104
Adult literacy rate: females as a % of males, 2000–2007	92
Enrolment and attendance ratios: females as a % of males, Net primary school 2000–2007, enrolled	100
Enrolment and attendance ratios: females as a % of males, Net primary school 2000–2007, attending	101
Enrolment and attendance ratios: females as a % of males, Net secondary school 2000–2007, enrolled	106
Enrolment and attendance ratios: females as a % of males, Net secondary school 2000–2007, attending	—
Contraceptive prevalence (%), 2000–2007	50
Antenatal care coverage (%), At least once, 2000–2007	99
Antenatal care coverage (%), At least four times, 2000–2007	—

Delivery care coverage (%), Skilled attendant at birth, 2000–2007	99
Delivery care coverage (%), Institutional delivery, 2000–2007	97
Maternal mortality ratio, 2000–2007 reported	—
Maternal mortality ratio, 2005, adjusted	—
Maternal mortality ratio, 2005, Lifetime risk of maternal death. 1 in:	—

The situation of women and children living in the occupied Arab territories has been the subject of increasing international concern since the beginning of the United Nations Decade for Women. At the World Conference of the International Women's Year, held at Mexico City in 1975, special attention was drawn to the specific needs of Palestinian women and children and measures to assist them.

Subsequently, the General Assembly, in paragraph 23 of the annex to its resolution 34/24 of 15 November 1979, had requested that "a study should be prepared in 1981 by the Commission on the Status of Women on the situation of women and children living under the racist minority regimes in southern Africa, especially under the *apartheid* regime, and of women and children living in the occupied Arab territories and other occupied territories".

The Assembly also adopted resolutions 34/160 and 34/161 of 17 December 1979, which resulted in the inclusion in the agenda of the World Conference of the United Nations Decade for Women: Equality, Development and Peace, held at Copenhagen in July 1980, of an item entitled "Effects of Israeli occupation on Palestinian women inside and outside the occupied territories: (a) Review of social and economic needs of Palestinian women; (b) Special measures for Palestinian women inside and outside the occupied territories", and in the submission under that item of reports on special measures of assistance to the Palestinian women (A/CONF. 94/4) and on the effects of the Israeli occupation on Palestinian women inside and outside the occupied territories (A/CONF/94/21 and Corr. 1). Both had been prepared by the Economic Commission for Western Asia (ECWA) and were considered at its regional preparatory meeting. The Programme of Action for the Second Half of the United Nations Decade for Women, adopted at the Copenhagen Conference, included proposals for assistance to Palestinian women inside and outside the occupied territories.

The Commission on the Status of Women, at its twenty-ninth session, recommended for adoption by the Economic and Social Council a draft resolution on the situation of women and children in the occupied Arab territories, which was subsequently adopted by the Council as resolution 1982/18 of 24 May 1982.

The provisional agenda for the thirtieth session recommended by the Commission and approved by the Council is its decision 1982:,123 of 7 May 1982 included an item on the participation of women is the struggle for the strengthening of international peace and security and against colonialism, racism, racial discrimination, foreign aggression and occupation and all firms of foreign domination. Under that item, the Commission had before it a report of the Secretary-General on the situation of women and children living under racist minority regimes and in the occupied Arab territories and other occupied territories (E/CN.6/1984/10).

The Commission took note of the report and recommended to the Economic and Social Council the adoption of a resolution on the situation of Palestinian women within and outside the occupied Arab territories, which was adopted by the Council as resolution 1984/18 of 24 May 1984.

The General Assembly, in its resolution 38/108 of 16 December 1983, considered that the World Conference to Review end Appraise the Achievements of the United Nations Decade for Women, within the framework of item 7 of the provisional agenda proposed by the Commission at its first session as the preparatory body for the Conference (A/CONF.116/PC/9 and corr. 1, chap. 1. sect. A, recommendation I), should pay particular attention to the problems of women in territories under racist colonial rule and in Territories under foreign occupation on the basis of appropriate documentation from the international conferences held at Mexico City and Copenhagen, with the theme “Equality, Development and Peace”.

The Commission, at its second session as the preparatory body for the Conference, adopted a draft decision recommending that the report of the Secretary-General on women and children living in the Arab occupied territories and other occupied territories (E/CN.6/1984/10) should be updated and submitted as basic documentation to the Conference (A/CONF.116/PC/19 and Corr. 1, chap. I, sect. A. draft decision II). This recommendation was approved by the Council is its decision 1984/125 of 24 Nay 1984.

The present chapter has been prepared in response to that recommendation. As no comprehensive study related to the status of Palestinian women has been prepared within the United Nations system during the last year, it draws exclusively on recent reports and other material dealing with various aspects of living conditions of Palestinian people in the Arab occupied territories, prepared by United

Nations bodies. Although none of these reports refer specially to the question of Palestinian women they describe the living conditions of the Palestinian population as a whole.

Since the Palestinian population has been dispersed all over the world, it is difficult to know exactly how many Palestinians there are altogether: estimates range from 3.6 pillion to 4.2 million for 1980 (E/ECWA/166/Add. 1, pp. 58-59). In 1981, the total population of the West Bank, with a land area of 5,500 square kilometres, was 707,300 and that of the Gaza Strip, with an area of 367 square kilometres, was 451,600. Some 50 per cent of the people living on the West Bank are refugees registered with the United Nations Relief and Works Agency for Palestine Refugees in the Wear East (UNRWA) and 85 per cent of those living in the Gala Strip are refugees.

Detailed information on the structure of the population in the occupied territories by sex and age is given in the following table.

West Bank and Gaza Strip: Population by Sex and Age

Age (years)	*Females (percentage)*	*Males (percentage)*	*Percentage of total*
0-14	43.2	48.0	45.6
15-29	28.4	30.2	29.3
30-44	14.3	9.6	11.9
45-64	11.3	9.2	10.3
65 and over	2.8	3.0	2.9

Source: See "The situation of women end children living under racist minority regimes and in the occupied Arab territories and other occupied territories: report of the Secretary-General" (E/CN.6/1984/10).

a. Based on a population of 707,300 for the West Bank and of 4,51,600 for the Gaza Strip, making a total of 1,158,900.

The high male migration rate resulted In a decline in the male population in the age brackets 30-44 years and 45-64 years and created a ratio of 80 males to 100 females. Since 1980, emigration has increased particularly for males aged 14-25 years. This increase further affects the demographic structure of the population, contributes to the growing number of dependences per wage earner and lowers the rates of labour-force participation.

West Bank and Gaza Strip: Migration

	West Bank		*Gaza Strip*	
Year	*Number of migrants*	*Rate per 1,000*	*Number of migrants*	*Rate per 1,000*
1967	-13,000	21.8	-12,300	32.0
1968	-15,800	27.0	-32,300	87.5
1969	+ 1,300	2.2	- 2,900	8.1
1970	- 5,000	8.3	- 3,300	9.0
1971	- 2,500	4.1	-2,400	6.5
1972	- 7,200	11.5	- 4,000	10.4
1973	+ 300	.3	+ 1,700	4.3
1974	- 2,800	4.2	- 1,900	4.7
1975	-15,100	22.5	- 3,500	8.3
1976	-14,400	21.2	- 4,200	9.7
1977	-10,400	14.7	- 2,900	6.5
1978	- 9,400	13.4	- 4,700	10.3
1979	-12,600	17.7	- 4,800	10.3
1980	-17,300	24.0	- 5,100	11.3
1981	-15,700	21.6	- 5,300	11.5

Source: See "Living conditions of the Palestinian people in the occupied Palestinian territories; report of the Secretary-General" (A/39/233-E/1984/79),

The policy of the occupying Powar uniformly effects men, women, youth and children as members of society. Despite countless resolutions of the Security Council, the General Assembly and other United Nations organs, emphasisimp the right of the Palestinian people to return to their homelqnd and the right of self-determination, calling for a:cessation of the; construction of settlements in the occupied territories (see, for example, General Assembly resolution; 35/79 C of 15 December 1983), the Government of Israel has been promulgating since 7 June 1967 a series of decrees, by which it has established a military administration for the West Bank and the Gaza Strip.* These Laws, particularly Decrees 1 and 2, constitute the basic for Israeli policy in the occupied territories.

The military administration has also reinstituted the Defence Emergency Laws of 1945, issued by the British Mandatory Government. These Laws enable the occupying Power to confiscate Arab lands and to prevent residents from returning to their village, and towns to claim their property, these laws and practices seriously affect the economic situation and living conditions of Palestinian families, often separating women and children from the male family members. The new income tax introduced by Israeli authorities in Gate end on the West Bank early in 1983, based on an estimate of all the property of Palestinian residents, including jewellery, furniture end the property of any sons, outside as well as in the territories, further diminished the living standard of many Palestinian families. People in the occupied territories are subject to two different judicial and local government systems. Civil law applies to the Israeli citizens; military law applies to Palestinians, their towns and villages, and is based on military administration and military orders, violations of which are tried by military Courts and cannot be appealed against.

The situation of Women has been aggravated under the Defence Emergency Laws, which have resulted in mass arrests, collective punishments, detentions without trial, deportations, and restrictions of freedom of association and expression. The life of the Palestinians in the occupied territories continues to be governed by these military regulations, since no new laws have been enacted to date.

1. Settlements

One of the first policy acts of the occupying Power was to confiscate Arab land cud create a network of settlements in which Israeli settlers reside. This policy, designed to force individual and mass transfers of the indigenous Arab population from the West Bank and Gaza, not only led to the continued strengthening and enlargements of existing settlements in 1983/84 but also to the illegal pursuit of the establishment of new settlements, whose, numbers are increasing continuously, despite international condemnation of Israeli settlements in the occupied territories as an obstacle to peace, for example in Security Council resolution 465 (1980) of March 1980 and funeral Assembly resolution ES-7/6 of 19 August 1982. In the period 1967-1982, 204 settlements were established in the occupied territories, including Jerusalem. An additional 83 were established between October 1982 and November 1983 or are under construction. The number of Israelis living in the settlements on the West Bank alone in 1984 was 35,000.

The settlements are primarily agricultural, though some are paramilitary and industrial, and they surround the major cities and villages in the West Bank and the Gaza Strip. They are often interconnected by water, electricity and communication and built mainly on high ground overlooking the countryside; their entrances are guarded to prevent Palestinian villagers from entering them. Recently, the Israeli occupying authorities have started a new phase of settlement policy by placing settlements within the central city of Hebron, surrounded by old, well-established Arab neighbourhoods. The Government of Israel has also announced its "Ben Porat Plan", a major feature of which is to demolish some of the camps and to relocate the refugees in proper houses in order to disperse Palestinians and to create a more homogeneous mosaic of Jewish settlements.

Dismantling the camps, which have become strongholds of Palestinian resistance, end disrupting Arab municipal communities, weakens women's everyday struggle against the assimilation and erosion of Palestinian national identity. The presence of Israeli citizens, who form a privileged group among the residents of the West Bank and the Gaza Strip, restricts communication and co-operation among the Palestinian people, adversely affects their social life and disrupts daily activities. The settlements are established in such a wanner that they fragment the demographic, geographical, economic and social unity of the occupied Arab territories and limit or impair the expansion of Palestinian towns and villages.

They hamper economic, social and cultural development, as well as diminishing the possibility of improving the status of women in all these spheres. The emergence of two societies subject to different legal systém:, with a different outlook, culture, religion and language, different customs, and differing standards in educational and health services and housing conditions causes deprivation, frustration and antagonism, and leads to violent incidents.

West Bank and Gaza Strip; Number of Settlements by Year of Establishment and Type of Settlement

Year	*Type of settlement*							
	Urban	*Community*	*Moshav*	*Kibbutz*	*Nahal*	*Centre*	*Park*	*Total*
1967-1970	6	-	5	6	-	2	1	20
1971-1973	5	-	6	1	1	-	-	13
1974-1976	-	4	6	-	-	1	-	11
1977	4	8	10	3	-	1	-	26
1978-1980	10	20	30	-	11	1	2	74
1981-1982	10	16	20		13	1	-	60
Total 1967-1982	35	48	77	10	25	6	3	204

Source: United Nations, Israeli Settlements in Gaza and the West Bank (including Jerusalem): their Nature and Purpose (1984), part two, p. 24.

The Israeli settlers have been granted permission to carry arms and to maintain law and order. There have recently been numerous instances of settlers, usually armed, entering the schools and disrupting classes or interfering in the refugee camps. The disruption of religious practices has assumed greater proportions in recent years; there have been acts of violence and Moslem and Christian religious sites have been desecrated. In 1984, two nuns were stabbed in the convent of the Russian Orthodox Church in Jerusalem.

The status of women is particularly affected by the diversion of natural water resources, the prohibition of the drilling of new wells by Palestinians and restrictions on the amount of water they are allowed to pump, because clean water is necessary for household use, for child care and for maintaining health and hygienic standards in the family. Curtailed electricity supplies create additional problems for them in carrying out household tasks and rearing children.

The fertile land is divided into small segments, rendering large-scale agricultural development difficult and restricting the sovereignty of the Arabs over-their own land. All these factors, have specifically negative effects on Palestinian women, for whom the family farm is a traditional source of livelihood and stability. The declining prospects for Palestinian farms seriously affect not only the economic status of women but also their social position and psychological well-being.

Losing a farm sometimes leads to separation of the family. According to UNRWA statistics for 1983 on registered Palestinian refugees, on the West Bank there were 27,226 female heads of household out of a total of 72,272 and in the Gaze Strip 14,567 out of a total of 72,296, a situation that creates many difficulties, since the majority of Palestinian women have not been prepared to live independently and to take decisions concerning every-day family life.

Oppressive Practices

Under the Defence Emergency Laws, activated on 7 June 1967, arrest, detention and other forms of oppression have continued to be applied to the Palestinian population: men, women and children alike. Examples of the oppressive practices by the military authorities in the occupied territories were reported by the Committee on the Exercise of the Inalienable Rights of the Palestinian People to have taken place between 1980: and 1984. In 1983, the military authorities responded to stone-throwing at vehicles by children and trainees on the West Bank by closing one

UNRWA vocational training centre for 48 days and three UNRWA schools for a period varying from 60 to 23 days.

There were also reports of the wounding of a young Palestinian at Jerusalem on 12 March 1983, and the subsequent beating of a Palestinian woman and her children who had come to his aid; of a break-in at the local school at the Shufat refugee camp by Israeli troops and attacks on students on the same day; of the closing of the Polytechnic Institute in retaliation for previous participation by students in anti-occupation demonstrations at Hebron, as well as at Al-Khalil University and schools at Halhoul, Yatte, Belt Sahour and Nablus; of continuing terrorization of the occupied population by the Israeli settlers at Yatte; and of Israeli occupation troops opening fire on Palestinian anti-occupation demonstrators — men, women and children alike — at Beit Sahour on 17 March 1983. In the period 1980-1984, restrictions on the population in the occupied territories increased, resulting in the dismissal of most of the elected municipal officials and the dissolution of the National Guidance Committee, which supervised socio-educational activity, some of its members, including female social activists, having been placed under house arrest. The restrictions caused further unrest, strikes in the municipalities and disruptions in the schools, involving the death of a few school children in the Gaza Strip.

The military authorities have imposed curfews in some camps and villages and restrictions on travel for selected residents. Palestinians have been also subjected to frequent security checks. Punitive demolition of the houses of those suspected or convicted of offences is continuing at an accelerated rate. In addition, the occupying authorities are carrying out a new punitive measure consisting in sealing houses or rooms with concrete. These forms of collective punishment affect equally all members of the family.

In 1983-84, residents of camps on the West Bank have suffered further serious hardships as a result of the blocking of camp entrances with bricks and cement by the Israeli authorities. In the Gaza Strip, 73 private rooms in Beach camp, owned by 35 Palestine families comprising over 200 persons, were demolished on the grounds that they contravened building regulations. The report of the Commissioner-General of the Unites Nations Relief Works Agency for Palestine Refugees in the Near East to the General Assembly at its thirty-ninth session provides further details. Furthermore, as a punitive measure in retaliation against families for acts said to have been committed by one or other of their members, the Israeli authorities demolished the housing of 12 refugee families in the Gaza Strip, resulting in 94 persons losing their homes. On the West Bank, two refugee shelters were demolished and several rooms in refugee shelters sealed.

West Bank and Gaza Strip: Number of Houses Demolished by the Occupying Authorities as a Punitive Measure, 1967-1982

Year	*Number of houses demolished*
1967	130
1968	140
1969	301
1970	191
1971	231
1972	35
1973	34
1974	61
1975	77

1976	24
1977	1
1978	2
1979	8
1980	24
1981	32
1982	55
Total	1,346

Source: See "Living conditions of the Palestinian People in the occupied Palestinian territories: report of the Secretary-General (A/39/233-E/1984/79)

Imprisonment and torture of Palestinian children on the West Bank and Gaza continues and inevitably affects not only the direct victim of these practices but also a whole new generation growing up under conditions of occupation.

Employment and Working Conditions

Since 1967, the West Bank and the Gaza Strip, as occupied territories, have registered a decline in their agricultural and economic development and the occupying Power has gradually incorporated their economy into that of Israel. These two factors, coupled with the never-ending expropriation of Palestinian lands and control of water resources by Israeli authorities, has led to a numbar of changes in the labour market that affect the economic status of women and change the existing pattern of women's employment.

In the period 1980-1984, Palestinian women from the occupied territories worked mainly in three categories of employment: as self-employed workers, as unskilled wage-workers in Israel and as employees in enterprises set up by Israelis in the occupied territories. The participation of women in the total labour force in 1980 was 18.7 per cent for the West Bank and 6.1 per cent for the Gaza Strip.

Self-employment: Self-employment, particularly through ownership of land, is still the most common form of women's work. Nearly two thirds of the female labour force on the West Bank, estimated at about 16,200, is self-employed. Approximately 90 per cent of the women are engaged in agriculture and mainly work on small family farms. It is estimated that nearly 45 per cent of the total agricultural work-force on the West Bank is female. The rest of the self-employed women work in small industries, on tasks such as sewing and embroidery. The reverse situation is found in the Gaza Strip, where only 8 per cent of the self-employed women are working in agriculture and two thirds are engaged in manufacturing. The fact that most of the Gaza Strip families are landless reduces the possibilities of work for women in traditional areas and results in a much lower participation of women in the labour force in the Gaza Strip than on the West Bank.

West Bank and Gaza Strip:
Distribution of Female Labour Force, 1980

	Women employed on the West Bank		*Women employed in the Gaza Strip*	
Occupation	*Number (thousands)*	*%*	*Number (thousands)*	*%*
Professional, technical, academic and related occupations	3.6	14.7	2.3	47.0
Administrators and managers	0.1	0.4	-	-
Clerical and related occupations	0.7	2.9	0.1	2.0
Sales occupations	0.5	2.0	0.2	4.1
Service occupations	1.0	4.1	0.3	6.1

Agricultural occupations	15.7	64.1	0.5	10.2
Skilled occupations in industry	2.5	10.2	1.4	28.6
Other occupations in industry and unskilled occupations	0.4	1.6	—	—
Total	24.5	100	4.9	100

Source: See TEAM/SP1/WP. 8.

Work for uses: Owing to a shortage of unskilled labourers, Israel began to employ Palestinians, including Palestinian women, from the occupied territories in 1968.* The flow of labour from the West Bank by 1981 reached 74,000 persons recruited through official channels. The actual number of Palestinians working in Israel is, however, much larger and covers those employed unofficially often including women and children working in seasonal agriculture.

Work in Israeli enterprises: In addition to being employed as migrant and agricultural workers, many women are employed in enterprises set up by Israelis in the occupied territories, which specialise in finishing goods imported from Israel. This is a prevalent practice in the garment industry. The wages received there are up to 50 per cent lower than wages for equivalent work in Israel. The comparative reluctance of women to move away has enabled entrepreneurs to depress the price of local female labour.

Working conditions: The majority of the Palestinian workers employed in Israel and in Israeli enterprises in the occupied territories work at the lower levels of the employment structure, in jobs that are mostly manual, unskilled and poorly paid. They have no job security and are employed on short-term work permits, which means that they are not entitled to unemployment benefits, compensation for illness etc. Palestinian women and children engaged on a short-term basis in Israel generally work under even more difficult conditions than Palestinian men, since they often work illegally. Many women and children are low-wage labourers engaged in seasonal work, harvesting crops or working in hotels and restaurants. They are exposed to various kinds of exploitation as well as to detention or interrogation, owing to their status as illegal workers, which prevents them from observing existing rules concerning work permits and staying off the work-site at night. Moreover, this type of work, which is contrary to the Palestinian tradition, is uprooting women from their traditional position in society, without giving them any guarantee of a permanent job or prospects for advancement. In addition, their absence (roe the house has adverse effects on the family and community life, on the education of children and on the preservation of traditions.

Education

The public educational system in the occupied territories covers elementary, preparatory and secondary· education provided by private, government schools run by UNRWA in conjunction with the United Nations Economic and Social Organisation (UNESCO). The UNRWA/UNESCO school system for refugee children goes up to the ninth grade. In 1983/84, enrolment on the West Bank totalled 39,593, pupils in 98 schools served by 1,281 teachers, and in the Gaza Strip 82,301 pupils in 143 schools, with a teaching force of 2,217. Fifty UNRWA/UNESCO schools on the West Bank and 92 schools in the Gaza Strip operated on a double shift. The double-shift system is, generally recognised as detrimental to the child's development. The much shorter school day also makes life more difficult for mothers, particularly in many cases where children from the same family attend different shifts. A lack of funds for capital expenditure has limited UNRWA/UNESCO school construction to the essential minimum.

The public educational system on the West Bank is based on the Jordanian system and in the Gaza Strip on the Egyptian system. Since 1967, both systems have been under the control of the military authorities. Since 1969, all textbooks newly prescribed or revised by host Governments have been submitted to UNESCO for approval before they are procured for UNRWA schools. On the West Bank and in the Gaza Strip, where Jordanian and Egyptian schoolbooks are used respectively, books are subject to the further requirement of a special import permit from the Israeli authorities. For example, for the academic year 1983/84 there were nine textbooks for the West Bank and 11 textbooks for Gaza that had been approved by UNESCO bet refused import permits by the occupying authorities. These restrictions referred especially to Palestinian history, geography and culture, hindering the transmission of knowledge of heritage, national history and tradition to Palestinian children and youth.

West Bank and Gaza Strip: Distribution of Refugee Pupils

	Number of Pupils	
Type of school	*West Bank*	*Gaza Strip*
Number of pupils in elementary classed at UNRWA schools:[a]		
Boys	13,122	32,282
Girls	15,172	28,677
Total	28,294	60,959

Number of pupi!s in preparatory clauses at UNRWA schools[a]		
Boys	5,417	11,099
Girls	5,882	10,243
Total	11,299	21,342
Number of refugee pupils in government schools	23,965	18,415
Number of refugee pupils in private schools	1,246	—
Total	25,111	18,415
Total number if refugee pupils known to receive education	64,704	1,00,716

Source: Based on the report of the Commissioner-General of the United Nations Relief and Works Agency for Palestine Refugees is the Near East to the General Assembly at its thirty-ninth session (*Official Records of the General Assembly, Thirty-ninth Session, Supplement No. 13* (A/39/13), p. 52.

On the West Bank 98 UNRWA schools, with 1,281 teachers, is the Gaza Strip, 143 UNRWA schools, with 2,217 teachers.

According to Israeli statistics, there were 13,988 children in kindergartens in 1981. Host of those children attended kindergartens sponsored by private institutions and Palestinian community organisations, although UNRWA operated 16 pre-school centres funded by the American Friends Service Committee in the Gaza Strip. A Serious shortage of this type of service is particularly felt by women who for financial reasons must work and have no place to leave their children.

In the period 1980-1984, there was a steady increase in overall enrolment, as well as in female enrolment at all levels of education. Male enrollment is higher at the

Preparatory and secondary levels, but women nevertheless perform better in the secondary examination (*tawjihi*). In 1981, of 13,489 students who completed Secondary education, 4,688 (34 per cent of the total) were females. At the university level, female enrolment represents more than 40 per cent of the total. This could be due to the high male drop-out rate in the 13-16 year age-group as a result of the need to work and to assist the family, and to the emigration or detention of the male youth.

Female College and University Enrolment in the Occupied Territories

	Number of students		
Institution	*Male*	*Female*	*Total*
Birzeit University	1,209	680	1,889
An-Najah University	1,580	942	2,522
Bethlehem University	626	522	1,148
Hebron University	637	664	1,301
Islamic University (Gaza)	1,311	367	1,878
Abu-Dis College of Sciences	28	32	60
College of Religious Fundamentals	139	98	237
Arab College for Medical Professions	14	138	157
Total	5,544	3,643	9,187

Source: TEAM/SD1/WP. 15, p. 46.

Academic life and teaching processes have continued to be seriously affected by restrictions on academic freedoms, programmes and research under the military administration. In 1983, there were numerous instances of universities being closed and teachers who refused to sign written undertakings linked to the military orders being expelled, cases of collective punishment and arrest of male and female students, and of soldiers opening fire at demonstrations, killing some students, including one female student at Hebron.

There are four types of vocational training institutions on the West Bank and in the Gaza Strip providing technical training to Palestinians, only two of which, the UNRWA/ UNESCO training centres and the private training centres, have large numbers of women trainees.

The Ramallah Women's Training Centre on the West Bank, run by UNRWA, offers two-year courses in secretarial and office skills, nursery and kindergarten training, administrative skills, medical technology, sewing, cosmetics and beauty care. In 1982-83, 165 graduates completed training in secretarial work (44); as laboratory technicians (19); in dressmaking (11); in clothing production (25); as infant leaders (39); in home and institutional management (15) and in hairdressing (12).

The private training centres have a low female enrolment, but many private Palestinian institutions, which have organised practical work-related short-term courses, train a large number of women. The secondary vocational public schools, which offer three-year courses in welding; carpentry, heating, radio and television repair, and the government training institutions have in practice an exclusively male enrolment.

UNRWA runs special activity programmes for refugee women and girls to develop the skills they need to raise their standard of living. Fourteen women's activity centres offer a varied afternoon programme of instruction in crafts, health education and child care, literacy classed and cultural and sporting activities. Two new centres were opened in the Gaza Strip in 1983/84 and work has begun on an extension to a third, which had been halted by the Israeli authorities. A more formal one-year course is offered at the 20 UNRWA sewing centres, in dressmaking, and hand and machine embroidery. At the end of the course, the successful graduates are awarded a diploma that helps them obtain employment.

The work of UNRWA schools, vocational courses and training programmes during the period 1980-1984 was disrupted by unrest and demonstrations, which began in the autumn of 1981 and continued for the reminder of the period, rsulting in the harassment of school pupils and teachers. For example, in December 1981, in one UNRWA centre, 246 female trainees and 6 staff were temporarily detained; 20 trainees were brought to trial and given suspended sentences.

In 1983, the Israeli military authorities entered the three UNRWA training centres on the West Bank (including the Ramallah Women's Training Centre). Two of them were closed for a few months, which affected the educational process.

Health

According to the report of the Special Committee of Experts Appointed to Study the Health Conditions of the Inhabitants of the Occupied Territories, submitted to the thirty-seventh World Health Assembly, health conditions in the occupied territories cannot be separated from the general socio-economic framework and its repercussions on the community and on individual men, women and children, manifested, for example, by the deterioration of mental well-being and an increase of mental diseases, particularly neuroses. The health conditions of the Arab population in the occupied territories, including Jerusalem, and the health system itself have remained unchanged. The management of the health programmes and budget is the task of Israeli authorities.

The improvements that have been made in the health services are far from being adequate to meet the needs of a growing population and to reflect the advances in medical science. As noted by the World Health Organisation (WHO) Special Committee of Experts, the insufficient number of hospital beds, the high cost of hospitalisation, antiquated diagnostic equipment, old buildings experiencing problems with electricity, heating and laundry facilities, and a shortage of essential medical equipment, staff and drugs remain serious obstacles to health protection. Although they effect the population as a whole, health conditions have greater significance for women, who bear and rear the children and look after the health and nutrition of the family.

There is also a higher percentage of adult women than of men in the occupied territories. The shortage of qualified staff in the medical professions, particularly specialists in mental disease and in the control of hygiene, poses a serious obstacle to the improvement of health care, which specifically affects women and children. At the same time, many male and female graduates, especially physicians, can find no employment in the public health care system of the occupied territories and either remain out of work or are forced to take other jobs.

The international community has endeavoured to overcome the shortage of qualified health staff, especially for mother and child care. UNRWA is carrying out extensive in-service training for its own staff; within the framework of a WHO-sponsored training and fellowship programme for health personnel, several fellowships are awarded annually to UNRWA personnel for post-graduate training courses. UNRWA also provides at its vocational training institutions paramedical courses to enable refugee students to become assistant pharmacists, laboratory technicians and public health inspectors. (In 1982/83, 39 girls trainees were attending paramedical courses at the Ramallah Women's Training Centre.)

On completing their training graduates may join UNRWA or the UNRWA Placement Office may help them to find employment in the region. In view of the fact that inflation is making it difficult for ordinary people in the occupied territories to obtain essential food, the WHO special committee or Experts during its 1984 mission paid specific attention to the question of nutrition as one of the most important factors affecting human life and, specifically, the health of women and children. The Committee was unable to make an objective evaluation of the nutritional status of the population in the absence of any statistics.

Nevertheless, it drew attention to birth-weight as the principal Indicator of the nutritional status of a community. Birth-weight as recorded in hospitals was below 2.5 kilograms for 6.8 per cent of the children born in 1983 on the West Bank and for 5.2 per cent of those born in Gaza. It also drew attention to the protein-calorie malnutrition commonly encountered in paediatric practices, in many cases requiring hospitalisation, which affects 7 per cent of the children aged 0-3 years In the refugee camps.

Preventive and curative medical care — both in-patient and out-patient— and dental services comprise an important part of the UNRWA health programme for Palestinian refugee women and children. They are provided by 32 UNWRA health units on the West Bank and nine in the Gets Strip, 22 Government clinics in the Gate Strip and one voluntary agency clinic on the West Bank, private health institutes and special health teams for children. UNRWA also operates dental clinics and central and clinical laboratories. On the West Bank, it runs a small hospital at Qalqiliya with 36 beds and, jointly with the local Public Health Department, a tuberculosis hospital with 70 beds in the Gate Strip. Other hospital and specialist services are subsidised by government, university and private health institutions.

With the changing demography of the refugee population, there is now a higher incidence of degenerative diseases, notably diabetes mellitus. A recent survey shows that this incidence is highest among middle—aged women who have borne more than one child. UNRWA is strengthening its specialist clinics to improve the diabetic service. The UNRWA nutrition rehabilitation clinics are directed particularly at the supervision, protection and promotion of the nutritional status of the most vulnerable groups of refugees: infants, pre-school and elementary school children, pregnant and nursing mothers, non-hospitalised tuberculosis patients and members of hardship families, the data collected through routine surveillance of the growth and development of children under five years of age who attend the child-health clinics show that their nutritional condition is well-maintained.

Nutritionally balanced midday meals are offered daily at UNRWA supplementary feeding centres to all children under six years of age and upon medical recommendation to older ones, sick adults end hardship cases. The nutritional status of the six-to-eight-year-olds may, however, be at risk and UNRWA would extend its supplementary feeding programme to this age-group if the funding were available. In addition to the UNRWA expanded programme on immunisation against the six target diseases — tuberculosis, diphtheria, pertussis, tetanus, poliomyelitis and measles — and the UNRWA environmental sanitation programme, the nutrition support of vulnerable groups and the health education activities among refugee communities contributes to the effective control of communicable diseases.

UNRWA provides maternal and child health services — pre-natal, natal and infant and child care — at its health units, supported by specialist and hospital referral services. In 1983-84 the Gaza Strip had six maternity wards attached to the UNRWA health centres; 28 per cent of the deliveries took place in these facilities, 48 per cent in the two government hospitals and 24 per cent at horns, usually with the aid of traditional birth attendants. On the West Bank, 70 per cent of the refugee children were delivered in hospitals and camp maternity centres and 30 per cent were born at home.

	West Bank	*Gaza Strip*
Pre-natal services		
Number of pre-natal clinics	24	9
Number of newly registered pregnant women	5,098	14,024
Average monthly attendance	1,514	4,370
Number of serological tests for syphilis (STS)	0	5,387
Number of positive cases	0	13
Number of home visits	48	272
Natal care		
Number of deliveries registered	5,769	13,370
At home	1,731	3,248
In camp maternity centres	86	3,670
In hospitals	3,932	6,452
Number of live births	5,731	13,377
Number of still births	64	138

Number of maternal deaths	1	0
Number of home visits (post-natal)	4,639	38,787
Child health care		
Number of child health clinics	23	9
Number of infants aged 0-1 year registered	4,812	13,756
Child health care (continued)		
Average monthly attendance	4,421	10,180
Number of children aged 1-2 years registered	5,315	11,555
Average bimonthly attendance	5,145	10,117
Number of children aged 2-3 years registered	5,066	10,298
Average trimonthly attendance	4,947	9,034

Source: United Nations Relief and Works Agency for Palestine Refugees in the Near East *Annual Report of the Director of Health. 1983*, p. 28,

Average incidence of underweight in infants and children registered in child health clinics

	First degree		*Second degree*		*Third degree*		*First, second and third degree*	
Area	*No.*	*%*	*No.*	*%*	*No.*	*%*	*No.*	*%*
Number and percentage of underweight infants aged 0-1 years								
West Bank	204	4.2	67	1.4	12	0.2	283	5.8
Gaza Strip	638	4.6	303	2.2	35	0.3	976	7.1
Number and percentage of underweight children (1-2 years)								
West Bank	184	1.6	56	0.7	3	0.2	243	2.5
Gaza Strip	739	6.4	397	3.4	18	0.2	1 154	10.0

Source: United Nations Relief and Works Agency for Palestine Refugees in the Near East, *annual Resort of the Director of Health, 1983*. pp. 29-30, table 8.8.

Family planning services are an integral part of the maternal and child health programme in the Gaza Strip, where a special programme on health and family life is included in the school curriculum for girls in the third preparatory class. The school health services at UNRWA schools were reorganised from the beginning of the school year 1983/84 with a view to developing an effective programme to monitor the health of pupils throughout the school cycle.

The extremely harsh life and poor health conditions in the refugee camps make their residents especially vulnerable to diseases and infections. Most of the camps have no covered water-supply system, the sewers are open and the toilets for common use are few in number and unsanitary. UNRWA is therefore paying special attention to the health protection of women and children, who are the ones most exposed to health hazards. UNRWA, with the co-operation of host Governments, municipalities and local councils, continues to provide basic community sanitation services to Palestinian refugees it camps. The services comprise the provision of adequate quantities of potable water, disposal of wastes, drainage of rainwater and control of insect and rodent vectors or diseases. Indoor water taps have been provided to all shelters in Bureij, Maghazi and Nuseirat camps on the Gaza Strip and private water connection schemes for Deir Ammar camp on the West Bank are being developed. The refuse collection system is being improved in the Gaza Strip. Surveys of sanitary facilities in the schools have been carried out and school health committees are being established to supervise major renovation projects.

Health education workers collaborate with camp health committees and other UNRWA staff members in health centres, schools and welfare centres to promote goods health practices. In particular, they give classes for women attending sewing centres. The medical and health preventive services and activities have suffered in the years 1981-1984 from frequent disturbences on the West Bank and in the Gaza Strip. The raids on camps have hindered efforts to improve their infrastructure, numerous acts by the police and military have affected the work of maternal and child health centres and other indoor and outdoor services for women and children.

Insufficient water supply, pollution of the drinking water, low standards of housing, sewage and waste disposal and the presence of rats remain the essential-problems of environmental health in the occupied territories. Gastro-enteritis, linked to environmental sanitation and community behaviour, continues to be a public health problem. Some 20 per cent of the Palestinian people in the occupied territories live in housing units with a density of three persons to a room, and for approximately 50 per cent of the population the average family household consists of seven or more members. Although electrical and plumbing facilities and the availability of running water have improved over the years, in some areas these basic services are inadequate. The housing problem is particularly difficult for women in the low-income categories, who are in need of adequate space and sanitary and cooking facilities to take proper care of their children and families. The occupying authorities have not taken any measures to help lower-income groups of the local population to acquire adequate housing. Absence of construction to replace substandard housing, restrictive practices as regards permits for private, public or municipal constructions and the transfer of funds from abroad have prevented Palestinian communities from improving the municipal services or providing new housing facilities.

Palestinian women's organisations date back as far as 1921. They have developed relief programmes, shelters for disabled persons, educational programmes for poor children, health and literacy centres, Workshops, and mother and child care units. They have also developed self-reliance, vocational training and income-generating programmes for women, relief programmes for refugees and committees (or the preservation Of heritage and culture. The broad spectrum of social activities undertaken by the contemporary Palestinian women's organisations are aimed at raising the living conditions and status of women in particular and of the Palestinian community in general. Among the women's organisations officially registered as charitable organisations are the following:

Names of Officially Registered Women's Charitable Societies

Name	*Location*	*Date of official registration*
Jerusalem governorate		
Ri'ayat al-Tifi Society	Ramallah	1945
Rawdat al-Zuhur Society (The Kindergarten of Flower)	Jerusalem	1932
Arab Women's Union - Beit Sahur	Beit Sahur	1936
Sayidat-al-Bishara Greek Catholic Women's Society (Lady of the Annunciation Greek Catholic Women's Society)	Jerusalem	1936
Arab Women's Union - Jerusalem	Jerusalem	1957
Old People's Home Society	Jerusalem	1951
Armenian Charitable Society for Women.	Jerusalem	1958
Jericho Women's Charitable Society	Jericho	1963
Arab Women's Society	Jerusalem	1965
Arab Women's Union - Bethlehem	Bethlehem	1965

Arab Women's Union - al-Birch	al-Birch	1965
Arab Women's Union - Ramallah	Ramallah	1965
Bisat al-Ruhman Greek Orthodox Women's Society	Bethlehem	1965
Dar-al-Tifl al-Arabi (Arab Children's Home)	Jerusalem	1965
Hamilat-al-Tib Greek Orthodox Society Bethlehem	1965	
Hamilat-al-Tib Greek Orthodox Society for the Relief of the Miserable Sick	Jerusalem	1965
In'ash al-Usra (Society for Family Revival	al-Bireh	1965
Ri'ayat al-Tifl Women's Society (Women's Society for the Care of Children)	Jerusalem	1965
Women's Revival Society	Ramallah	1965
Bir Zeit Women's Charitable Society	Birzeit	1970
Society for the Training of Young Women	Bethlehem	1973
Muslim Young Women's Society	Jerusalem	1979
Nablus governorate		
Jordanian Red Crescent Society-Tulkarm	Tulkarm	1947
Arab Women's Union - Tulkarm	Tulkarm	1953
Society for the Care of Children and the Guidance of Mothers	Nablus	1954
Al-Mirabitat Charitaple Society	Qalqilia	1960
Arab Orphan's Home - Tulkarm	Tulkarm	1961
Charitable Society of Huwara	Huwara	1963
Arab Women's Union - Nablus	Nablus	1965
Charitable Society of Burin	Burin	1965
Women's Charitable Society of Salfit	Ṣalfit	1965
Charitable Society of Burqin	Burqin	1971

Charitable Society of Jenin	Jenin	1976
Women's Charitable Society of Anabta	Anabta	
Hebron governorate		
Women's Charitable Society of Halhoul	Halhoul	1964
Women's Charitable Society of Hebron	Hebron	1965
The Society for the Revival of Village Girls	Doura	1965
Women's Society for Social Development of Arroub	Arroub	1973

The resolution of the Palestinians problem remains one of the main international political issues for the numerous organs and divisions of the United Nations and the specialised agencies in the political, social, economic and humanitarian spheres. In connection with the humanitarian aspects of the Palestinians problem, international oganisations have been and are undertaking two kinds of activities: (a) the preparation of various studies and reports, and the convening of conferences that bring the attention of the world community to the situation of the Palestinian people in the occupied Arab territories, all of which serve as a basis for the preparation of their assistance programmes; and (b) the directing of humanitarian assistance to the Palestinian people by and through various United Nations offices and the specialised agencies. The mandate for assistance is based on Economic and Social Council resolution 2026 (LXI) of 4 August 1976, in which the Council invited United Nations bodies to intensify their efforts to identify social and economic needs and requested their co-operation in establishing and implementing projects to ensure improvement of the social and economic conditions of the Palestinian people. Another form of activity was initiated by the Committee on the Exercise of the Inalienable Rights of the Palestinian People, which convened a series of regional seminars on various aspects of the inalienable rights of the Palestinian people during the period from 1981 to 1983. The Committee also organises every rear the International Day of solidarity with the Palestinian People. Under the guidance of the Committee, the Division, for Palestinian Rights has prepared a number of studies md publications on the issue. The Palestinian problem was also discussed at the regional preparatory meetings for the International Conference on the Question of Palestine, held at Geneva from 29 August to 7 September 1983.

The Latin American Regional Preparatory Meeting, held at Managua, was the only such meeting to pay specific attention to the question of Palestinian women; it requested the secretariat of the conference to prepare a study on the conditions of women and children in all the occupied territories and to encourage various non-governmental organisations to investigate that matter as well as to undertake relevant joint action with their Palestinian counterparts. At the International Conference, various aspects of the Palestinian problem were analysed.

The relevant conclusions and recommendations are contained in the Geneva Declaration on Palestine and the Programme of Action for the Achievement of Palestinian Rights. Among the various activities undertaken by the United Nations system to assist Palestinian women, those of UNRWA are particularly noteworthy, focusing as they do on measures to implement the Programme of Action for the Second Half of the United Nations Decade for Women; Equality, Development and Peace.

These measures are mainly concentrated on education, relief, health and vocational training in the entire school system. UNRWA is continuing its special training programmes, mainly attended by women, on the feeding of nutritionally vulnerable groups, including mothers and small children.

It organises, women's and youth activities centres, modest activity programmes for pre-school children, youth and women, a welfare counselling service and adult craft training courses. The UNRWA relief programme is mainly concentrated on the most needy among the refugee population, including widows and orphans. Supplementary feeding is provided for young children, pregnant woman and nursing mothers, environmental sanitation is provided and families in special need are given help in repairing their houses. UNESCO plays an important role in education, and shares with UNRWA the task of preparing school curricula and programmes (as well as teacher training and vocational training) for the entire school system. It is continuing to second 20 specialists (men and women) to the UNRWA/UNESCO Education Department to plan and supervise the operation of schools and technical and vocational training centres situated on the West Bank and the Gaza Strip.

Steps have been taken to ensure the effective implementation of resolution 14.1 on educational and cultural institutions in the occupied Arab territories adopted by the General Conference of UNESCO at its twenty-first session in 1983, to help the population of these territories to exercise their right to education and culture. In view of the specific role of Palestinian women in the preservation of the national tradition and heritage, it is of special relevance for them. The United Nations Children's Fund (UNICEF) provides its major assistance, comprising health services, vocational and pre-school training, to mothers and children.

WHO contributes to the organisation of health services, especially in the field of professional training and preventive and curative courses and activities. WHO is also responsible for the technical supervision of the UNRWA health services and provides sir senior staff who manage the services. Traditionally, WHO also studies the health conditions of the inhabitants of the occupied territories, drawing the attention of the international community in its annual report to the possibilities of improving those conditions. UNDP has developed several projects related to the promotion of pre-primary, technical, vocational and higher education, as well as assistance to primary and secondary education in the Gaza Strip and training programmes in agricultural development. The two projects on women's institutions and children's institutions are of special interest to women. Its future programme of assistance also foresees the training of specialists in glass and ceramic engineering technology and assistance to women's institutions.

In accordance with Economic and Social Council resolution 1983/43 and General Assembly resolution 38/145, UNDP has set up a Special Programme of Assistance to the Palestinian, People, which is centered in the West Bank and the Gaza Strip. The United Nations Conference on Trade and Development (UNCTAD) provides in its 1983 report entitled "Palestine: options for development" a broad evaluation of the potential for and constraints on the economic and social development of Palestinian people in the occupied territories and directives for the comprehensive survey on this subject TD/B/960). Pursuant to resolution 146 (VI) of 2 July 1983, adopted by the General Conference of UNCTAD at its sixth session, the UNCTAD secretariat is setting up a special economic unit to monitor and investigate the policies of the Israeli occupying authorities hampering the economic development of the occupied Palestinian territories.

The International Labour Office designated an expert who participated in the preparation of a project designed to promote the vocational training opportunities offered by Palestinian women's institutions and community development centres. The project identified the following objectives to be pursued: technical assistance for the development and marketing of handicraft products, the evaluation of the social service needs of the community development centres, the granting of fellowships in the fields of administration, social work, community development and vocational training, the promotion of basic education programmes and the acquisition of income-producing skills.

The International Labour Office indicated its willingness to collaborate with UNDP in elaborating project documents concerting the provision of suitable assistance to Palestinian women in its spheres of competence, such as the promotion of long-term vocational training facilities at more advanced levels (technical schools for girls on the West Bank), the promotion of vocational training courses in income-producing skills (at the elementary and intermediate levels), the reinforcement and expansion of the educational activities of the best organised and most effective women's organisations and support of handicraft production activities experiencing difficulties or threatened with disappearance. In the context of its programme of work and priorities for 1983/84 the Economic Commission for Western Asia (ECWA) carried out numerous activities related to the situation of Palestinian people, including publication of summary data for 1983, reflecting among other things, demographic changes in the occupied territories.

The Commission is also preparing a study on food security in the occupied territories, which deals with the development of food production and consumption on the

West Bank and in the Gaza Strip since the Israeli occupation, in order to recommend the ways of promoting food production and raising nutritional standards under prevailing conditions. The Food and Agriculture Organisation of the United Nations, the United Nations Industrial Development Organisation, and the Commission on Human Rights have also mentioned in various reports the assistance they are providing to Palestinian women. To conclude, it is worth mentioning

5

Women in Bangladesh

> "In a country well governed, poverty is something to be ashamed of. In a country badly governed, wealth is something to be ashamed of."
>
> —*Confucius*

Bangladesh as a sovereign nation-state came into existence only in 1971. The position of women in Bangladesh is similar to colonial Bengali society. It is remarkable that despite being Muslim dominated country, Bangladesh can boast of having two women prime ministers—Begam Sheikh Hasina and Begum Khaleda Zia. In the field of literature many women writers have made debut; Taslima Nasreen is one among them.

In the following pages we have made an attempt to portray the actual position of women of Bangladesh.

It is difficult to write about the women of Bangladesh. Little published material is available on women. Statistical data are outdated because the last census was taken in 1961. The vast majority of Bangladesh's 35 million women live in *purdah,* and little is being said or written about their problems. This lack of data on women is partially explained by the difficulties that researchers (usually male) face in studying women in a *purdah*-dominated society.

Additionally, as women are nonvisible and unorganised, their problems are not articulated and hence they fail to draw the attention of researchers. But the fact that nothing is being written about the problems of women in Bangladesh does not mean that the problems do not exist. Indeed the women of Bangladesh are among the most oppressed in the world. This paper attempts to highlight this oppression and to analyse some of the problems they face today.

Rural and Urban Women

To describe the lifestyles of women in Bangladesh, one has to distinguish between those of rural and urban women. The overwhelming majority of Bangali women are rural; only about 5 per cent of the population is urbanised. While most of the rural women can be broadly classified as traditional, not all urban women can be called modern. If modernity is defined in terms of literacy, urbanisation, and adoption of a modern occupation, then only a small fraction of Bangali women can be classified as modern. Of 35 million women in Bangladesh, only 1.75 million are urban; of these urban women a mere 32 per cent are literate and only about 1.27 per cent adopt a modern occupation. As modern women constitute a miniscule minority of Bangali women, it is useful to describe in some detail the lifestyle of rural women who form the mass of the women in Bangladesh. If generalisations are ever to be made about the women of Bangladesh, it has to be done in terms of the rural women.

Rural Women

A brief description of a rural woman's life from birth to death facilitates an understanding of her lifestyle. In the rural areas the birth of a girl is rarely celebrated by parents and relatives, unless she happens to be the first daughter after four or five sons. That usually no *azan* [call for prayer] is given when a girl is born symbolises the community's disinterest in the girl's arrival. From early childhood on, girls are made fully conscious of the feeling that, unlike their brothers, they are liabilities. Girls are taught the two virtues—patience and sacrifice—of ideal Bangali womenhood. They also learn to accept the essentially inferior status of women in society. As girls grow up they perceive the preferential treatment given to the male members of the family, and they are told that getting less of everything and not complaining about it is the ideal behavior of good women.

In a *milieu* of scarcity, whatever is available—food, clothing, or opportunities for education and health care—is offered first to the men. If the family can afford good food i.e. meat or milk, the father and sons have the first and major share. If the family has enough resources to send children to school, boys get preference over girls, even if the girls are brighter. From her childhood a girl is trained to fit into the only socially acceptable role, that of wife and mother. By the time a girl reaches the age of five or six, her mother has produced two or three additional children; and the young girl has to look after them. She also helps her mother in other households chores, i.e. looking, cleaning, sewing, etc. In rural areas few girls are sent to school. According to the 1961 census, only 21.9 per cent of rural females between the ages 5 to 14 (compared to 46.7 per cent of males) were enrolled in school. Girls are given some schooling only by economically and socially established families. And that schooling usually Consists of learning to read and recite the *Quran* [the Holy Book] and four or five years of formal school attendance. The major purpose of formal schooling is Very similar to that of the girl's informal learning at home i.e. training her to he a good wife and mother.

A girl's stock in the marriage market goes up if she has some formal schooling (Ahmad 1966). Educated men prefer wives who can at least read and write letters and keep basic accounts. "Respectable" families in rural areas therefore give their daughters some formal schooling so that they can be married to educated men employed in urban areas. Village girls usually drop out of school after the fifth or sixth grade. Only 1.7 per cent of rural women above the age of fifteen are enrolled in school, compared to 20.8 per cent of men. Girls discontinue schooling at an early age for two main reasons. First, by the time a girl is in the fifth or sixth grade, she has completed basic training in reading, writing, and arithmetic, and any further education is regarded as unnecessary, if not harmful for a happy married life. Second, after she reaches the age of 12 or 13, a girl has to drop out of school for *purdah* considerations. Few villages have high schools for girls, and the village *samaj* frowns upon girls attending coeducational schools after they have reached puberty. Also because many villages do not have boys' schools, girls' enrollment rigidly enforced outside her own village (Ahmed 1966).

While it is difficult for a girl to study in a boys' high school in her own village, it is nearly impossible for her to go to a neighboring village to study. In rural areas it is customary for girls to go in *purdah* when they reach puberty But even before that, a girl is made aware of the two separate worlds of men and women. A woman's world is her home, while the man's world is outside the home. Separation of the two worlds is enforced by the pervasive *purdah* system. Women perform tasks at home (cooking, cleaning, nursing children, sewing, etc.), and men negotiate with the outside world (working in the fields, shopping etc.)

Only in very rare cases does a man help his wife in her household tasks, and few women work in the fields, no matter how poor the family is. Here Muslim society in Bangladesh differs from other Muslim countries, e.g. Indonesia, where women work freely in the field and in the market place. However, Bangali rural women do share in tasks that involve earning family income. Women clean and husk rice, prepare fuel, make sugar, and tend the kitchen garden, but their rile in earning family income ins never acknowledge. Farming is a "two-person" occupation (Papanek 1973) where the wife's role is non-paid and non-recognised. Thus while the two worlds of men and women are interdependent, a woman's world is always regarded as inferior to the man's world. The rigidity of *purdah* observance, like the extent of schooling, depends very much on the socioeconomic status of the family. An easy index of the rising socioeconomic status of the family is the increasing rigidity of *purdah* observance. Economic status and *purdah* observance are correlated because only prosperous families can afford to put their women in *purdah*. *Purdah* observance involves two kinds of restrictions on women's movements (Papanek 1971). The first is spatial: women are confined within the walls of their homes, a separate women's wing, separate tank for women's bathing and cleaning facilities, and separate toilet facilities for women.

The second type of restriction allows a woman to move out of her home, but only if she is veiled in *burqah* [tent-like veiled clothing for women] or travels in veiled transports (carts, boats, or rickshaws with heavy curtains drawn around them). To ensure spatial restriction on women's mobility, the family has to be relatively wealthy, so that it can allocate enough living. The second category of restriction also requires money. Only rich farmers can afford to buy *burqah* for their women; average rural women have only one or two saris. In poorer rural families, the women have to leave their households and go to the houses of rich farmers to fetch water, to bathe, and to work as part-time household help. When leaving their houses, these women cover their heads with their sari to. symbolise their, *purdah* observance. And when they visit relatives in the neighboring villages,' they go walking in the evening and use umbrellas as veils.

Thus, while the rigidity of *purdah* observance varies among families, at puberty all girls are required to start observing some *purdah,* whether total seclusion at home or imposition of some restrictions on contact with men. At puberty, not only are girls put in *purdah* but their marriages are also arranged by their families. In rural areas girls are usually married between the ages of 12 and 15. Girls are married early because by 11 or 12 they complete all the informal and formal training necessary for their only socially acceptable roles—those of housewife and mother. Furthermore, after a girl reaches puberty she is regarded as "vulnerable," needing "shelter," and the safest course open to her family is to arrange a marriage for her so that she can move into a permanent shelter (Papanek 1871).

Marriages are always arranged, and the father and other male members of the family have the dominant say in the matter. As the marriage arrangement requires negotiations with the outside world, it is handled by the male guardians of the girl (Ahmed 1966).

In Muslim marriage, a girl's consent is mandatory, but the consent is a mere formality. After her marriage, a girl moves to her husband's household. In the first few years of marriage, her position is very insecure. In her husband's house, a bride has to observe a stricter purdah, her mobility is even more curtailed, her work load increases, and the two virtues of Bangali womanhood—patience and sacrifice—instilled in her as a child, are put to a hard test. Her position is inferior to that of the other women of her husband's house, i.e. her mother-in-law and sister-in-law. The only way she can get security in her husband's household is by producing a male heir.

The more male children she has, the greater is her security and acceptance. On the average, a rural woman has eleven or twelve pregnancies. She may have one or two miscarriages, two or three of her children may die young, and Six or seven children may survive. She has little control over her body the decision to have children is totally her husband's. Rarely does a rural woman practice any form of birth control. A survey in Comilla indicated that after six years of widespread publicity about family planning, only about 4 per cent of women practiced some measures of birth control (Stoeckel and Chowdhury 1973).

Abortion as a means of birth control is sometimes practiced by the poorer section of the rural population but it is considered a sin. By the time a woman reaches the age of thirty, she is often a grand-mother and is regarded as an old woman. Divorce and remarriage are more frequent in rural areas, especially among poor farmers. According to one study of a village in Comilla, approximately 16.5 per cent of all marriages ended in divorce (Peter Bertocci, personal communications). In socially established families, divorce is frowned upon. A divorced woman, if she is young, is usually remarried, because an unattached woman, be she single, widowed, or divorced, has no social standing. Additionally she is a financial burden.

Young widows are also remarried, sometimes to their brothers-in-law to keep the family property intact. After a certain age, however, it is difficult for widows and divorced women to get married. *The master survey of agriculture,* published in 1961, listed a sharp increase in the number of widowed females after the age of 34, with no such corresponding increase in the number of widowed males, which only indicates that while Bangali men can and do remarry at all ages, women can not (East Pakistan Bureau of Statistics 1961).

If a widow or a divorced woman remains unmarried, she has to live under the guardianship of either her father or brother, or father-in-law or brother-in-law. In short, a woman is never regarded as capable of taking care of herself. Before marriage her father is her guardian, after marriage her husband takes that role, and after her husband's death her son becomes her guardian.

Urban Women

In urban areas, there are sharp differences in the lifestyles of various categories of women. Here we would distinguish between two: working-class and middle-class women. There is a third group of westernised women, but they are small-in number and play a marginal role in society.

The lifestyle of urban working-class women is not very different from that of rural women, the only difference being the relaxation of *purdah* observance in an urban setting. The majority of urban working-class women are new migrants to cities and they maintain close rural ties. As in rural areas, the birth of a girl is unwelcome and the early socialisation process is very similar.

Girls from working-class families are also made aware of the separate worlds of men and women, though their housing is conducive to relaxation of *purdah* observance. From childhood, working-class girls are trained to be housewives and mothers. They have to carry the major burden of household chores, including care of baby brothers and sisters, because their mothers go outside to work. The literacy and school enrollment rates among working-class women are low. Most girls leave school after fifth or sixth grade.

The drop-out rate is high partly because the family cannot afford to send the children to school and partly because women's education in working-class families is not customary. Working-class women are married early, ordinarily by the age of 15 or 16. Marriages are usually arranged by parents, but as there is a greater scope for contact between the sexes, some love matches do take place. Divorce and remarriage are frequent.

Like rural women, urban working-class women have little say over such a vital matter as the decision to have children. They have nearly as many pregnancies, miscarriages, and surviving children as the rural women. Working-class women cannot observe strict *purdah,* but they do not repudiate the concept of *purdah.* Indeed, in their *minds purdah* is associated with respectability, and they do observe *purdah* when their economic status becomes more secure. When asked whether they would want their daughters to observe *purdah,* the majority of working-class women answered in the affirmative (personal interview). *Purdah,* in the sense of modesty, restriction on contact between the sexes, and shelter for women, is a universally accepted value in Bangladesh.

Of all the categories of women, only among urban

working-class women do we find many women who are their own guardians. Even in cases where there are male guardians, the women are more assertive. This deviant behavior pattern is explained by their being wage earners. Compared to their rural sisters, working-class women are more politically conscious and organised. Working class women constitute the bulk of all the women's processions brought out by political parties. But while their rate of political participation is high, they are not feminists.

"Modern" Bangali women are urban middle-class women, whose lifestyles are visibly different from that of rural women or working-class women.

Ostensibly the modern woman has an easier life and more leisure, but like all modern women in a traditional society, she lives in two worlds. While rural women are more blatantly oppressed and discriminated against, the oppression of and discrimination against urban women is subtle. The birth of a girl is not a happy event even in an urban middle-class family, though her parents quickly become reconciled to a daughter. She is socialised differently from a rural girl. She grows up in a nuclear family; has greater contact with her brothers, father, and other male members of the family; and her opportunities for education are nearly equal to those of her brothers. The informal learning process at home, 'where she is taught how to cook, clean, sew, and look after babies, does not start as early for an urban girl. And she is expected to finish school before she is married. Urban middle-class women do not observe rigid *purdah,* but they do live in a separate world of women. Segregation of sexes starts at puberty.

Girls may not wear the veil, but restrictions are put on their mobility and on their contact with males. Between the ages of 11 and 17, boys and girls go' to separate schools; and though the university is coeducational, contact between male and female students is restricted. Here again, separate space is allocated for women: there are separate reading rooms and lounges and in classrooms women students occupy separate seats (usually the first two or three rows).

A woman may spend four years in a coeducational institution and not exchange four sentences with her male classmates. Indeed, the less contact she has with males, the better her reputation as a good woman.

Marriages are arranged for urban middle-class women. Most women are married between the ages of 19 and 24. Only in rare cases does a woman remain single beyond 24. Single women have no social status even in urban areas, and a good marriage is regarded as the ultimate goal of a woman's life. An overwhelming majority of urban, educated women still accept and prefer arranged marriages because there is little opportunity to meet members of the opposite sex. Girls also have little confidence in their own abilities to find established husbands and they trust their fathers' judgment in arranging suitable matches for them. Nearly all the university students who were interviewed showed an anxiety over security and preferred arranged marriages.

A small percentage of urban middle-class women adopt a career. In a recent survey of a part of the Dacca municipal area, about 10 per cent of urban women were found to be working, though nearly 34.4 per cent of these women are university graduates. Women's career choices are very much determined by the *purdah* society's imperative of two separate worlds. Papanek (1971) argues that teaching and medicine are regarded as the two most respectable occupations for women because of the presence of a large female clientele. In a *purdah* society women are preferred as doctors for female patients and as teachers for female students, and hence there is a great demand for women in these occupations. Similarly occupations that bring women in contact with men, e.g. nursing and secretarial work, are regarded as non-respectable. In contrast to the pattern in Western countries, many more women go into medicine than into such women's occupations as nursing and secretarial work.

A women's career choice is also determined by her family. Her father usually will decide whether she should study and what she should study. It is again her father or her husband who decides whether she should have a job and what type of a job she should have.

An urban middle-class woman, if she has a job, has some say in the couple's decision to have babies. She often practices some form of birth-control. Career women usually have fewer children than a housewife, who tends to have five to six children. The notion of a planned family appears to be acceptable only to the younger generation of urban women. Divorce and remarriage are rare among the urban middle class. Divorce brings disrepute to the whole family and hence is looked down upon. Thus an urban middle-class woman's life is different from a rural woman's in that she has greater opportunities for education and a career. But she can enter a man's world only by exploiting another class of women—maidservants, mothers, and mothers-in-law—who' take over her household tasks and thus provide her with the free time needed for outside work.

Even in an urban middle-class family the household tasks are not shared by the husband of a career woman, except for the care of babies, in which the younger generation of men show an interest. Men refuse to share in household work because it is regarded as women's work and hence inferior. That a woman's status should be inferior to a man's is a thesis universally accepted by Bangali men. In a recent survey of two localities—one rural and one urban—70 per cent of rural men and 80 per cent of urban men, compared to 39 per cent of urban women; agree with the statement that "It is natural and right for women to have inferior status to men". Interestingly enough, on the question of whether women should participate in politics, 52 per cent of urban women approved of women's participation compared to 55 per cent of rural mm and 64 per cent of urban men. Thus the response of urban men is inconsistent. While 64 per cent of urban men support women's participation in politics only about 20 per cent of them regard 'women as equals. Their deep bias against women is obvious.

An urban middle-class woman is considered as vulnerable as a rural woman, as much in need of male protection and shelter. She is rarely her own guardian; almost always a male relative is the guardian. Thus the basic relationship between men and women remains constant in rural and urban areas. An urban woman has greater mobility, but she can achieve and retain that mobility by not challenging the superior social status of men.

Legal, Economic, Political and Social Status

Much is said and written about the legal status of Muslim women, and indeed, compared to the other South Asian religion, Hinduism, Islamic women are treated more equally by the *sharia* (Islamic personal laws). But there is a great difference between the legal status and the socioeconomic status of women. Their insecure socioeconomic status prevents women from exercising their legal rights.

Three noteworthy legal rights are given to Muslim women by *sharia:* rights regarding marriage, divorce, and inheritance. In Islam marriage is a contract, and the consent of both partners in front of witnesses is required. Because marriage is a contract, divorce is allowed. The marriage contract itself enumerates the conditions under which each partner may initiate divorce proceedings. In the marriage contract provision is made for *Mehr*—a fixed sum of money, part of which is payable to the bride after the wedding ceremony and the rest payable only in case of a divorce. Both the husband and the wife can start divorce proceedings, but it is by far much easier for a husband to divorce his wife. Islamic law allows a man to divorce his wife by simply pronouncing his intention to do so in front of witnesses. A woman is allowed to obtain a divorce by returning the *Mehr*.

Such divorces—known as *Khul*—are rarely practiced these days. At the time of divorce, a woman who has minor children can get custody of them, but she can never get their guardianship, which remains with the husband. Another much publicised legal right of Muslim women is their right it, inherit property. After a man's death, his widow inherits one-eighth of his property; and if he dies childless, she inherits one-fourth; daughters inherit one-half of the sons' shares. But though the law recognises women's rights in marriage, divorce, and inheritance, in practice women can rarely take full advantage of these rights. As mentioned earlier, a woman's marriage is arranged by her father or other male guardians and she usually consents to such arrangements.

Only in rare cases would a woman stand up against the expressed wishes of her guardians. In cases of divorce, men usually take the initiative. Though the Muslim Family Laws ordinance, passed in 1961, put a number of restrictions on the male's *sharia* rights regarding polygamy and divorce, in practice prevailing social norms still permit men greater freedom to practice polygamy and initiate divorce. Women initiate divorce only among the poorer sections of population, but here, too, the initiative is taken by the woman's father or other male guardians. Among the poor, *Mehr* is regarded as a bride-price, and the bride's male guardian demands payment of part of the *Mehr* after the wedding ceremony. Often a woman is married several times so that her male guardian can collect.

Among the middle class, the actual payment of *Mehr* is rarely made. Even when a woman is divorced, *Mehr* is renounced because that improves the chances of her remarriage. Men are reluctant to marry divorced women who demand *Mehr* (Ahmed 1966).

Few middle-class women initiate divorce, because it involves litigation and is regarded as a disreputable act. There is a similar gap between a woman's inheritance rights and the actual practice. Widows always demand inheritance, but it is used by their sons. If a widow demands inheritance, she is expected to five in her husband's household and not to return to her parents. It is customary for daughters to renounce inheritance in favor of brothers unless the family is either very rich or very poor. Daughters give up inheritance in exchange for *naior* (Ahmad 1966)—the right to visit the father's house once or twice a year after the father's death. Women give up inheritance for a number of reasons. Partly it is a social custom.

The majority of women interviewed argued that they gave up inheritance to be on good terms with their brothers. In case of divorce or widowhood, they would need their brothers' assistance, guardian protection and sometimes they would come back (especially in case of divorce) to live in their natal homestead. So they did not want to strain relations with their brothers by claiming their inheritance, which was their legal due, and thus risk being rejected by their brothers.

Additionally, women who give up inheritance in favor of *naior* indicate their preference for mobility. For a woman, *naior* days are the only days of vacation in a year. In her father's house, a woman has greater mobility, *purdah* observance is less strict, and she is relieved of her household chores. Thus, renouncing inheritance for *naior* appears to be a fair exchange, because inheritance is used by the husband but *naior* is a woman's exclusive vacation. In a social system where a woman; always needs a guardian, her legal rights are exercised by the guardian on her behalf.

Economic Status

It is pertinent to note that being a wife and a mother is the only goal of a Bangali woman, and few take up a career. Roughly 10 per cent of women are in the civilian labor force and only about 1 per cent of these adopt a modern occupation. Out of 2,553,212 women in the civilian labor force in 1961, only 214,715 were in the nonagricultural labour force; the rest were in agricultural labor force. Thus the overwhelming majority of working women live in the rural areas. In urban areas, the largest number of women are employed in factories; Table 14.1 indicates that nearly half of the female nonagricultural labour force were in manufacturing and mechanical occupations. Urban women are employed in such low-paid jobs as factory labor, street cleaning, and construction work, as well as in professional and technical occupations, e.g.; teaching, medicine, and nursing. Middle-class women usually enter teaching, nursing, sales work, research and other related professional "women's" occupations. Further very few women enter traditionally male occupations. In 1961, while there were 3,541 female teachers and 2,986 nurses and midwives, there were only 11 architects and engineers, 13 scientists, 200 physicians, 11 lawyers and judges, and 20 public service administrators. In contrast to women in such South East Asian countries as Burma and Thailand and in East and West Africa, few Bangali women go into business. In 196!, only 185 women, as compared to 30,627 men, were classified as proprietors and managers of industrial and business offices. Only 67 women, versus 15,707 men, were in retail trade, and this number might be even smaller—men often register businesses in their wives' or sisters' or mothers' names to publicly cover the real ownership

Similar to women's occupational patterns in other countries, the majority of women are employed in low and middle-salaried jobs, with very few women in top administrative or decision-making posts. As the top administrative posts are manned by ex-C.S.P. (Civil Service of Pakistan) and ex-E.P.C.S. (East Pakistan Civil Service) members, organisations where women's participation was restricted, women have little input in decision-making processes. Unlike India, where women compete in the foreign service and administrative service examinations, in Bangladesh women were barred from these jobs during the Pakistani days. There is no woman in the Bangladesh foreign service, or in the higher echelons of the various ministeries and the Planning Commission of the Bangladesh government. Administration and planning in Bangladesh are all-male affairs. The pyramidal structure of the women's employment pattern is also visible in educational institutions. More women are employed as lecturers than as principals of colleges, chairpersons of departments, or deans of various faculties in the universities. In Dacca University during the 1972-1973 session, of a faculty of 566 there were 86 women.

There were 166 male Ph.D.s and only 9 women Ph.D.s; 5 women professors and associate professors, and only two women chairpersons of departments. None of the deans were women. It is, however, interesting to note that few women feel job discrimination. None of the women interviewed, especially those in middle-class occupations, felt that they were discriminated against on the basis of sex in recruitment, in salary distribution, or in promotion.

This is an expected response. In other countries, also, women felt little job discrimination before their consciousness about it was raised. Another reason appears to be that since there are only a few women in various jobs, they are usually not in a competitive position with men and hence do not pose a threat. Additionally, even when a woman takes up a career, she keeps to her place.

Except for the time she puts in her job, she remains in the women's world and does not question the socially sanctified superior status of men. A career woman is therefore no threat to a man's ego; rather she is a financial asset, as her income helps balance the family budget. Quite frequently an educated, urban man proudly introduces his wife as "my wife who is an M.A. and a professor," or the like. In a society where education is universally valued, having an educated wife enhances a husband's social status. In sum, very few Bangali women take up an occupation, especially a modern occupation. But once they are in a job, particularly a middle-class job, they face little discrimination. It is difficult for women to break the barriers of tradition, but after they break them, there is greater acceptance.

Political Status

Notably, Bengali women won their basic political right, the right to vote, without a fight. It was granted to them by the British colonial government at the same time as it was granted to Bangali men. In all elections from 1937 on, women constituted nearly half of the country's electorate, but their only political role consisted of casting their ballots. Bangali women's participation in the movement for Pakistan was marginal. In the hierarchy of the Muslim League there was no woman. There was a separate women's wing of the party, and the major function of women in the Muslim League was to recruit the support of Muslim women for electoral purposes.

No attempt was made to organise the women on feminist issues or even to get a pledge of the male leadership on such issues. In a *purdah* society, the ethos of separate worlds for men and women permeates even politics. Thus separate seats are reserved for women in the parliament and in the political parties women work only in the women's wings. The Bangladesh Constitution provides for; 15 reserved seats for women in the Parliament. These women are to be elected, not by the female electorate of the country, but by the three hundred male members of parliament. The constitution does not prohibit women from campaigning for general seats. Indeed, two women contested but failed to win general seats in the March, 1973, election.

The reserved seats deter political parties from nominating women for the general seats, as the prominent party women can easily be accommodated in the reserved seats. Similarly; because of the existence of separate women's wings in the parties, the top post a woman can aspire to in any party hierarchy is that of women's secretary. In only one of the existing political parties does a woman hold the post of organising secretary (Mrs. Motia Chowdhury of National Awami Party, Muzaffer group). There were no women in the first two cabinets, and the two women ministers of state predictably hold the traditionally female portfolios of education and social welfare. Women are still far from being politically organised. They played a marginal role in the various political movements of the country in the last two decades. Few women took active part in the national liberation movement. While thousands of young men were recruited in the Mukti Bahini (freedom fighters), only a handful of women took arms training, and a few hundred women worked as nurses and teachers in the freedom fighters' hospitals and refugee camps.

Only as the victims of the liberation war did the Bangali women receive world-wide publicity. Soon after Liberation, the government of Bangladesh disclosed that thousands of Bangali women who had been raped by the Pakistani soldiers were then made social outcasts. The failure of the various women's organisations to mobilise public support or, for that matter, women's support for the raped women indicates the weak politicisation of Bangali women.

Social Status

In fact, a woman's social status is separate from, and inferior to, a man's. The religious community takes little notice of the existence of women. Women do not participate in any congregational prayers—e.g. the Friday prayer, the *I'd* prayer (one of the Muslim holidays), or the funeral prayer. Women are deeply religious, but they practice the various forms of prayer individually and in private.

Although the idea of *umma* [community] is important to Muslims, women are excluded from any community celebrations. In some of the Muslim countries of the Middle

East, women do participate in separate women's congregational prayers, but Bangali Muslim women do not. *Purdah,* the social imperative of sexual segregation, isolates women and confines them to their individual homes. Papanek (1971) argues persuasively that because *purdah* society regards women as highly vulnerable, there is a need to "shelter" them and to control their impulses. "Impulse control is achieved with the help of restraining social institutions, in ways which are closer to 'shame' mechanisms of social control than those associated with 'guilt". (1971: 519) The non-acceptance of raped women in Bangladesh is a good illustration of the operation of the "shame" mechanism. If a woman is raped and it can be kept a secret from her social circle, then she is acceptable. It is not raping *per se,* but the *samaj's* knowledge about it that brings disrepute to the family. When a woman is violated, the family is more concerned about the loss of face than about her physical and mental health. One organisation, which worked with the war-affected women in Bangladesh (the National Board of Bangladesh Women's Rehabilitation programme), informed the author that it maintained strict secrecy about the cases of violated women because their chances of social acceptance depended on it. Where parents were alive, a violated daughter was always accepted back by the parents. Only in rare cases were women who had been in Pakistani army camps taken back by their husbands. These women were not acceptable because the fact of their violation was known by the *samaj.* But many women whose violations were not publicised were accepted back by their husbands after they underwent secret abortions. The National Board of Bangladesh Women's Rehabilitation in Dacca received 22,500 applications from raped women. Of them 19,500 were illiterate and 3,000 were literate; 15,030 were rural and the rest were urban. The majority of cases were not reported because of the family's desire to maintain secrecy. This anxiety over secrecy is illustrated by the reluctance of Bangali women to talk about the problem of the women who were violated during the war. The majority of women interviewed stated that, while they were agitated by the problem, they rarely discussed it. The father of the nation reflected the same anxiety when he coined the term "war heroines" for women raped by Pakistani soldiers.

The term camouflages the state of these women and is less disreputable and shocking than the term "violated" women. The fate of these war-affected women, together with the failure of the non-affected women to mobilise support for the acceptance of these women, reflects the totally vulnerable social status of women.

Women's Movements and Women's Organisations in Bangladesh

The movement for the emancipation of Muslim women in Bengal started in the 1920's. The emancipation of women was closely associated with the modernist movement among the Muslims, and it received sympathy and support from the modernist men. In the twenties and thirties, the movement was primarily concerned with women's literacy, and did not raise questions about employment opportunities of the equal status of women. These questions came up only at the later phase of the movement. Roughly, the movement for women's emancipation in Bengal can be divided into three periods. The first phase (1910-1947) saw the questioning of rigid *purdah* observance and the demand for women's literacy and school enrollment. The 1920's and 1930's were the periods of *Khilafat* movement and the development of Muslim nationalism in India.

The movement for the emancipation of Turkish women

and other Middle Eastern women at this time inspired Muslim modernists in Bengal to agitate for women's emancipation at home. The leadership in the first phase belonged to women from traditional landlord families, many of whom were Calcutta-based and nonvernacular but who later achieved fluency in the vernacular. The movement for women's emancipation was started by a woman from a traditional, landlord family who was married to a "modernist" civil servant.

Rokeya Sakhawat Hussain (1880-1932) was not only the pioneer of the women's emancipation movement, she was a true feminist. Indeed, she is the only feminist in the leadership of the women's movement. None of the women who came after her could be called feminists. Rokeya Sakhawat Hussain keenly felt the oppression of the rigid *purdah* system. In her father's and husband's houses she lived in *purdah,* and she had to fight against heavy odds to educate herself. Rokeya felt that the only way a woman could be emancipated was through education, which 'would enable her to achieve economic independence and to renounce strict *purdah.* Rokeya was both a publicist and an activist. She wrote a number of short stories, articles, and a novel, all of which depict the stultifying life of women in a *purdah* society. In all her writings, she made scathing attacks on the unequal relationship between men and women and propagated the cause of women's emancipation. In *Sultana's dream* (1905) Rokeya portrays a social system where men are kept in seclusion and women handle all the traditionally male jobs.

In 1911, Rokeya established the first Muslim girls' school in Calcutta, which started with eight students. For twenty years she worked in the school despite bitter criticisms from orthodox Muslims, At the time of her death in 1932, the school had 123 students. In 1916, Rokeya also established a women's organisation, Anjuman-e-Khawatein-Islam, which was essentially meant to draw out the Muslim women from traditional families.

After Rokeya's death in 1932, there was not a single woman who made the cause of women's emancipation her lifelong interest. In the thirties and forties, there was a small group of Muslim literary women who wrote occasional pieces on women, but these women served more as models for women's emancipation than as active participants in a movement. The 1947 partition of India and Bengal marked a radical change in women's status and role. The second phase of the women's movement (1947-1970) saw the growth of women's organisations in urban areas. Muslim women took the place of Hindu women in all the women's organisations. In the second phase, though women's organisational activities increased, there was no recognisable movement for the emancipation of women.

During this period a large number of women were emancipated, but their emancipation was the result of the general process of modernisation and was not due to any feminist movement. There was less of a women's movement in the second phase than there had been in the first. The most important women's organisation that developed during this phase was the All Pakistan Women's Association (APWA). The APWA in Bangladesh was a branch of the central APWA, which had local branches in all the districts and subdivisions. The APWA had very close ties with the government and the power structure of the country. The leaders were the wives of powerful political and administrative figures. In the districts and subdivisions, the wives of district and subdivisional officers were invariably the presidents of the APWA. In Dacca the APWA presidency shifted between the wife of the chief minister and the wife of the governor, depending on the relative power of their husbands in the political system. As the APWA leadership changed with the administration, the organisation failed to develop leadership among women. The APWA was very much like a social club of elite women which arranged social and cultural get-togethers. In Dacca APWA women did some voluntary work; they ran schools and managed sewing and handicraft centers. But the APWA's major activities were still confined to the concept of neighborhood women's clubs. The APWA's major role was to act as a meeting place for middle-class Muslim women who had been in strict *purdah* and were not even used to meeting other women in an organisation.

The decades of the 1950's and 1960's saw a rapid increase in women's literacy and school enrollment. As Table 14.3 shows, the rate of increase in female enrollment in schools and universities was much greater than the rate of increase for male students. These rates are of course deceptive, because the base for women was so low at first. The increase in the number of career women was also substantial. As a result, a number of women's organisations developed, especially in the capital, Dacca. In addition to the APWA, nine other women's organisations were established in Dacca at this time. Many were neighborhood women's clubs, e.g. Gandaria Mahila Samity (formed in 1950), Wan Mahila Samity (formed in 1954), and Purana Paltan Ladies Club. All these associations were formed by the "enlightened" ladies (to quote one woman long associated with women's organisations) of these localities, who wanted to improve the socioeconomic condition of lower-middle-class and poor women.

Their usual activities included running a neighborhood

primary school and sewing or handicraft center. It is interesting to note that these associations were formed in the established and affluent neighborhoods of Dacca in the fifties, e.g. Gandaria, Wan, and Purana Paltan. The motivating force behind these associations was the feeling among the "enlightened" women that they should work FOR and not 'WITH their less enlightened sisters in the neighborhood. Apart from these three neighborhood associations, which were run by vernacular-speaking Bangali women, there were two organisations for non-Bangali and non-vernacular speaking Bangali women, the Anjuman Falah Muslim Khawateen and Baitul Athfab-e-Sabiyya (orphanage for Muslim girls).

In the 1960's the more westernised women formed a number of women's organisations to achieve specific goals. The Business and Career Women's Club was formed in 1960 to look after the interests of career women, i.e. to establish hostels for working women, childcare centers for working mothers, and programmes to encourage and train women from lower-class groups to take up an occupation, etc. The leaders of this organisation were mostly non-Bangali women. Bangali women associated with the Career Women's Club were different from the women in the *mahila samity* who were mostly housewives and rarely career women. In 1960 the House Wives Association was formed for the "meeting of minds and sharing of experiences" by housewives. Here, too, the women were more westernised than were the *samity* women. Two other women's organisations of the 1960's were the Women's Voluntary Association (WVA) and the Zonta club.

Foreign women resident in Bangladesh took the initiative in establishing the WVA. Wives of the diplomatic community played an active but less publicised role. WVA's major purpose is social work—to raise funds for specific projects. Unlike the APWA, Samity, or Career Women's club, WVA did not have regular social and cultural get-togethers. Instead duties were assigned to individual members and the group met specifically to discuss projects. The Zonta club is the Dacca branch of an international club, very similar to the Lions and the Rotary clubs. Its major purpose is to motivate women from affluent families to donate voluntary service or money for the poorer section of society.

The modes of operation and the leadership patterns of these various women's organisations differed from each other. Roughly speaking, the leaders of the neighborhood *samities* were Bangali middle-class women, while the APWA and the organisations of the 1960's—the Career Women's club, WVA, and Zonta—were dominated by non-Bangali and upper middle-class women. In many ways the varied women's leadership of the two decades reflected the sociopolitical reality of the country, which saw a transfer of power from Bangali lawyer-type politicians to non-Bangali bureaucrats. The role of the Bangali women in the organisations of the 1960's was that of intermediaries, the same role the Bangali political-administrative leadership was playing in the country.

The organisations of the 1950's and the 1960's did not differ fundamentally Groups were especially involved with girls' schools, women's sewing and handicraft centers, and women's career-trainings programmes. While the *samity* women raised funds by organising cultural evenings at the Begum Club, the APWA, WVA, Zonta women raised funds by oganising *meena bazaars* at the Dacca Club or Grand balls at the *Hotel Inter Continental* and the *Purbani.* The third phase of the women's movement, in the post-liberation period in Bangladesh, is marked by a growing awareness among the women about women's problems, though no concrete programme or organisational leadership has yet come forward. The liberation movement, the fate of the violated and other war-affected women, and the vulnerable position of women in the post-liberation period of lawlessness have led women to raise questions (not publicly) about the stability of the "shelter" provided by men. The women of Bangladesh have found themselves in a state of semi permanent seige by male aggression—the incidence of abduction and raping of women has increased tremendously since liberation, as have other acts of lawlessness such as robbery and murder, which has severely restricted women's mobility. All this has made feminists of many women of the younger generation, but the women's leadership is lagging far behind. The post-liberation period saw a scramble by Bangali women to move into the positions of organisational leadership left vacant by the departure of non-Bangali women.

The APWA was renamed Bangladesh Mahila Samity, and the Awami League women moved into its leadership positions; in the Business and Career Women's club and the WVA, Bangali women are filling the 'slots left empty by non-Bangali women. Since 1970, many women have become very active in Mahila Parishad. Its leadership is in the hands of women with leftist (especially pro-Moscow) leanings, and it has branches in various districts outside Dacca. Mahila Parishad leadership partly resembles the old *samity* leadership of middle-class and vernacular Muslim women. In part, it consists of ex-student leaders who were active in student politics or party politics. Of all the women's organisations, Parishad is the most political; it concerns itself with women's problems and it has a systematic programme to recruit the support of the larger masses of women.

Still, there is no women's movement in Bangladesh at present. There are no feminist leaders or feminist journals, or feminist writings. The absence of a movement or leadership has not prevented a growing number of Bangali women from seeking their emancipation. However the process is understandably slow since the rate of social change and modernisation is slow. Only an active women's movement with a feminist leadership can expedite the emancipation of Bangali women. To conclude, Bengali women, both rural and urban, traditional and modern, live in a social system that sanctifies an unequal and inferior status for women. *Sharia* laws grant Muslim women a number of limited rights, but prevailing social norms prevent them from taking full advantage of even these limited rights. So far, the women's emancipation movement has concerned itself with such basic issues as literacy and employment for women. The unequal relationship between men and women is not yet questioned. There has been no serious movement to modify the legal system to give women equal rights of inheritance, guardianship, or marriage and divorce.

The small number of women who are educated and seek careers can easily be accommodated by the social system, especially because these women do not challenge the basic rules of the system. The elite women can participate and hence there is no dissatisfied elite group to lead a women's movement. In the absence of a movement, consciousness about the oppression of women is low. In Bangladesh the movement for women's emancipation is part of the process of social change and not a revolutionary movement.

To sum up, despite being an Islamic society, women in Bangladesh are more awakened and enlightened than their counterparts in Pakistan. This is perhaps due to advancement and vision of awakened Bengali society of colonial period.

REFERENCES

Ahmad, Taherunnessa, 1996, *Palli anganader jemon dekhecki* [Rural women as I saw them]. Comilla: PARD.

Bangladesh Bureau of Statistics, 1970-1971, *Statistical digest of Bangladesh.*

East Pakistan Bureau of Statistics, 1961 The master survey of agriculture in East Pakistan. *Sixth Round, Table 2.4 (A), page 18.*

Government of Pakistan, 1947-1967, Twenty years of Pakistan in statistics. *Ministry of Economic Affairs, Central Statistical Office.*

1961, Census of Pakistan, volume four. Ministry of Home and Kashmir Affairs (Home Affairs Division).

Hussain, Rokeya Sakhawat, 1905, *Sultana's dream.*

Papanek, Hanna, 1971, Purdah in Pakistan: seclusion and modern occupations for women. *Journal of Marriage and the Family.* (August): 517-530.

Qadir, S.A., 1968, *Modernisation of an agrarian society.* Rural sociology research Report 1, Mymensingh: Agricultural University.

Stoeckel, John, Moqbul A. Chowdhury, 1973, *Fertility, infant mortality, and family planning in rural Bangladesh.* Dacca: Oxford.

6

Women in Thailand

FACTS ABOUT WOMEN

Life expectancy: females as a % of males, 2007	113
Adult literacy rate: females as a % of males, 2000–2007	97
Enrolment and attendance ratios: females as a % of males, Net primary school 2000–2007, enrolled	99
Enrolment and attendance ratios: females as a % of males, Net primary school 2000–2007, attending	100
Enrolment and attendance ratios: females as a % of males, Net secondary school 2000–2007, enrolled	111
Enrolment and attendance ratios: females as a % of males, Net secondary school 2000–2007, attending	109
Contraceptive prevalence (%), 2000–2007	77
Antenatal care coverage (%), At least once, 2000–2007	98
Antenatal care coverage (%), At least four times, 2000–2007	-
Delivery care coverage (%), Skilled attendant at birth, 2000–2007	97
Delivery care coverage (%), Institutional delivery, 2000–2007	97
Maternal mortality ratio, 2000–2007 reported	12
Maternal mortality ratio, 2005, adjusted	110
Maternal mortality ratio, 2005, Lifetime risk of maternal death. 1 in:	500

Under the absolute monarchy, member of the royalty in Thailand were in theory a world apart from commoners. In terms of Siamese law, aside from a host of finely-graded sumptuary rights which they had to observe, their royal status was reinforced by two privileges: they could not be tried in any judicial court except those of Krom Wang (the Palace Department), and they could not be sold into slavery. The rationale of the Palatine Laws is the protection of the dignity of the royal family, and the security of the Palace.

Where royal women were concerned, this meant the observation of strict limits on their mobility and communications, there being no distinction made between their personal and public conduct. These women upheld the sanctity of the royal family by denying any accessibility to their selves by unauthorised men. They were the repository of the honour of their families, and hence had to he confined, for possession of their bodies would give men the claim of having partaken of a royal object. According to the Palatine Law, even attendants of the Inner Palace would be put to death if they were found to be in receipt of, or sending messages to men. If palace women (ying chaowang) were party to an illicit sexual liaison, the death sentence was awaited them; palace men who were their liaison received fifty lashes of the whip. Where marriage was concerned, needless to say, female members of the royal family were forbidden to demean themselves and their lineage by marrying beneath their status

The impression given by reading the Palatine Laws would lend credence to two influential portrayals of the life of palace women. Anna Leonowens' *Siamese Harem Life* condemns what she claimed was the stifled, repressed, loveless and terror-filled lives of the palace-women whose very meaning of existence had to be for the sole purpose of serving the king's will; on the other hand, *Si phaendin* highlighted the security, spiritual fulfilment and sense of service that being a member of the royal household gave to the women. When one looks at the records of the Palace court, however, the isolation from the world outside of the palace that typify the lives of both Leonowens and Khukrit's characters, the great divide between the restrictions of palace life and the permissiveness the commoners' existence is found to be overstated, especially for the lower levels of royalty, where the restrictions on palace women applied, but were hardly enforced seriously until their cases appear before the Palace courts. A duplicates of the Inner Palace where no male over the age of eleven save the King was permitted, the households of princes where the distinction between the Inner and Outer quarters were observed, cases of legal infractions that involved palace women show that their lives were far from being static. They were not unaffected by nor incognizant of the societal forces that grew out of the larger policies which the kings had adopted. This was so especially for the women of "marginal royalty" as Khukrit Pramoj glossed the MR title before his name—formally speaking, those who held the rank below that of **momchao,** namely **momratchawong** and **momluang,** but also those of higher rank who could not afford to maintain royal way of life. Two court cases involving such marginally royal women will be examined for the insights that they lend to the meaning of being a member of the royal family where they were concerned.

At the same time, a couple of the court cases also suggest that commoner women who served or had access to the palace were attuned to the vulnerabilities of their countrymen and women in the Fifth Reign, a period which saw greater degrees of bureaucratisation, penetration of capital, and the presence of Western consulates in Bangkok. These lowly serving women can be seen as the antithesis of that paragon of the female palace official, Thao Worachan, the highest-ranking official position in the palace, whose task it was to maintain and preserve protocol and tradition in the Inner Palace, in other words, to keep the world beyond at bay. In the two cases examined here, the women tried in their own ways to elude the separation between the inside and outside when they played on their claims to have palace connections to mediate between the larger social, economic and political developments, and individuals who were either the victims of these forces, or who were empowered by them.

In brief; **wang** (palace) and **muang** (city, town) exemplify two polar positions: the "inside" and the "outside", tradition and modernity, privilege and politics **(kanmuang).** The four women discussed here have left traces of their lives in the records of the Palace court of justice which showed that they moved between **wang** and **muang** illicitly; the fact that their records exist is on account of their failure to negotiate this slippage successfully. Nevertheless, we can gather from the records the possibilities that they, and perhaps other women, discerned were inherent in their time and place.

Marriage and Marginal Royalty Case I—the Price of Being Momchaoying

In 1893 the Palace Court heard the case of Momchao On, the wife of a commoner **(phrai)** who like him and their daughter, was a debt slave. Momchao On was the daughter of Phraongchao Renu, a son of Rama II. He had died in the Third Reign, following which On, then age 9, entered the service of her mother's niece in the Grand Palace, and later, of a half-sister. It was in the latter's residence that she met Saeng, his brother and sister-in-law, all of whom were debt slaves in the household. Momchao On left the palace to live with Saeng as a debt slave, and assumed the identity of his sister-in-law on her death. All the while, she continued collecting her yearly stipend from the palace. Her situation came to light when she fell ill, ran away from their creditor of 11 years, and sought refuge in the palace of a relative. She was then 60 years old, and her daughter, 25.

The case of Momchao On marrying an impoverished commoner and becoming a debt slave caused consternation among the council of princes who heard the case as they found that records which contained the prescribed punishment for this breach of the palace laws were not available. They were certain that the Fourth Reign had laid down clearly that **chao** (royalty) could marry only **chao;** that **momchao** were not allowed out of the palace walls, and they were in agreement that she had indeed demeaned the dignity of the royal family, and should be stripped of any claims to royal status. The question was whether she should be imprisoned, sent to work as a **khlon,** performing the most menial tasks in the kitchen, or as a **phrai** in the palace sewing room.

A number of the princes saw mitigating circumstances in the case. Prince Sawat noted that as a **momchao,** On had little leeway to improve her livelihood, and did not have the legal option of becoming a debt slave. Moreover, On did not sign the debt papers as a **momchao,** but passed off as a **phrai.** He was supported by Prince Chaiyan, who claimed that there were a good many cases such as Momchao On's, for **momchaoying** on the whole did not receive adequate stipends, which were paid annually, and unless they had wealthy patrons, or were very industrious, they would fall into debt once they have exhausted the money, which had to last a year. Similarly, Prince Naret thought that it was not right to inflict harsh punishment on On for becoming a debt slave, for impoverished female **momchao** performing menial tasks because of indebtedness was common; unlike On, however, they were mindful of their royal status and worked only in the households of royalty and nobility. However, Naret could find no redeeming arguments for her marriage a commoner Prince Narathip raised the point that though she had married a **phrai,** Momchao On was not adulterous, unlike one Momchaoying Sawat, who had a number of husbands. Also, On was already 60 years old; she had lived with Saeng for about twenty-five years. The council could not reach a decision on the punishment for On, and referred the case to King Chulalongkorn. Princes Chaiyan and Sawat each added an addendum: the former recommended that all **momchao** who were in On's situation should also be punished; the latter, that they should plead for clemency, and their allowances should be raised.

King Chulalongkorn pronounced that On should be stripped of her royal rank, and imprisoned in the Palace.

The case of Momchao On illustrates that for female marginal royalty a life of discreet poverty and spinsterhood was a very real prospect. In all probability, On left the palace with Saeng on becoming pregnant, this at the age of 35. On's "disappearance" could not have been unnoticed; for twenty-five years she turned up regularly at the Palace to collect her annual stipend, yet no one brought this to the attention of the authorities until she absconded from her creditor, and it was the latter who, afraid of being punished for having royalty as a debt slave, alerted the Palace court. A **momchaoying** who confirmed to the court that On was indeed the daughter of Prince Renu mentioned that aside from the yearly collecting of stipends, she hardly saw On as the latter was poor. As is evident from the statements of the princes, On's slippage from the domain of the **wang** to **muang**—the inside to the outside—did not alter her circumstances significantly. When the princes were confronted with her case, a number of them were in fact were sympathetic to the financial plight of the many women in her position, but they were far less forgiving of her marriage to a **phrai.**

While King Mongkut's oft-cited decree of 1854 permitted "all Lady Consorts serving the Inner Palace, Middle Palace and Outer Palace...as well as Ladies in Waiting of all ranks, Ladies chaperons and chaperons and all Palace dances and concubines" to resign and "reside in the palace of a prince or the castle of a noble or to return home to their parents, or to dispel such discomfort by the company of a private husband and children", women born into the royal family could not resign from it. Mongkut also widened the web of the royal family when he established the lower ranks of **momnratchawong** and **momluang.**

Marriage and Marginal Royalty Case II: Momratchawongying and Modernisation

A copy of a lengthy love letter written by Nai Liab, age 29, a clerk in the Klang Mahasombat to Momratchawong Sa-ing was the evidence presented to the Palace court in 1903 in the case against him for the seduction of a member of the royal family. This letter was a response to Sa-ing's correspondence to him, which laid down her expectations and conditions on his behaviour in return for her love. His reply was that not only would he gladly and manfully abide by her wishes, he himself had added clauses to the code of good behaviour that would govern his life as her husband.

Her first injunction was that he should not indulge in

gambling; during the festive season, he could seek her permission to do so. Nai Liab in his letter agreed with her that gambling was a vice which led to greed, impoverishment and recklessness, put one under the control of fellow gamblers, and made a man unfit to provide for his wife and children. He assured her that he had never been addicted to gambling, though he did bet on horse and buffalo races, but this was a very recent development, and grew out of frustration more than anything else. At that time, he was without proper guidance, but now that she, a person of wisdom and goodness had taken him under her command, he would gratefully celebrate the glory of royal power and goodness **(chalong pradech prakhun)** and trod the righteous path.

Secondly, she forbade him to indulge in alcohol, except at **"dinner".** Liab agreed wholeheartedly to this, for he recognised that drunkenness would lead to dereliction of government service (**sermsia nai ratchakan**). However, official dinners have become popular as they were good for the morale of the officials and the people; drinking to the cheer of **"hip hip horray"** heightened the esprit de corp of his brother officers of the crown who were of the same uniform **("fom offit").** He would drink only in such situations, and not even accept her waiver granted for illness as he did not believe in alcohol's efficacy as medicine. He went on in the letter to list six dire consequences of inebriety as he understood them.

Momratchawong Sa-ing also wanted Nai Liab to agree that he would be constant and caring. To this he proclaimed in his letter in the name of overflowing royal power and goodness **(phradech prakhun pen-lonklao hathisut midai)** that she would his only love for all time for he was under the command of her royalty **(chaonai).** If he himself were ever to bully her, this would constitute the degradation of the power of his very own patron, and would therefore render her unable to extend protection to him, which would be against his interest.

To her condition that she would accompany him to all his official postings, he gladly agreed, but he would like to spare her in instances of hardship posts.

Nai Liab pledged to ask Momratchawongying Sa-ing's mother for her daughter's hand. He also unilaterally added a number of clauses to the contract that he signed, one of which stated that he would venerate her sister and her as being of the highest rank **(yothabandasak).** He also vowed not to quarrel with her when perchance she was in an angry mood, and admonished that she too should observe this practice as forbearance would lead to **samakkhi** (unity) which was the path towards lasting **"civilai".**

The Palace court found that there were a number of grey areas in the case. In particular it was difficult to claim that Momratchawong Sa-ing's father's household (he was a *phraongchao*) observed the "inner sanctuary" prohibition, for Sa-ing was allowed to bathe at the river by herself; nor were there guards who prevented outsiders like Nai Liab from having easy access to her room. Members of the Mahatlek similarly went in and out of the house freely. Also he had indeed spoken to her mother about his intentions. Prince Damrong, who was consulted on the case, even noted that the Palace codes did not apply to **momratchawong;** it was entirely up to the king to pronounce on the case. The court initially put pressure on Nai Liab to enter the monkhood, but he refused on grounds that he was not ready to renounce the world, and that at least there was an end to a prison sentence.

King Chulalongkorn had Nai Liab put in chains and

imprisoned till he reformed; after four months in prison, he pleaded for clemency, and admitted that he had aspired beyond his position in society **(makyai fai soong)** in daring to fall in love with Momratchawong Sa-ing. The king also ordered that Sa-ing be imprisoned in the Inner Palace until she learnt the errors of her ways.

Nai Liab's lengthy missive to Momratchawong Sa-ing offers an insight into the ideal notions of love and marriage that one young woman of marginal royalty harboured: it could be argued that the sentiments could be entertained only by women of such position. Those of higher status would be much more restricted in their options to even contemplate a future that was not already charted by tradition and custom without having to reckon with severe retribution; commoners on the other hand conceivably would not need to communicate surreptitiously with their intended lover, nor need they self-consciously formalise their thoughts, hopes and fantasies on paper. Other illicit messages that have been intercepted normally are a couple of sentences long, and are cryptic notes on how much the writer admires the addressee, and plans on arranging for an assignation.

Momratchawong Sa-ing and even Nai Liab were certainly naive, as it turned out to think that their marriage would have been socially acceptable. Yet their naivety may have been encouraged by certain expectations that were linked to developments in the Fifth Reign. Nai Liab expressed his love for Sa-ing in terms of faithful royal service. He was a clerk in the Phra Khlang Mahasombat, and was assigned to Prachinburi, where her father was the Superintendent Commissioner. As is evident from their discussion on alcohol, he was very proud of his service uniform, used a sprinkling of English words **("dinner", "hip hip hurray", "form offit")** and most significantly, argued that fidelity, love and forbearance would lead to samakkhi, which would lead to civilisation—a distinct echo of King Chulalongkorn's **"Phraboromarachaowat lae phraboromarachathibai ruang samakkhi"** (The Royal Discourse on Unity) delivered in 1903, the same year that the couple engaged in profuse correspondence. Nai Liab evidently presented his situation as a microcosm of principles on which the Crown professed to operate.

To him, it was manly to agree to Sa-ing's conditions even though she was a woman for she was royalty, and thus superior in terms of wisdom— hence he elevated her in his letter to the highest royal status. In fact, King Mongkut had decreed in 1864 that **momratchawong** and **momluang** would not be considered as **chao.** Doing her bidding was **"chalong phradech phrakhun".** Nevertheless, he asserted his manliness by "improving" on the conditions that she had laid down. For instance, he waived the dispensations that she made for him to consume alcohol as medicine; elaborated on her points about the importance of **"dinner";** reiterated her disapproval on gambling by stating what he saw as its disastrous consequences; and as a climax, coaxed her to appreciate that the way they conducted their future relationship as man and wife would be a demonstration of the attainment of civilisation. In the end, the new breed of (male) civil servants (low-ranking though he was) emerges as superior to female royalty. Sa-ing's letter has not survived, and we only learn of her ideas through Liab's reference to them in his letter. From this perspective, her demands appear to be those of a woman whose only concern was domestic bliss and personal happiness, while it was he who elevated her views into moral principles an higher sense of duty and service.

Sa-ing's injunctions that the man she marries should eschew gambling and drinking, and polygamy, have resonances in the Western discourses on mid-nineteenth century Siam, especially missionary-run newspapers such as the *Siamese Repository,* and in the response to them by the Siamese male elite ***Kitchanukit,*** wherein they argue in relation to polygamy that "the Buddha did not absolutely forbid it, because he could not say there was any actual wrong in a man having a number of wives properly acquired. it. It is a moot point whether the missionaries influenced views such as Sa-ing's or that there was a coincidence; more pertinent is that hers is the voice of a Siamese woman of marginal royalty who thought that she was in a position to choose, and her choices were patently not in favour of what were deemed as commonplace practices of Thai men.

Sa-ing might also have derived the notion that she could move from the traditions of the wang and into the modern sphere of the **muang** from the physical mobility that had been brought about by the administrative reforms of the Fifth Reign. She had mentioned accompanying Liab on his postings. He father was sent to Prachinburi, accompanied by his household where, as the Prince Damrong note there seemed to be an absence of vigilance in enforcing the Inner and Outer spatial distinctions. Sa-in was not constantly chaperoned; Nai Liab could enter her chamber with impunity on her invitation; office was a stone's throw away from the Superintendent Commissioner's residence. In fact, the relationship came to light only when Sa-ing's mother spoke to her husband about Liab's proposal when the Superintendent Commissioner returned from a trip to Bangkok. It was in his absence that Sa-ing arranged for Liab to visit her at night. She had written him 214 letters in three years (1901-1903). Yet while the physical distance between **wang** and **muang** may have been breached to some degree, the social distance between the two poles which Liab had thought he could overcome as a civil servant remained as insurmountable as ever in the eyes of Sa-ing's father, and King Chulalongkorn.

There is a twist in the story of Momratchawong Sa-ing and Nai Liab. On investigation, the court discovered that he was actually named Ubon. He had a wife and a five-year old son whom he left in Bangkok to go to Prachinburi. Sa-ing passed him her first letter when he was in fact setting out on a trip to Bangkok to receive treatment for venereal disease. She had fallen for his suave selling of the **muang** that he held out to her: conjugal bliss based on a monogamous marriage, equal partnership, mutual respect and responsibility. The outside was far from being modernised and liberating as she had envisaged.

Palace and Power: One Amdaeng's Access

In June 1902, three men reported to the police that they had been swindled of 222 baht by one Amdaeng (form of addressing female commoners) Chom. They had been involved in a land dispute with the Siam Lands, Canal and Irrigation Company. Six years earlier, the company had obtained a court order evicting them from the land; the Court of Appeal had also ruled against them. Amdaeng Chom claimed to have access to the Queen, and promised to help them seek redress by handing their petition to Her Majesty. On the appointed day, their wives entered the Grand Palace with Amdaeng Chom, while the men waited outside. Amdaeng Chom told the women that the were not allowed to look at the Queen (the traditional practice was that commoners had to look away when the king appeared in public, but this had been rescinded by King Mongkut); they obligingly shut their eyes when "Her Majesty" came into the room, and Amdaeng Chom presented their case. After that, Amdaeng Chom gave them eleven envelopes bearing what looked like Royal Seals. The men were so overjoyed that they 'and the other households whom they represented held a huge celebration, only to find out later that the seals were those of the Royal Survey Department. Chom's husband, a coolie in the Department, had collected the crests from damaged, discarded maps. Inside one envelope was half a land registration form; another contained the Department's application form for leave. Among the men who fell for the scam was 50-year old Nai Sang, who was the headman **(phuyaiban)** of the community.

Amdaeng Chom had access to the Palace (at least in the sense that she was permitted to enter it) as well as the newly-developed settlements which were the outgrowth of the penetration of capital in Bangkok and its vicinity. She connected **wang** and **muang** by proffering the former as the appeal of last resort which could ameliorate the dislocations that were engulfing the latter. That the Queen could put things right, over-ruling courts of law, impersonal rules and regulations, and the profit-oriented imperatives of the Company was a credible proposition that Amdaeng Chom held out: as a woman, Her Majesty would sympathise with the human condition, especially when it was pleaded by other women, which courts of law would discount. And the Queen had been the Regent in 1897, when King Chulalongkorn went on a tour of Europe, so she certainly she would have great political clout. The power of the Palace as represented by the queen was considered at once feminine and masculine—it could be personal an compassionate to one party by being firm and official to the other. The **wang** was perceived to be the fortress against the intrusion of the ways of the **muang.**

Palace and Alternative Power-centres: One Amdaeng's Counterweight

Amdaeng Chaem, whose husband was a **momratchawong,** was a brothel owner whose establishment was well-known among men of rank for its refined prostitutes. One day in 1895, she sent a proxy to tell Tunkaew, age 21, who was a serving woman in the palace of Chao Dararasami in the Grand Palace that both a high-ranking prince and a noble of **phraya** rank would like to have her for a wife. Tunkaew expressed preference for the prince. Amdaeng Chaem managed to sneak her out to her house near the Palace. Tunkaew then voiced her apprehension that the prince would not take good care of her as he already had a number of wives. Amdaeng Chaem told her not to worry, for she could set up her own establishment instead of living in the Prince's palace. Tunkaew then waited as Amdaeng Chaem purportedly went to make arrangements for the Prince to fetch her. However, she returned with the message that one of the Prince's children was ill, and he would come **for** her only in a couple of days. In fact, she had hesitated at the Palace gate, for fear that the Prince would reprimand her for abducting women from the Grand Palace.

Amdaeng Chaem then made arrangements with the British consul's housekeeper to have Tunkaew stay at the consulate. When they duly went to the consulate that evening as arranged, however, they were told that the consul was out, and would only be back the next morning. The housekeeper said that the Consul was not interested in taking a Thai wife, but would allow Tunkaew to stay. She was to spend the night in the house of the housekeeper and his wife, and they would get her into the Consulate early the next morning. Later that night, however, Amdaeng

Chaem brought Tunkaew back on the insistence of her husband, who feared that she would abscond. They were apprehended by palace officials the next morning.

Reading the testimonies of the defendants, the whole affair seemed rather farcical—Amdaeng Chaem, for all her years of experience as a brothel-keeper arranged for Tunkaew to sneak out of the palace, but didn't quite know what to do with her, and ended up shuttling her around. The two women attributed the idea of going to the British Consul to one another. It is unclear whether they saw the Consulate as a temporary haven or that they expected the Consul to take her into his household on a long-term basis. Either way, they assumed that the foreign dignitary would be a counterweight to the **wang** from where she had fled, and presumably, he would be sympathetic to the plight of a woman. The foreign consulates had been granted extra-territorial rights since the Bowring Treaty of 1855, and were regarded as a shelter against Thai law by those who claimed to be subjects who were born in the colonies. In theory, its jurisdiction would also cover Siamese women married to Western men.

The women in this case viewed the British Consul as unlike any other institution in Siam in that it could grant immunity against the palace. Yet, at the same time, they also assumed that as any man, the consul would not be averse to the proffering of a young and attractive woman. Tunkaew, was tempted by the prospect of a more central role for herself in the **wang** as one of the wives of a high-ranking prince. She failed in her bid, and saw the way out of losing her standing as even a palace serving-woman as being the rejection of the authority of the **wang,** and seeking the protection of alternative centres in the **muang.** It is extremely unlikely that the British consul would have had the slightest interest in getting involved in the tangle, but the women must have thought differently. A **farang** man was their solution, the more powerful, the better.

Police and Court Flies as Materials for Social History

The records in the police and court case files of the Fifth Reign are a potential source of material for researching into topics relating to social history, but they require the historian to yoke otherwise unrelated and disparate cases together by considering how, when fit into a series, they might reinforce or raise questions about the image of the past that could be derived from reading one document or another. This is necessary as there is but one case in the records where a **momchao** manages to live as a debt slave for twenty-five years, only one case in which a palace serving woman throws herself at the doorstep of the British consulate. This paper juxtaposed the cases to contrast the choices available to the two women who were trying to escape from their life in the palace; they we also related to the dream of Momratchawong Sa-ing, and the schemes and machinations of Amdaeng Chom in that they all share the idea that they can better their lives whether it be by leaving the palace, or by taking advantage of their relationship with it in terms of the changes that the institution, and the society outside it, were undergoing,. No matter how these four cases are shuffled around, they fall into the same deck of cards.

However, they are able to resonate with other cases as well. For instance, the case of Tunkaew sits well with those of Siamese women who were (or in some cases, claimed to be) married to Western men and who had cause to appear before the law. Amdaeng Chom's use of the printed seals of the Royal Survey Department brings to mind cases where men sold forged certificates of exemption from corvee using similar tactics, and even the by far more sophisticated attempt at counterfeiting by a high-ranking prince and a Japanese printer. Amdaeng Chom's taking advantage of her "royal connections" has echoes in low-ranking official who convinced a foreign jeweller to let his wife sell the merchandise in the Inner Palace, where she had relatives, only to abscond with the valuables.

In themselves, the cases mentioned are unique. Placed in a series, they permit attempts to produce essays on various aspects of social history where the material are scarce and fragmentary, in comparison to societies for which diaries, literary works, art, the popular press, statistics and treatises and manuals on agriculture, medicine, manners, etc. which cover a century and more exist.

The specificities of the cases examined in this paper we certainly not mere "description". They we set out in this paper at some length as it is the very concreteness, immediacy and almost matter-of-fact tone of their narration (and those of witnesses and victims) to the investigating officers that permits the human dimension of the individuals involved to emerge in their social context. They we neither necessarily heroes nor villains, nor simply predators or victims, but people who gave thought to what their lives were about. In this, they are certainly not special; yet because traces of their lives have survived in the records, the historian can draw on them for a sense of their time and place. Not as representative, typical or even case studies from which generalisations and theories can be drawn: simply as manifestations of the complexities of life faced by women related marginally to the Palace which were wrought by the condition of society in a liminal period.

In the present chapter we have described the status of women of Royal and elite class. With the emergence of modern Thailand, great changes have come in Thai society. The status of women is pitiable not better than the traditional women of yore day. Thailand is a popular tourism destination, attracting a large number of tourism from all over the world. Sex tourism is popular in Thailand. As such women are badly exploited for prostitution. The facts furnished at the beginning of this chapter put ample light on the status of women in modern Thailand.

REFERENCES

1. Akin Rabibhadana, *The Organisation of Thai Society in the Early Bangkok Period, 1782-1873,* Data Paper no. 74, Southeast Asian Studies Programme (Ithaca: Cornell, 1969), p. 101.
2. *Ruang kotmai trasamduang* (the Three Seals Law Code), kotmonthianban (Palatine Laws), Clause 132 (Bangkok, Department of Fine Arts, republished 1978), p. 59.
3. Anna Leonowens, *The Romance of the Harem* (Charlottesville: University of Virginia, first published, 1872, reprinted, 1991).
4. Momratchawong Khukrit Pramoj, *Siphaendin* (our Reigns), (Bangkok, Kaona, 8th printing 1975, first published 1953).
5. Prince Dhani Nivat, *Prawat Thao Worachan* (A history of Thao Worachan), Cremation volume of Thao Worachan (Wad), (Bangkok, 1941).
6. National Archives of Thailand, Yuthitham 13/8 Ruang momchao pen that laemi phuaphrai (The case of a momchao who is a slave and has a commoner for a husband) 17 April—29 August 1983)
7. Cited from A King Of Siam Speaks, ed. M.R Seni Pramoj and M.R. Kukrit Pramoj (Bangkok: The Siam Society, 1987), p. 197.
8. Damrong Rajanubhab, *Ruang Chaloem Phrayot Chaonai* (In honour of the establishment of royal titles), (Bangkok, 1929), cited in Akin Rabibhadana, *The Organisation of Thai Society,*

p. 99.

9. National Archives of Thailand, Yuthitham 13.3/13 Nai Liab thamchu kab Momratchawong Sa-ing (Nai Liab commits adultery with Momratchawong Sa-ing)

10. Cited in Eiji Murashima, *Journal of Southeast Asian Studies,* vol. XIX no. 1 (March 1988), p. 88.

11. King Mongkut, *Prachumprakat Ratchakan thi si* (Collected Decrees of the Fourth Reign), (Bangkok: Khurusapha, 1961), Decree no. 255, p. 235.

12. Henry Alabaster, *The Wheel of the Law: Buddhism Illustrated from Siamaese Sources* (Farnborough: Gregg International, 1871, reprint edition 1971), p. 65).

13. National Archives of Thailand, Nakhonban 36/231 klong 14, Chab Amdaeng Chom phanraya Nai Sung angwa pen khonprodnai Somdetphrarachininat kab phakphuak lokluang ngern rasadon khwaeng Thanyaburi (The arrest of Amdaeng Chom, wife of Nai Sung, who claimed to be a favourite of Her Majesty the Queen, and who, with her group, cheated the money of the residents of Thanyaburi).

14. National Archives of Thailand, Yuthitham 13/24 Khamprueksathod ruang Amdaeng Chaem Raphai chakpha Tunkaew okchak phraborommaharatchawong (Consultations on the case of Amdaeng Chaem and Paphai who got Tunkaew to leave the Grand Palace) 25 July 1895.

7

Cuban Women and Society

> "If there must be warfare in the world, let it be between good and evil and not between nations."

The socioeconomic structure existing before the Revolution and the plunder of imperialism with the wealth of Cuba, had a decisive influence in the working and living conditions of the people. The economic delay brought about the social backwardness. Illiteracy constituted a chronic illness because of the lack of instruction, schools and teachers. Diseases were spread due to the lack of medical assistance and hospitals, specially in the rural zones.

These conditions, that affected the whole Cuban people, were more acute in the case of women; moreover a significant influence of social inherited prejudices was exerted upon women, as well as the ancestral conceptions that place them forever in a position of inferiority. During the colonial period, women neither participated in the political life of the country not had the right to vote concerning the familiar aspect, women's inferiority regarding men was made clear in the civil code with establishment of several articles with different ways of women's dependent to men, such as: woman's nationality depending on husband's nationality, the disposition to obey men, the dependence to the paternal and judicial authority, the preference of the female, the regulation of adultery, the setting up of limitations for second weddings, fixing time of waiting and losing the patri-potestas.

Before the triumph of the Revolution, there were 19400 employed women, 70% in domestic jobs; it was common to see in the newspaper long lists of classified announcements of women offering their services as maids for a very low salary without being protect any law.

Women suffered salary discrimination in industry as as well as in commerce. Regarding the women employed in agriculture, the situation was even worst. They worked without being considered salaries workers but as auxiliar member of the family, deprived of the right of social legislation of the epoch. Besides the worst and poorly remunerated job, that unjust society had reserved for women an even more terrible way: prostitution.

The discontent and indignation of the working women in front of exploitation they were facing, their apprehensions and reivindications, were in correspondence with the interests of their class comrades, based on the increased exploitation of the salaried labour in benefit of the monopolis and bosses.

Within the working class, the women formed one of the categories on which influenced, besides of the exploitation that the workers suffered in general, all kinds of discriminations and also the evident injustice in wages, employment and other demands granted as reivindications. The content of the laws nor always answered to their implementation because laws were not fulfilled in practice. Constantly the trade unions and their workers struggled against the violation committed by the proper State and bosses.

The Maternity Security presented limitations. A great number of workers could never enjoy such benefits, the presently was excluded. The hospital services excluded in the Maternity Security did not cover the regions placed far from the capitals of the provinces. To the eventual or alternate working women, submitted to these conditions because of the imposibility of seeking a fixed job, it was difficult to enjoy the benefits established by that law.

The great majority of children were born in their homes in the hands of the private midvives, in occasions they were under the attention of their own relatives or persons without training. And sometimes not even this. There were many Cuban women that saw their children dying because of the lack of medical assistance, or that saw then graving up illiterate due to the lack of schools or means to means to sand them to these.

Notably, there were many others that had to sleep in the middle of the way without shelter because of the slogments and dispossessions committed by the landowners who obliged them to do it. However, the most exploited and the most humiliated undoubtedly were black womens, because, besides of all prejudices suffered by the women of that society, they also paced the racial discrimination that kindered the opportunity of finding a respectful job.

The principle "equal pay equal work" was not respected. The jobs occupied by women were undervalued. They were classified in male jobs and female jobs, being the female jobs the ones that perceived the lowest salaries. In the Census of 1953, there were almost 2 million persons as active population, that is the population of over 14 years old that were working or looking for jobs. The 87.4% of this active population was composed by males and only the

13.7% embraced woman that were working or looking for jobs. That is 86.3% of women were not working and without conditions for seeking a job.

There were 200,000 huts and hovels in Cuba, 400,000 families in the country side and in the cities lived cramped in huts and tenements without even the minimum sanitary requirements. The main food of the peasant families was rice, beans and some viands; only 11% drank milk, 4% consumed eggs; being calculated the nutritional deficit in 100 daily calories. No less than 36% of the population was noticed as parasitic, while a significant preportion suffered or had suffered tuberculosis.

From 2,132,000 women over 10 years old, a 20% was illiterate, 71% subscholarized and only a 2% had completed the Senior and Junior High Education' the university level did not reach 1%.

Unemployment, misery, starvation, prostitution, the administrative abandon, and the distortion of our economy in the hands of the foreign capitals were the illness that Cuba complained in the pre-revolutionary epoch. This environment was found and rapidly transformed by the Revolution that triumph on January 1, of 1959, in which the Cuban women had actively participated.

The national historical legacy and ,the end of more than 100 years of struggle with the triumph of the Revolution in 1959 show us that the battle for the real emancipation of women can only be achieved with a profound transformation of the social, political and economic structures that make possible the immediate incorporation of women to the process of development. Extraordinary changes have taken place in the whole country, changes that are expression of the development program stated by the direction of the

Revolution; changes that pass beyond the economic relations, social environment; changes that exert into interaction and generate valuable experiences, reached in the revolutionary proceed and by the conquest of the political power by our people.

The transformation that is taken place in the field of construction which is materialised in practice, and the implementation of new of exploitation of resources is more clear every day the same form, the mining, dock and sugar regions or territories, and mainly our towns in which the 37% of the population lives in, and transformed.

Since the very beginning of the Revolution, it was stated the integration of women to the building of the new society, hence to create conditions that enable them to be incorporated to the general development process of the country. In Cuba, it is a great achievement the presence of women at all levels and sectors of the country: in the planning process: in industry, agriculture, education and others. The situation of 24 years ago has been essentially changed. Women constitute half of our population. Her no participation in the development process not only would mean an squndering of human resources, but also it is reflected in it in an apposite form.

The socioeconomic and political structures influence in a decisive form in women conditions. An example of this, is that in the socialist countries, no matter the degree of the development reached, the judicial and social condition of women has been considerably raised in regard to equality. In Cuba nowadays, about 920,000 women are incorporated to the socially and useful labour, this represents 34% of the total amount of workers in our country. In some is high, reaching 64.6% and 68.6% in the branches of education, science and health.

In other economic sectors, the amount of women incorporated is not so high however, it is manifested a notorious increase if we compare it with the figures before the Revolution, mainly in some branches of construction in which there were not women incorporation. In industry women represent 24.6% of that total amount of workers; in transportation 12.6% in the agricultural sector 14.6% in construction 9.8% and 40.7% in commerce. The growing participation of women in the economic life of the country has favoured the increase of the amount of women leaders in the working movement.

In the last electoral process, women were elected as deputies to the National Assembly of the People's Power. These achievement do not hinder our struggle to reach the full equality of women in our society, although we can affirm that never before in the history of our country women's representation has been so wide at the levels of direction. It should be pointed out that in the traditionally most backward rural areas, women represent today the 31% of the total amount of women peasants incorporated to the cooperatives which belong to the great agricultural plans to achieve highest forms of production.

Since the vary beginning. The Cuban state has created institutions and services to help women in their incorporation to the social labour. In 1961 the first day-care centres were opened, institutions created by the Revolution and whose objective is to facilitate incorporation to work and to the tasks assigned by the Revolution; and also to help in the development of their personality.

In 1980 there were 832 day care centres with a final enrollment of 91,736 children under 6 years old. Besides, the amount of mothers benefited with this service is about

82,941. On the other hand, these institutions follow the recommendations of child care teachers and advisers that promote the education and development of the enrolled children whose ages are between 45 days and 6 years old.

The semi-boarding primary school is a service given to working women that have children from 6 years old on. Now-a-days, more than 278,575 children enjoy this service, receiving education, food and in accordance with the mother's working schedule they are also given extra-school recreational attention. The scholarship plans have been increased, reaching in the school period 80-81 the figure of 580-612 scholarship students in the levels of Education. These students perceive free of charge education, study materials, food, medical and hospital assistance, recreation etc. The achievements attained by our Socialist Revolution in regard to the social, political and economic order have made possible for our women to receive the benefits of an adequate and necessary judicial protection, hence they can achieve active participation in the development process of the country.

The Maternity Law of the working women guarantees medical care for her and for her child, assuring a 6 week pre-and 12 week post-natal paid of absence, together with the right of occupying the same poet and salary she had before. The Family Code establishes the absolute equality of right for men and women in marriage as well as their common duties and responsibilities in regard to the created family. The constitution of our Republic establishes the equality of rights of women in marriage in work, salary, education and in all fields of the social, political and economic life of the country, reflecting the manifested desire of struggling through education, culture and mass media against the prejudices that still exist in some women's and men's mentalites and which are remains of old conceptions on the role of women in the framework of society.

An example of the achievements attained in this concern, is the presence of women in the different levels and types of education. If before the Revolution they represented more than the half of the illiterate people all over the country, today they represent about the 47.5% of the total amount of students of the primary level, the 50.8% of the intermediate level and the 50.8% in the superior education, as well as the 43.8% in the adult education plans. Healt services in Cuba are available to the whole population without any type discrimination. The curative preventive integral character of the social medicine in Cuba has substantially modified our country's health situations. The vaccination programs have eradicated communicable diseases as poliomyelitis and diphtheria, modified our country's health situation. The vaccination programs have eradicated communicable diseases and poliomyelitis and dipteris. With the consolidation of the structure of the National Health System, the activities concerning mother and child attention were aimed at the formation of a Mother-child attention program, that immediately became an important task of the Revolution. The 98.6% of delivers and accomplished in medical state institutions. This indicator places our country in the first levels at a world scale.

Before the triumph of the Revolution in 1958, the estimated infant mortality rate was 60% per each one thousand live birth, while in 1980 the rate was 19.6% and the mother mortality registered 5.2% deaths per each 10,000 live births. Among the activities directed to reduce infant and mother mortality, as well as the promotion and health prevention of mother and child, it can be distinguished the continues improvement of the labour technical norms in pediatrics and obstetrics, pre- the diagnostic and care fo the pregnant woman and the increase of institutional deliveries.

The pregnant women receive socio-prophylactic preparation for deliveries and dental care attention, they are also incorporated to a wide prevention programme of disease through vaccination. The successes and advances that the Cuban women have obtained in the judicial protection and her improvements in the necessary material conditions to accomplish her incorporation to the different spheres of economy, are very close related to the work of the Federation of Cuban Women. Due to the process of transformation initiated at the triumph of the Revolution on January 1st., 1959 an to women's enthusiasm and desire of participating in this process, the Federation of Cuban Women was founded in August, 23rd 1960. The F.C.W. whose main objective is the integral development of women regarding their full and effective incorporation to the building of the now society. The FCW comprises the best struggle traditions of the women movement in our country. It carried out its work aware of the fact that the true women emancipation can only be achieved in the liberation process of all the people and the way she actively participates in this process and also in the social cultural, political and economic life of the country. That is why, the content of work of our organization has gone at the same rhythm of development of our Revolution, and because of the simple organizational forms and tasks of the firsts moments, the CW has become a strong and powerful organization able to carry out the most complex tasks assigned by the Revolution. At present, the CW has 2,514,095 members which represents 91% of the feminine population over 14 years old.

Remarkably, among the objectives of the CW we can mention: to exalt women before herself and before society, making her aware of the value of her participation in the social process; to raise her ideological, political and cultural level in order to enable her to play the part that is her right as a constructor of the new society: to take notes of the concerns womens have, submitting them to the party and state institutions to find the necessary solutions; to give the Revolution all possible contribution to the development of the national economy: and at the sometime to practice solidarity and proletarian in internationalism.

Cuban women have realised that in a society free of exploiters and exploited it is possible its foundation, the FCW has carried out a systematic work to raise the cultural level of women, not only in the urban but also in the rural zones; achieving substantial advancements in this field. It has graduated thousands of women in the sixth grade and great number of them are studying in courses medium and superior and levels. It also develops a broad plan for technical training.

Regarding this, thousands of women are incorporated to different courses of qualified workers in the different sectors of the national economy organised in 13,628 brigades of Militant Mothers for Education, 1,574,000 women develop several activities in support to schools where their children study: for example to collaborate in the accomplishment of political and recreational activities, to help to maintain in good conditions the didactic materials, to include correct habits in the norms of social life and the respect and care of the social property. Our organization also developed a broad work in the program of the integral attention to women and child through the work of the Health Brigades which in the daily work with polyclinics, respond with great efficiency to the requirements of the communitary medicine, carrying out several plans of vaccination in the infant and feminine population—At present we have 65,370 health brigadists.

In rural areas the FCW works in coordination with the Farmers Association: and we asses we valuable the collaboration given by women to the national economy through the voluntary work in agriculture, industry and services as well as their work in the cooperatives of agricultural production. In the work of the FCW it has always been present the militant solidarity with all the peoples of the world; and example of this, are the friendship brigades that function at the grass root levels in our organization, which are dedicated the study of the history, cultural traditions, costumes, habits of brother countries, developing activities of solidarity and celebrating the significant historical dates of the country they study.

Now-a-days there are 32,311 friendship brigades. A great number of Cuban Women have honourably fulfilled with the high principles of proletariat internationalism in the military and civil fields as constructors, doctors, nurses and technicians. In all the achievement and successes scored by the FCW we can see the courage, responsibility and enthusiasm of our Cuban women in the whole country and the decisive and consequent support of our government and party regarding women's concerns.

The increasing boom of the women movement in Latin America has been characterized by the economic, political and social situation of the countries that belong to, it. The existence of repressive and dictatorial regimes have sharpened the socio-political situation of the peoples of Central America in which we observe with satisfaction the growing participation of women in the vanguard progressive movements in the struggle to achieve the true national independence and with this the break of old socio-economic structures that promote the relations of dependence and exploitation in regard to the North American imperialism.

In this context the women organization coordinate and strengthen their work and intensify the actions taking into account the specific characteristics of each country. In the western hemisphere, an important group of countries are suffering bloody dictatorships and their peoples write true pages of heroism in the struggle for the conquest of their independence, others suffer the effects of exploitation and imperialist economic dependence, some of them with correct positions concerning the rescue of their rights upon their territories with the defence of the material resources maintaining a frontal battle for the respect and sovereignty of their countries.

Nicaragua and Grenada, engaged in the national reconstruction of their countries, are victims of th attacks and maneuvers of imperialism. In front of these facts and of the increase fo the struggle of Latin American peoples, women have not rested. This was shown in the Women Continental Meeting "National Independence and Peace" that represented a significant platform in which several womens organization raised their voices in support to the struggle of the peoples of El Salvador and Guatemala, to reject the aggressive plans against Cuba.

Nicaragua and Grenada: they expressed their desire of peace for the region and the world; and also called for urgent actions of solidarity with the creation of a coordination body named Women's Continental Front Against Intervention "composed by outstanding women of the region that belong to different representative political forces of Latin America and the Caribbean. Women International Democratic Federation gathers today a strong feminine force able to carry out multiple actions in favour to the struggle of National Independence, Peace and Equality. Its Regional Headquarter in Havana has enabled the affiliated national organizations to undertake the training of their leaders through three-month courses for women leaders of Latin America and the Caribbean. In the scope of the Movement of the Non-Aligned Countries, the women of the region also provided their efforts in the elaboration, approval and implementation of the Action Programme. About the Role of Women in the Development of the Non-Aligned Countries and other developing countries approved in Havana from May 25-27 of 1981.

The Program represented a valuable contribution for women's integration to development of their countries which can only be achieved when the people can choose by themselves the most convenient way of development. Today we can affirm that women from Latin America and the Caribbean engaged in the struggle for National Independence, social equality and sovereignty constitute an unbreakable force against imperialism, colonialism and neo-colonialism. With their peoples, they sing the anthem of struggle, and with the world th songs of peace: because they know its price and understand that only a peace for all the peoples will permit to direct all our actions towards a better world and a happy future for humanity.

As of now some changes have come in cuban society. And women are enjoying some better status. The impact of globalisation is being felt there also.

8

Women in Nigeria: Issues & Challenges

BASIC FACTS

Life expectancy: females as a % of males, 2007	102
Adult literacy rate: females as a % of males, 2000–2007	80
Enrolment and attendance ratios: females as a % of males, Net primary school 2000–2007, enrolled	86
Enrolment and attendance ratios: females as a % of males, Net primary school 2000–2007, attending	88
Enrolment and attendance ratios: females as a % of males, Net secondary school 2000–2007, enrolled	84
Enrolment and attendance ratios: females as a % of males, Net secondary school 2000–2007, attending	87
Contraceptive prevalence (%), 2000–2007	13
Antenatal care coverage (%), At least once, 2000–2007	58
Antenatal care coverage (%), At least four times, 2000–2007	47
Delivery care coverage (%), Skilled attendant at birth, 2000–2007	35
Delivery care coverage (%), Institutional delivery, 2000–2007	33
Maternal mortality ratio, 2000–2007 reported	-
Maternal mortality ratio, 2005, adjusted	1100
Maternal mortality ratio, 2005, Lifetime risk of maternal death. 1 in:	18

Over the last many decades, researchers have paid more and more attention to the rote that women can play in social change and in the transition of a society from a rural agricultural state to a modern industrial one. Associated with such change—which, in a fluid and dynamic society like that of Nigeria, leads to a transformation of the social and economic systems—is culturally a change in which women, in their roles as wives and mothers, play a very important part as innovators and as transmitters of culture.

Culture here is to be understood as including not only social institutions and their derivative forms of learned behaviour (behaviour that is not instinctive, innate, or biologically determined) but also those manifestations of human creativity whereby new and distinctively individual forms are produced within the range of traditional patterns (Herskovits and Bascom 1959: 1,6). It is therefore pertinent to examine the traditional roles of women in the development of culture in Nigerian society and the degree to which women in modern Nigerian society transform these roles. This examination is of great importance, as the conventional wisdom in Western liberal circles maintains that women in traditional and modern African societies comprise a deprived group, incapable of giving focus and direction to cultural development, of low status, economically dependent on men, with few legal rights and no political responsibilities. This widely held viewpoint is, of course, a projection on African women of the experience of nineteenth century Western women, a projection that ignores the fundamental differences between the various cultures and the roles that women have played in them. It should not be surprising, therefore, to find that in Nigeria, as in many other African countries south of the Sahara, women have played and still play a very important role in the cultural process. In fact, as mothers in the nuclear or extended family, their role is central, for they help to conserve those vital elements that make Nigerian culture distinctive.

Like women the world over, they are responsible for transmitting the indigenous language to their children. They are also responsible, in great part, for handing down the oral literature and history, especially to children, through the vehicle of moonlight stories. In many parts of Nigeria, after the evening meal women tell stories of heroes and villains, of might and prowess, to their own children and to children from neighboring compounds.

These stories feature the traditional norms of society, and through them children unconsciously assimilate the traditions of the societies to which they belong and learn quite early in life what sanctions await them if they do not conform to these norms. As transmitters of the culture, women also ensure that there is no radical break with the past and that the process of change is gradual. It might be thought, for example, that modern Nigerian women, with Western-type education, would repudiate the bonds that link the nuclear family with its kin. However, these women realize that Western notions of social relations cannot be applied so readily to Nigerian society and that the nuclear family is not in a position to repudiate the obligations of family and kinship (cf. Wilson 1961:111). The Nigerian woman has safeguarded the ties between the nuclear family and its kith and kin by insisting that the husband observe family and kinship obligations (e.g. contributing cash for ritual and ceremonial occasions, education, clothing, and other expenses), even if this stretches to their limits the budget and harmony of the nuclear family. The attitude of women, no matter how highly educated and modern, toward marriage customs also illuminates the role of Nigerian women in the process of change. For marriages to be accepted as legal in most Nigerian societies, a marriage payment, however small, must be made, and bridal gifts must be exchanged. As field observations have shown, it is usually the women of the elite, not the men, who insist on these payments and gifts in order to ensure that their daughters are PROPERLY married. Recently, a highly educated Western Ibo woman told me that the most important thing that had happened to her in the previous year was her husband's decision, after eight years of marriage, to buy her a sewing machine.

When I asked her why she herself had not bought the machine if she needed it, as she was a well-paid business executive, her answer was prompt and unexpected: "Custom requires that my husband should, as part of his gift to me during marriage, buy me a sewing machine." Here is a striking example of the role that women play in preserving the distinctiveness of Nigerian culture. In addition to functioning as the main transmitter of the culture, the Nigerian Woman has shown herself to be an innovator in spheres that are ordinarily held to be unrewarding for cultural innovation. These include food preparation, hairdressing, pottery manufacture, cloth weaving, and dressmaking, which in Nigeria are dominated by women. To understand the current cultural significance of these activities it must be remembered that Nigeria, like most other sub-Saharan African countries, has only recently made the transition from colonial to independent status. Under colonialism, one expression of cultural domination by the British metropole was the adoption by the emerging Nigerian elite of Western norms in food, dress, and toiletry. Western foods like potatoes and baked beans were preferred to nutritionally similar but indigenous foods like yams and *ewa,* because the Western foods displayed the degree of

Western acculturation of the elite, with the power and prestige that this conferred. But with the emergence from the colonial situation and the necessity of creating and stressing a national image and personality, the elite were forced to rediscover their roots in the traditions, customs, and practices of their own people. Three spheres in which it was relatively easy to "boycott the boycottables," to use a slogan current in Nigeria in the early fifties, were those of food preparation, toiletry, and dress.

Thanks to the quick response and inventiveness of the womenfolk, Nigerian dishes soon took their proper place at state parties and other functions, albeit with a considerable improvement in their preparation and variety. To the standard dishes of village fare were added new dishes based on traditional foods. Plantain crispies took the place of potato crispies; salad was made from ocally grown fruits and vegetables; yam balls (a fried mixture of mashed yam and meat) and *moi moi* (a pudding of bean flour with eggs, beef, pepper, and onions) appeared on the tables of the elite. The distinctively Nigerian cuisine that emerged could take its place beside the cuisine of any other nation. A similar development can also be traced in the evolution of hairdressing among the elite in Nigeria. In the 1930's Sylvia Leith-Ross noted the intricate hairstyles of the Owerri Ibo women, yet from 1940 to 1960 hair straightening by pomades or hot iron combs was the fashion among the women of the elite (Leith-Ross 1965:95).

Since then, however, the situation has turned full circle and today, when a primary goal of most developing countries is an accelerated economic growth rate, with the concomitant rapid assimilation of Western technology, traditional hair styles have come back into their own, against the competition of Western styles and wigs. Many women of the elite prefer traditional-hairstyles for their durability and beauty. In offices, markets, recreation clubs, and meetings, in streets and homes, in rural and urban areas, women are wearing traditional hair styles, and women hairdressers are hard at work, improving former hairstyles and inventing new ones. Moreover, an important aspect of the yearly Festival of the arts competition is hairdressing, and traditional hair fashions were decreased as standard for the Second All-Africa Games, which were held recently in Lagos. Traditionally, pottery manufacture is exclusively a woman's domain. Throughout Nigeria women make pots and other household utensils of various sizes, shapes, and qualities, to suit every taste and purse. Despite the severe competition of imported china and enamel ware, these potters still remain very active. In the rural areas particularly, and to some extent in the semiurban towns, women prepare meals, expecially sauces, in traditional clay pots.

Clay pots are also preferred for the storage of water because they keep the water cool in the absence of refrigerators. In some areas, such as Abuja, in Northern Nigeria, the standard of workmanship is so high that the pottery has attracted national and international attention. The governments of the federation have had to take an interest in and give support to such work, as these wares have given Nigeria a craft which is distinctive and of very high aesthetic quality. Traditional weaving and dyeing, dominated by women, have also lately come into their own, despite the increased and severe competition of foreign machine-made textiles which are dumped on the Nigerian market and which imitate traditional designs and colours. These foreign textiles, however, have only strengthened the traditional homemade textile industry. The demand for the *Akwete* [cloth woven by the Akwete women of East

Central Nigeria] by both foreigners and Nigerians has been remarkable and has naturally resulted in a price increase. Almost the same can be said of the *asho oke* [cloth woven by Yoruba men] which is also much sought after and quite expensive. The increased popularity of these traditional cloths can be traced in part to the patronage given them by prominent Nigerian women. But by far the greater part of this popularity is attributable to the imagination and taste that women dress designers like Shade Thomas, trained in Western Europe and North America, have put into their creations, which have won them and these cloths an international reputation. An equally important role is played by Nigerian women in the dyeing industry. Barth, visiting Kano in the 1830's, remarked that dyeing was by far the most important industry there (Barth 1965:512*)*. The Yoruba woman has brought this art to near perfection, introducing varied patterns in order to achieve an attractive, distinctive effect. Visitors to Nigeria now readily admit that whether the *akwete* is used as an evening or cocktail dress, the *asho oke* as a wedding outfit with the *onilegogoro* head tie to attract attention, or the *adire* [dyed cloth] as a shirt or dress, they all have a charm that is uniquely Nigerian. Less well known is the important role that women play in the economic activities of Nigeria. In agriculture, which is the main economic activity, farm work in many Nigerian societies is shared by men and women. Some crops, like yams, are produced by men, while others, like cocoyams and cassava, are produced by women. Both men and women provide food for the family, and many an erring husband in the rural areas finds himself being starved into submission when his offended wife refuses to provide her portion of the family meal. Furthermore, as Green (1964:170-171) has pointed out, the part that women play in Nigeria's economic life has meant that, where they do not occupy public positions, they have much quiet power, because they are often the chief breadwinners, supplying the lion's share of the family food, buying such extras as salt and fish with their own money, and providing their husbands with funds to finance their multifarious activities. This gives women, both individually and collectively, a lever by which they can bring pressure to bear on their men. Thus the notion that women are economically dependent on men, when viewed in the actual operation of Nigerian society, is easily recognized as a myth.

The Nigerian woman, whether as mother, tiller of the soil, or trader, has her own quiet dignity and commands respect not only from her husband but also from her family and her community. Nowhere is this real power better exemplified than in the markets, which are dominated by women whose archetype is the proverbial "market mammy." In the lives of Nigerian women, markets have a central function and have always been important. As Hodder points out:

> Women rather than men are concerned in rural marketing activities. Rarely will a rural periodic day market contain more than a handful of men... To Yoruba women, moreover, marketing, petty-trading or at least attending a market, forms part of their way of life, and their reward lies as much in the social life offered by the markets as in their cash profits.

Besides their economic functions, these markets (most of which are periodic day or night markets) act as meeting places and as channels of communication for friends and relatives, where the latest news and gossip can be discussed. The market is also a place for displaying wealth. In many Ibo towns and villages, women who have taken titles come to their local markets accompanied by friends and relatives, to display their *erulu* [coral beads] and *odu* [elephant tusk armbands], local emblems of wealth. Furthermore in some parts of Benin and Ishan divisions, a mother brings her newborn baby to the local market after her obligatory rest period of a few weeks following delivery. Accompanied by friends and relatives, the mother dances around the market, receiving congratulations and presents from the other women. Markets are also advertising grounds for new dances. Dances—especially women's dances like the age group dances in Eastern Nigeria—are not sanctioned for display to the public until they have been taken through the market and approved by the market women. Even dance competitions, which have recently been encouraged by women's groups to strengthen and develop this aspect of Nigerian culture, take place in these rural towns on market days. In the urban areas, too, women's societies organize and encourage dance festivals and competitions.

Girls in secondary schools are encouraged to enter their traditional dances in arts festivals and competitions, which not only consolidate what is traditional and uniquely Nigerian, but also refine and improve dance styles and techniques. Paradoxically, in the realm of economic attitudes, where men have had the greatest degree of direct acculturative experience, it is the women who have changed most. Among the Afikpo Ibo, for example, although wealth has long been an index of personal importance and distinction for both men and women, the economic aspirations of women have changed in recent years (Ottenberg 1959).

Afikpo men, having achieved a high consumption level—with cars, bicycles, radios, European furniture, and certain European foods and smoking habits—still regard taking titles as the most valid form of investment. While many women believe taking titles represents the best disposition of wealth, a number of them, both literate and illiterate, give first consideration to a standard of living that includes clothing, adequate nutrition, and the education of their children. Thus the number of women taking titles has declined, even when business conditions are good. Instead of living on a near-starvation diet in order to save money for a title, many women now consider it bad "not to eat in one's house' in order to take unnecessary titles. In fact, among women a higher standard of living and better education for children are replacing titles as symbols of status, and sometimes profit, although the principle underlying both the old and the new forms of distinction, achievement, and prestige, have remained the same (Ottenberg 1959:216-217). However, it is not only in the economic affairs of the nation that women play an important role. They are also a force to be reckoned with in politics. Those who think that Nigerian women are passive, lethargic, and uninterested in the political life of their communities need only he reminded of the role they played in the Women's Riot of 1929-1930. The British colonial government in Nigeria introduced taxation of men in 1926. In 1929 women in the Owerri and Calabar areas learned that the government was preparing to tax women. The women were, of course, enraged by this, as it ran counter to all culture and tradition, "How can they tax the seed that bears fruit?" they asked. "We cannot buy food or clothes, how shall we get money to pay tax?" (Aba Commission, 11-12).

Word spread, especially during market days, when the women had the opportunity to exchange views, and soon the women rose like an army in massive protest against this injustice, looting European trading stores and banks, breaking into prisons to release prisoners, and beating chiefs and court messengers. The British district officers, fearing for their lives and hoping to reestablish law and order, sent for the police and troops. To their eternal disgrace and shame, they actually opened fire and killed or wounded over thirty of these angry but defenseless women (Leith-Ross 1965:23-30). Since then, governments in Nigeria have been extremely chary of taxing women, and it is only within the last twenty years that working women have had to pay tax. As recently as the early 1940's Abeokuta women in Western Nigeria revolted under the leadership of Mrs. Fumilayo Ransome-Kuti, a well-known member of the Nigerian Woman's Union. This uprising protesting the taxation of women led to the temporary self-exile of the *Alake* of Abeokuta, Oba Ademola II, by the Abeokuta Native Authority, which was headed by the *Alake* [king] of Egbaland (Sklar 1963:25).

Thus Nigerian women can and do exercise great political influence. But in many traditional Nigerian societies women also exercise considerable power and authority, participating fully in decision making at most levels. Among the Ibos of Midwestern Nigeria, for example, the villages and rural towns are ruled jointly by the *obi* [the male king] and the *omu* [the female counterpart of the king]. The *omu* is not the wife of the *obi* and is in no way related to him. The rules for succeeding to the positions of *obi* and *omu* are different. In the case of the *obi,* succession to the throne is hereditary and lies with the eldest male child. A regent is appointed if the child is not yet of age. In the case of the *omu*, succession is not hereditary and the *omu's* eldest daughter has no claim to her throne. The *omu* is appointed from certain lineages; in some of these lineages she is selected by the *umuaka* [all adult daughters of the lineage).

The *omu* is thus appointed by her kith and kin and she is always a woman past child-bearing age. The *omu*, rules in conjunction with the *obi.* A clear division of functions exists between them, and neither is inferior to the other. The *omu* rules the women just as the *obi* rules the men, and the *omu* has the onerous duty of seeing that the women abide by tradition. With the help of her advisers, she judges cases, metes out punishments in cases of adultery, stealing, or other infractions of local law and custom, and gives advice in the spirit of the age-old traditions. She also presides over and encourages title-taking among the women. Women are thus responsible for maintaining law and order among their own sex, and they participate in making decisions that affect the life of the whole community.

In the local government reforms that swept over Nigeria from 1950 to 1960, very little cognizance was taken of this institution and of the traditional role that women play in government. This is perhaps not too surprising, because the designers of the proposals seem to have based their recommendations not on the principle of modernizing the traditional political systems, but rather on that of copying the British local government system, paying deference here and there to local tradition. The result has been that even these recent political adaptations of government forms do not exhibit the congruence between political structure and political culture that is expected of a properly functioning political system.

As such we can conclude

> African women, by and large, have a high social position: legal rights, religious and political responsibility, economic independence.... Women in Africa are not, in short, a deprived group as they were in the nineteenth century Western world. (Bohannan and Curtin 1971: 107-108).

Notably, they are, in fact, a driving force in the search for cultural regeneration and a national identity. In Nigeria women have succeeded in their own way in creating forms and fashions that are uniquely Nigerian and that grow organically from the traditional culture, They have thus helped to lessen the psychological frustration engendered by the colonial and neocolonial experience. They have built up poles of creativity and aesthetic invention which are essentially Nigerian and have thus given purpose and direction in the search for a new Nigerian cultural identity in the postcolonial era.

REFERENCES

Aba Commission, n.d., *Report of the Commission of Enquiry Appointed to Inquire into the Disturbances in the Calabar and Owerri Provinces.*

Afigbo, A.E., 1972, *The warrant chiefs: indirect rule in South-Eastern Nigeria 1891-1929.* London: Longmans.

Amucheazi, Flochukwu, 1973, Local government and traditional legitimacy: divisional administration in the East Central State. *Quarterly Journal of Administration* 7(4): 439-450. Ife: University of Ife, Institute of Administration.

Bohannan, P., P. Curtin, 1971, *Africa and Africans.* New York: Doubleday.

Barth, Heinrich, 1965, *Travels and discoveries in North and Central Africa (1849-1855)* (centenary edition), first volume 444. London: Frank Cass.

Green, M.M., 1964, *Igbo village affairs* (second edition). London: Frank Cass.

Herskovits, M.J., W.R. Bascom, 1959, "The problem of stability and change in African culture," in *Continuity and change in African cultures.* Edited by M.J. Herskovits and W.R. Bascom. Chicago: University of Chicago Press.

Hodder, B.W., 1961, Rural periodic day markets in parts of Yorubaland. *Institute of British Geographers Transactions and Papers* 29.

Leith-Ross, S., 1965, *African women* (second edition). London: Routledge and Kegan Paul.

Ottenberg, P.V., 1959, "The changing economic position of women among the Afikpo Ibo," in *Continuity and change in African cultures.* Edited by M.J. Herskovits and W.R. Bascom. Chicago: University of Chicago Press.

Sklar, L.R., 1963, *Nigerian political parties.* Princeton: Princeton University Press.

Thomas, Northcote W., 1969, *Ibo speaking peoples of Nigeria* (second reprint). New York: Negro Universities Press.

Wilson, G., 1961, "Mombasa—a modern colonial municipality," in *Social change in modern Africa.* Edited by A. Southall. London: Oxford University Press.

9

Women in China

> "Waste is worth than loss. The time is coming when every person who lays claim to ability will keep the question of waste before him constantly. The scope of thrift is limitless.."
>
> —*Thomas E. Edison*

NOTABLE BASIC FACTS

Life expectancy: females as a % of males, 2007	105
Adult literacy rate: females as a % of males, 2000–2007	93
Enrolment and attendance ratios: females as a % of males, Net primary school 2000–2007, enrolled	100
Enrolment and attendance ratios: females as a % of males, Net primary school 2000–2007, attending	-
Enrolment and attendance ratios: females as a % of males, Net secondary school 2000–2007, enrolled	-
Enrolment and attendance ratios: females as a % of males, Net secondary school 2000–2007, attending	-
Contraceptive prevalence (%), 2000–2007	85
Antenatal care coverage (%), At least once, 2000–2007	90
Antenatal care coverage (%), At least four times, 2000–2007	-
Delivery care coverage (%), Skilled attendant at birth, 2000–2007	98
Delivery care coverage (%), Institutional delivery, 2000–2007	88

Maternal mortality ratio, 2000–2007 reported	41
Maternal mortality ratio, 2005, adjusted	45
Maternal mortality ratio, 2005, Lifetime risk of maternal death. 1 in:	1300

The Fourth United Nations International Conference on Women in Beijing, China in September, 1995, and the United Nations International Conference on Population and Development (ICPD) in Cairo, Egypt in September, 1995, have changed the world's perception of the roles of women globally, in general, and in China, in particular. Ironically, plans were made to hold the next International Conference in 1998 in Seneca Falls, New York, southeast of Rochester, in celebration of the sesquicentennial of the world's first organised movement in behalf of women inaugurated in 1848 at a small chapel in the sleepy village of Seneca Falls, New York, now the home of the National Women's Hall of Fame and Museum.

Here our intention is four-fold: *first*, and most important, it deals with cultural and legal definitions of *violence against women; second*, the *development of population policies*, in the context of health, empowerment and rights; *third*, the formulation by and for *health policies* for women, in the areas of reproduction, fertility, gender selection and contraception, and *fourth,* women's *political action*, as representatives of and in the development of their own futures.

Women and men are networking through conferences, legislatures and the information super-highway to provide "equality and equity" in their human/humane treatment around the world. This paper addresses some of these developments.

The Constitution of the People's Republic of China was

adopted by the First National People's Congress of the People's Republic of China on 20 September, 1954, virtually five years after the founding of the People's Republic on 1 October, 1949. Chapter III: "Fundamental Rights and Duties of Citizens" clearly states in Articles 85, 86 and 96 that women are equal to men, constitutionally:

> *Article 85*: Citizens of the People's Republic of China are equal before the law.
> *Article 86*: Citizens of the People's Republic of China who have reached the age of eighteen whatever their nationality, race, *sex* [emphasis added], occupation, social origin, religious belie, education, property status, or length of residence except insane persons and persons deprived by law of the fight to vote and stand for election.
>
> Women have equal fights with men to vote and stand for election.
>
> *Article 96*: Women in the People's Republic of China enjoy equal fights with men in all spheres of political, economic, cultural, social and domestic life.
>
> The state protects marriage, the family, and the mother and child. (Li, 298-9)

With the possible caveat of "except insane persons" in Article 86, the protection appears to be equal and equitable. What follows, in the context of the above noted four categories of *violence against women, population policies, health policies*, and *political action* deviates from this "theory" as it has been applied during the past forty years of "practice."

The basic thesis of Margery Wolf's *Revolution Postponed: Women in Contemporary* China, published a decade ago, is "...the frequency which a revolutionary government has stepped aside from one of its most earnestly stated goals, gender equality (Wolf, 26)." She notes that:

> Even though women were held up as 'the other half

> of the sky' with important contributions to socialist construction, their release from 'backbreaking manual labor and tedious housework' was to be gradual. In the meantime, a double burden was clearly stated. 'Women workers, commune members and women scientists and technicians need to work hard and study, but they have to spend a considerable portion of the time tending to housework and children (Wolf, 26).

Discussion of male participation in balancing the familial responsibilities is notably absent. The emphasis on *gradual* release is put forth with no notation of gradual release to or from something and/or someone! "...(W)hat the revolution had promised (women) was a stable family life in the traditional (Confucian) patriarchal style (Stacey, 155-57)."

> Women...bear the brunt of the birth-control effort, which has been enforced vigorously under the reforms. The PRC's extraordinary strict and successful birth-control programme places the responsibility for limiting births overwhelmingly on women.... In addition, reports from China indicate that the old practice of kidnaping women and selling them to men who want a spouse has revived and is spreading.... In sum, it appears that on balance women's positions in society have suffered under the reforms. Like men, of course, women enjoy an improved overall standard of living as the economy grows; nevertheless, their position *relative* to men has in some important ways deteriorated (Liberthal, 310).

Female infanticide has been a curious problem since the revolution in 1949. Initially shunned, it has increased since the imposition of the new family planning policy of "one child per family" and in 1992

> the authorities were stunned by the results of a new government-sponsored survey which showed

> that the sex ratio for newborn infants had reached 118.5 boys for every 100 girls. If the norm is taken to be 105.5, then more than 12 per cent of all Chinese baby girls go missing each year. That adds up to more than 1.7 million missing girls annually (Kristof, 229).

Although Family Planning Minister Peng Peiyun proclaimed "in no case is coercion allowed as a means of implementing family planning policy" (Sen, 98), government imposes fines, withholds medical and housing benefits and other privileges to "force compliance" with state policy. Such violence against women, in practice, is chronicled more today than when the theory of equality was propounded in 1949 verbally and in 1954 constitutionally. Such theoretical principles still exist in Articles 48 and 49 of "the Constitution of the People's Republic of China" promulgated by the National People's Congress on 4 December, 1982, with two interesting revisions over the 20 September, 1954 version:

> *Article 48:* . . .the state protects the rights and interests of women, applies the principle of equal pay for equal work to men and women alike and trains and selects cadres from among women.
>
> *Article 49:* . . .Both husband and wife have the duty to practice family planning. . .and children who have come of age have the duty to support and assist their parents (Lieberthal, 365).

As the theory gets more explicit, the practice appears to get less supportive, with increased examples of violence.

Sexual rights and family planning are key to *population policies*, in the context of health, empowerment and rights The U.N. Conference in Beijing defined sexual rights as "the right of a women to decide when and with whom to have sex; the right of a couple to decide when to have children (Brauchli, B1)." The International Women's Health Coalition (IWHC) and the Harvard Center for Population and Development Studies under an arrangement with the Swedish International Development Authority (SIDA) in March 1994, published a monograph entitled *Population Policies Reconsidered: Health. Empowerment, and Rights* which focuses globally on the United Nations Conference on Population and Development held in Cairo in September 1994. *The Cairo Consensus: The Right Agenda for the Right Time* at this conference of 184 governments, for the first time agreed that "the reproductive and sexual health and reproductive rights of women are central to an international agreement on population (Germain, 3)."

Population policies, as addressed by the above three organisations, were based upon "...the universally accepted goals of health, empowerment and human rights...(Sen, xiii)."

> This new vision of population policies does not call for a retreat from government intervention in population affairs. Rather, it seeks a quality of life and the services that could advance human well-being and freedom for the next century (Sen, 11).

In the 1950s, Mao Zedong encouraged a population policy that more babies would make for a more powerful China. When the communists came to power the population of China approximated 550 million. By 1979, it had almost doubled to 971 million (Dietrich, 292). The imposition of a birth limitation program was put in place in 1979, yet even with the so-called "one-child per family" policy in place the population is projected to 1.5 billion, a three-fold increase, by 2030 over 1949 (Lii, 27).

In sum, the birth planning program that promises

> so much for women is also run at their expense. They must take responsibility for the contraceptive devices that they may or may not wish to make use of... The child is in her body, so she must be to blame....(what) about male sterilisation. The usual answer was that men were not willing, but many said vasectomies 'weakened' men, and since they must work for the family it was better to have the women sterilised... One can only assume that the government agrees with the male farmer...that women are expendable, men are not, and that was why vasectomies were rarely performed (Wolf, 259).

It is obvious that tradition still dictates the future of modern China, as it did in the past 4694 years of the Chinese calendar. Empowerment and rights will likely be driven by the economic engine that continues to view men as more important than women. Women, if they choose to ride this 21st century mechanism, will have to adjust to that reality.

The formulation of health policies for women in the areas of reproduction, fertility, gender selection and contraception will also rest on their shoulders as noted:

> Couples who have serious hereditary diseases including psychosis, mental deficiency, and malformation must not be allowed to bear children. Those who are already pregnant must terminate the pregnancy.
>
> Fertile couples must use reliable birth control according to the provisions. In case of pregnancies in default of the plan, measures must be taken to terminate them.
>
> All fertile couples who are conformable to the criteria of child-bearing must adopt birth control measures without exception. Birth control should be practiced

> by contraception as a principle. Conceptions against family planning caused by the failure of contraception measures must be ended (Sen, 98).

The provincial policies propounded between 1987 and 1991 in Sichuan, Zhejiang and Jilin, respectively, place responsibility on families, in general, and women, in particular, through financial penalties that foster the Five Goods Movement: (1) unite with the neighborhood families for mutual aid, (2) do housework well, (3) educate children well, (4) encourage family production, study, and work, and (5) study well themselves (Andors, 33). The growth of the economy in a harmonic atmosphere, whether through male or female workers, is still based on the "family values" system reminiscent of age-old Confucianism as the ultimate stabiliser of the society, the culture and the nation. Individual freedoms are predicated on this framework, because the economy supersedes political pronouncements, former or otherwise.

In fact, this political action, whether in China or through international channels, is reflective of a more relaxed policy of economic advancement over the past decade and a half:

> Women face greater economic opportunity than they did under Mao but also more discrimination; they can find work more easily, but many of the jobs are on the assembly lines in the noisiest, dirtiest industries; they may drive buses and taxis, but they usually take only one-third of the spots in the universities; they enjoy excellent maternity benefits, but they are the first workers fired during times of economic austerity; while they are sometimes allocated land in the countryside, valued possessions are handed down from generation to generation through the male line. Worst of all, the rising market economy now embraces women themselves

> as tradable commodities. A huge market emerged in the 1980s in the trafficking of women and children.... In 1978, 11.1 per cent of the Central Committee members and their alternates were women; the proportion (by the early 1990s) is 7.5. In 1993, the government selected women for just three out of the forty-one ministerial jobs, and there are indications that the proportion of female party members has dropped (Kristof, 216-22).

Further, the theory appears equitable; the practice is less than ideal. The changing roles of women in China appear to be gravitating backwards to the more traditional model of Confucianism. Couple this with the decrease in next generation family members to take care of their elders as is the past and the lot of women "under the sky" will be anything less than equal! No doubt, despite a closed society modern wave of LPG has brought in great change in all spheres of Chinese society and women are not untouched with it.

REFERENCES

Andors, Phyllis (1983). *The Unfinished Liberation of Chinese Women. 1949-1980*. Bloomington: Indiana University Press.

Brauchli, Marcus and Kathy Chen (1995). "Women Play Political Scrabble to Spell Out the Issues." *The Wall Street Journal*, September 11.

Chen, Kathy and Joseph Kahn (1995), "China's Reform March Growing Longer: Foreign, Domestic Crises Make Leadership Go Slow." *The Wall Street Journal*, April 7.

Dietrich, Craig (1986). *People's China: A Brief History* New York: Oxford University Press.

Germain, Adrienne and Rachel Kyte (1995). *The Cairo Consensus: The Right Agenda for the Right Time*. New York: International Women's' Health Coalition.

Gilmartin, Christina, Gail Hershatter, Lisa Rofel and Tyrene White. *Engendering China: Women. Culture, and the State*. Cambridge: Harvard University Press, 1994.

Kristof, Nicholas D. And Sheryl WuDunn. *China Wakes: The Struggle for the Soul of a Rising Power*. New York: Random House, 1994.

Li, Dun J. *The Road to Communism: China Since 1912*. New York: VanNostrand Reinhold, 1969.

Lieberthal, Kenneth. *Governing China*. New York: W.W. Norton, 1995.

Lii, Jane H. "Boom at a Glance" *The New York Times Magazine*. February 18, 1996/Section 6.

Sen, Gita, Adrienne Germain and Lincoln C. Chen (1994). *Population Policies Reconsidered: Health. Empowerment, and Rights*. Boston: Harvard School of Public Health.

Spence, Jonathan D. (1981), *The Gate of Heavenly Peace: The Chinese and Their Revolution. 1895-1980*. New York: Penguin Books.

________(1990). *The Search for Modern China*. New York: W.W. Norton.

Stacey, Judith (1983). *Patriarchy and Socialist Revolution in China*. Berkeley and Los Angeles: University of California Press.

Wickeri, Philip L. (1988). *Seeking the Common Ground: Protestant Christianity. the Three-Self Movement, and China's United Front*. Maryknoll, New York: Orbis Books.

Wolf, Margery (1985). *Revolution Postponed: Women in Contemporary China*. Stanford: Stanford University Press.

10

Women in the West

"Fame like a river is narrowest at its source and broadest after of."

—Ancient Proverb

West hemisphere of the globe is considered to be more civilized, advanced and prosperous in terms of sociology, economics and polity. No doubt, modern wave of feminism started from the west and many movements were launched therefrom. But so far the status of women is concerned, despite the tall talks of equality, social justice etc., discrimination against women still exists there in one form or other with varying magnitude.

Here in the present cahpter, an attempt is made to portray the women in West from an analytical angle.

If a girl were asked before birth whether she would like to be born in the East or the West, she would probably reply" "And why must I be born at all?" True it is that woman's condition in all countries is one of sad servitude. The vast majority of men too are in a state of moral, intellectual, economic and political bondage all over the world. But woman occupies a still lower position. In her case, the old Oriental form of obsequious address acquires a fearfully literal significance:—"The slave of a slave."

One thing is certain, as this article will demonstrate, and that is that there is not much to choose between the East and the West in this respect. Missionaries and self-complacent Europeans and Americans declare that woman occupies an exalted social position in the West, that she is respected and honoured as man's equal, that she ennobles and purifies society by her presence, that she enjoys true freedom and great opportunities for education, and that she is immeasurably happier, cleverer and nobler in the West than in the backward ignorant Asiatic countries. All this talk is very fine and inspiring, but it has only one small defect: it is false.

Burke exclaimed on hearing of the execution of Marie Antoinette, Queen of France, in 1793:—"The age of chivalry is gone." He was wrong; the age of chivalry had never existed. All this cant about man's respect and love for woman in the West is a disgusting lie. As regards woman, man is the same gross brutal egoist everywhere. In going from Turkey to England, a woman changes her geographical but not her social position. If Western women are free form some evils that afflict their Eastern sisters, there are others perhaps greater evils from which they suffer in the "enlightened" countries, to which Asiatic youths are taught to look for their ideals. Slight differences of condition make no radical change. Advantages are counterbalanced by disadvantages. And beneath all masks and disguises peers forth the same old figure of the unchivalrous disdainful indifferent man-brute, and the stunted, weak, timid, dependent, and ignorant slave woman. The boasted "higher" position of woman in the West is a myth. It is an instance of hypotism by auto-suggestion in the case of many European men and women.

It is worth mentioning here that opinions expressed in

this article are based on personal observation of social life in several countries and among all classes, corrected and supplemented by the testimony of representative thinkers and the still more eloquent evidence of facts. One fact is worth a thousand fibs. And seeing is believing.

For the purpose of discussion, we shall divide the women of Europe and America into two sharply marked classes: the working class, and the upper classes. This latter category includes the "middle classes," which control the politics of Europe, and the few fortunate or unfortunate adventures who are called "the upper ten," because they have drawn some prizes in the lottery of business or birth. we shall try to describe the condition of the women of each class, and leave my readers to judge if a social system, which tolerates such injustice and misery, and wnich condemns its delicate women to a life of such servitude and degradation, can be said to be permeated with the spirit of chivalry or even ordinary respect for woman. By their fruits, ye shall judge them. And the Western man is to be judged by his actions, individual and collective, and not by his professions. Hypocrites and tyrants have always been adepts in the use of the vocabulary of benevolence and virtue. Let us not be deceived by words.

We will begin with the upper classes first, as they are supposed to provide ideal conditions for women, and boast of education, freedom, and self-respect for them in the hearing of the whole world. It is this rotten class, that is the object of the simple Oriental scholar's envy and admiration, when he considers the question of the position of woman. He sees the ladies go to college, play the piano, read the newest books, deliver lectures and write novels; and he is enraptured at the sight. He immediately accepts the formula of the "higher position" of woman in the West, which has been patented for export of Asia by missionaries and other apostles of "civilisation."

He does not see the hypocrisy, the misery, the contempt, the awful cruelty that are concealed beneath this fair show to beauty and accomplishments. He does not know that all this refinement is an additional insult to woman, and is the product of circumstances involving the acutest suffering to all women, and the denial of common human rights to them by this society of gallant men. He cannot realise that this middle class and upper society is like unto a whitened sepulchre.

He does not see its hidden machinery of lies, cruelties, insults and agonies, which is crushing the women every moment under its monstrous wheels. He cannot hear the wail of the maiden between the tunes of the piano, or see the tears of the wife on her smiling face, rubbed and scrubbed and polished for social decorum. Appearances are deceptive, as they say; but nowhere are they so misleading and mendacious, so infernally false and faithless, as in this same educated and cultured European society in which woman is said to occupy an incomparably "higher" position than in Morocco or Kordofan.

In this society, the life of a woman between the age of 15 and her death is one continual crucifixion. And why is this so? Because of the extreme difficulty of economic support for women. Woman must eat and drink and wear clothes, and she must therefore find some man to keep her. For under our present social system, that is the only way for a woman to escape starvation. Man is the master of food, and its sole dispenser. Now this great civilised society is exquisitely ruthless in its arrangements for this necessary provision for woman. That is the starting-point of every living creature's life—the search for means to live, for food, fuel, clothing and medicine. Even the most angelic ladies cannot live on air or ether. So with this all-important question of marriage, the tragedy of woman's life begins. It is a sadder tragedy in the West than in the East, for in the East, the duty of finding a bread-winner devolve on the girl's parents.

The young maiden has not to go in search of a home. society does her the service of anticipating her greatest need. But here, by a strange refinement of cruelty, a girl in her teens is left to herself to find some one in the wide world to "love" her as the high-sounding phrase goes. What it really means is that the poor lonely girl is to hunt for herself in the dark jungle of tea-parties, dances, "church-parades," friendly dinners and summer-resorts for meat and drink for her life. What cruelty in the name of "freedom of choice" in marriage! What ghostly sacrifices are offered under the pretext of "love!" Carlyle once said in the bitterness of his heart: "Freedom is a divine' thing. Freedom to die of starvation is not so divine"

That is exactly how the average European girl feels, or ought to feel, when she is complimented on the possession of "freedom" in her lover affairs. And here comes the utility of music, and college education, and dancing, and instruction in "deportment." It will surprise my readers to learn that there are professors of "deportment" in all towns in Europe. Now what does this "department" mean? Is it possible that young ladies, who are brought up in cultured middle-class homes, do not know how to behave themselves in society? Is it probable that they have not been taught by their mothers that it is improper to bite one's nails, or blow one's nose, or interrupt another person in conversation, or have dirty-hands at the dinner-table? What is the business of these professors of "deportment.?" As a matter of fact, this art of deportment does not refer to such social amenities as we understand, and as we all learn at our mother's knees. It is the art of appearing very attractive and bewitching in society. It is the art of baiting the hook with the biggest fly. It is an education in conquetry and artificial behaviour.

It is surprising to think how and why this lady can *suddenly* begin to smile and look so funny, when she greets others, even perfect strangers. And then it flashed in my mind that all this facial contortion was part of the "deportment," which had been learned as such cost at the professor's. The lady was trying to look charming and fascinating! That was all. But as she was rather ugly, her efforts made her more ridiculous than beautiful.

Similarly the piano-thrumming is an institution, not because all European girls have a musical ear, or because all European gentlemen like this intolerable drawing-room screeching, but because it is an "accomplishment," *i.e.,* it is a weapon in the marriage-hunt, or a bid in the marriage-market. Marriage is secured by woman in Europe in two ways:—By a hunt, or by purchase. The later is often the more merciful method. Now it is clear that a hunter must have good weapons. And this music and dancing are really the girl's trade. She learns them, not because the Europeans love a refined domestic life, but because these things constitute her business. She persecutes the piano, as her brother joins the technical institute or the college of arts and sciences. In both cases, the object is not human improvement or development, but that bugbear of mortal man and woman in our civilisation, that tyrant of our boyhood and youth, our middle-age and our declining years, that lord of our affections, opinions, principles, beliefs and actions, that master of our speech and our silence, our love and our hate,—Beard and Butter.

Marriage is for woman what a profession is for a man. An unmarried woman is in the ranks of "the unemployed." And every girls is taught and schooled and drilled for this necessary object. To show that my interpretation of the value of this superficial veneer of "refinement" in European society is not a libel invented by my cynical fancy, I shall quote a few lines from Bernard Shaw's famous play, *"Man and Superman."* Mr. Shaw is on of the foremost writers and thinkers of England. He introduces a man and his friend's wife talking in hell after death—,

> "*Don Fuan*— Come, Ana! do not look shocked: you know better than any of us that marriage is a mantrap be baited with simulated accomplishments and delusive idealisations. When your sainted mother, by dint of scoldings and punishments, forced you to learn how to play half-a-dozen pieces on the spinet—which she hated as much as you did—had she any other purpose than to delude your suitors into the belief that your husband would have in his home an angel who would fill it with melody or at least play him to sleep after dinner? You married my friend Ottavio: well, did you ever open the spinet from the hour when the Church united him to you?
>
> *Ana.*—You are a fool, Juan. A young married woman has something else to do than sit at the spinet without any support for her back so she gets out of the habit of playing.
>
> *Don Fuan.*— Not if she loves music. No: believe me, she only throws away the bait when the bird is in the net.

What a story of slavery is implied in these pathetic

words! The poor child was not developing her genuis for music, for she had none of it. She was a slave victim of man's sexual market, wasting her life in a dark room, her weary fingers wandering listlessly over the keys, her ears ringing with the confused noise that she was making; while the flowers and the sun-shine called her to play in the garden, and wonderful books recording the marvels of science beckoned to her with mute appeal, and her whole nature craved for growth, for freedom, for play and frolic, or life and its unfoldment.

It this is not slavery, what is it? O the hecatombs of victims prepared for the marriage-market, where men come and examine the fair girls put up for sale, as the Moors examine the slaves they buy. The only difference is that the Moor only wants a round supple form, or though sinews for domestic labour, but the European exacts more—a knowledge of reading and writing, and of a thousand artificial blan-dishments and utterly useless trivialities, which have to be acquired by the girls before they can hope to find a husband. And thus all their talent is wasted, all their natural sweetness disappears, and cunning and affectation become second nature to them. *All* girls are passed through *the same* mill, are stamped with *the same* trade-mark of conventionality and respectability, are provided with *the same* outfit of abominable music, awkward dancing, unsuitable education, artificial manners, absurd notions of propriety, and degrading forms of vanity and ostentation, so that the gentleman customer, whoever he may be, may be sure of the genuine article in his transaction.

Any marks of individuality, any traits of eccentricity, would ruin, the woman's chances for ever, for no wise man will "buy a pig in a poke," as the familiar saying puts it, Thus does Europe waste its womanhood, Europe which is so anxious to preserve her coal supply and her foreign commerce! But the worst is not yet told. We are in the first act of the tragedy, which consists in the crushing out of all that is most valuable in every girl's personality and forcing her through a stupid discipline calculated to increase her chances in the marriage-hunt or the marriage-market.

Then comes the actual period of suspense and misery. Her youth is spent in frivolity and social dissipation, when she should be improving her mind, forming her views on great questions of religion and politics, and rounding off her personality to beautiful, self-evolved whole. But how can she do so, when the problem of bread faces her first? So she must fatigue herself by attending tea parties and private concerts, and going to live in boarding-houses in the holiday seasons. The Moors and the Soudanese have at least provided a public slave-market, where all can meet. But this society is not so considerate for its women. The market is not in one specious building like the Stock Exchange, or the Employment Agency. It consists of an endless series of "social functions," dances and parties, where young men and women meet.

So the poor girls have to go to all these tedious gatherings. It is sad to see these poor girls dressing for these parties, and tiring themselves out evening after evening, or at longer intervals when in their heart of heats they simply hate the while show, and curse their fate. It is not implied that every girls reasons in this way. But that is the true inwardness of the affair. The slaves on the plantations did not think of the iniquities of the system under which they lived every moment of their lives; many of them did not and *could* not think at all. They only did the day's work, bore the pain and the toil, and danced away the night in mirth and glee. For the victims of servitude hug their chains, or at least their sensibility is dulled and blunted. Similarly these unlucky girls do not argue in their minds. But that does not change the truth one jot. When a girl begins to play the piano, because her mamma tells her, she does not ask, "And why should I play the piano? Why should I not go out and look at the flowers and drink in the sunshine with the rose and the linnet?" If she were wise enough to ask such questions mamma would curtly reply: "Because you have to capture a husband when you are twenty, my child. Nature and knowledge and true development are all fine things, but they will not give you food and clothing and a roof to sleep under.

You are not being prepared for true, abounding, natural well-developed life, but for the marriage-market. You cannot be true to yourself, my girl, for then you may starve. So we have to follow the directions issued by the controllers of the market. We can't help it, so go and learn that Highlanders' march, dear, and don't be silly. Do." Then after cruelty in childhood comes contempt in youth, on the part of man in his relations to woman. This marriage hunt is a weary struggle indeed, suitor after suitor passes by, indifferent or disdainful.

The girls try all their arts of fascination. For a young man can wait for a wife, but a young woman cannot wait for a husband, both for economic and psychological reasons. Women want bread but they want love too. And above all, they want children to fill the void in their hearts. But this system does not care for these primary rights of woman. She has to shift for herself, and find bread, love and a child by degrading herself to the position of a flatterer, buffoon and a fiddler.

A child is even more precious to her than a vote. But this hopeless search embitters so many lives, blasts so many womanly virtues. How often I have seen unmarried women of twenty-five and thirty looking wistfully at the couples that enter in at the church-door or pass them on the promenade. I could almost feel that a sigh escaped their lips. And I have seen this ignoble marriage-hunt in operation. I have noticed all its shamelessness, it brutality, its gross injustice.

Young women must try to insinuate themselves into the good graces of young men by desperate means. And if they are ugly, they become veritable butterflies. Poor things, are they to blame? The call of motherhood, even more than the need of maintenance, sounds loud and clear within them. But they cannot have these blessings until they find favour in the sight of some man: Can tyranny go further.

In fact, no pen can describe the anguish of those women who cannot find purchasers in the market or who fail to bag some game in this hunt. They are stranded, and no one pities them Their lot is one of terrible hardship in these upper classes. They become mere human wrecks, the refuse of the market, which the managers throw into the garbage box.

Am I drawing on my imagination? Alas no! Here is a confession from a woman herself as to the yearning for marriage implanted in the hearts of all women:—

> "These is not one woman in a million who would not be married if... she could have a chance. How do I know? Just as I know that the stars are now shining in the sky, though it is high noon. I never saw a star at noonday, but it is the nature of stars to shine in the sky, and of the sky to hold its stars." (Gail Hamilton.)

George Bernard Shaw lifts the mask a little to show

what is passing in this apparently cultured and civilised society which bestows an "exalted" position on woman. He says:—

> "Look at fashionable society as you know it. What does it pretend to be? An exquisite dance of nymphs. What is it? A horrible procession of wretched girls, each in the claws of a cynical, cunning, avaricious, disillusioned, ignorantly experienced, foul-minded old woman whom she calls mother, and whose duty it is to corrupt her mind and sell her to the highest bidder. Why do these unhappy slaves marry anybody, however old and vile, sooner than not marry at all? Because marriage is their only means of escape from these decrepit fiends who hide their selfish ambitions, their jealous hatreds of the young rivals who have supplanted them, under the mask of maternal duty and family affection. Such things are abominable."

Rudyard Kipling for once blurts out the truth even in the midst of his eternal cant about "the white man's burden" and the "Lord of hosts" of these modern Israelites of England. The young man has received a letter from his lady-love, telling him that she cannot marry him unless he gives up the habit of smoking. This ultimatum sets him thinking. He says to himself:—"A woman is a woman, but a cigar is a smoke." And finally he decides to stick to his cigar, for, says he,—

> "Open the old cigar-box—let me consder anew,—
> Old friends, and who is Maggie that I should abandon you?
> And a woman is a woman, but a good cigar is a smoke."

—(Kipling's "The Betrothed").

Mr. August Bebel, the leader of the German Socialist party, and one of the greatest orators of the world, says:—

> "Woman is at the present day chiefly an object of enjoyment for man: her pecuniary circumstances oblige her to look to marriage for support; she thus becomes dependent on man... Her position is rendered still more unfavourable by the fact that the number of women is as a rule larger that of men.... This disproportion, which is further augmented by those men who for one reason or other remain unmarried, heightens the competitive struggle among women, and forces them to pay the greatest attention to the attractions of their personal appearance, if they are to have any chance of successful emulation with their fellow-women in the favour of men....

A man is free from a number of restrictions which a woman is bound to observe. He alone, thanks to his position as ruler, has the right of exercising choice in love, a right which is limited only by social considerations. The nature of marriage as a means of subsistence, the numeric excess of women, and custom conjoin in forbidding a woman to express her desires it is her lot to wait till she is sought, and to accept her fate whatever it may be. As a rule, she seizes the first opportunity that presents itself for securing a maintainer, who rescues her from the social proscription and contempt which is the portion of the unfortunate old maid." Is not the condition of the Oriental woman, who finds a husband, a home, and assured maintenance provided for her as soon as she reaches maturity, a hundred times better than that of these pitiable scramblers in the matrimonial market, where, to add to their troubles, the supply far exceeds the demand? Marriage here being a personal affair, and not a social duty, many men do not marry. Others want to be very wealthy before marrying.

An anonymous writer, who describes himself as a "Christian philanthropist" thus enumerates the causes that lead to the disproportion in the numbers of marriageable men and women:—

> "But few young men are born to large fortunes, which these times of extravagance require for the fashionable maintenance of a family; and those who are rich are not always the most prompt to marry. They prefer to spend their early manhood in dissipation, and are unwilling to bow to the yoke of wedlock till they begin to feel the infirmities of age; while the poor man must devote several years of his majority to toil before he becomes able to assume matrimonial expenses. After men have arrived at adult manhood, and have acquired the means of supporting a family, many of them refuse marriage. Some have outlived their youthful desires, and have acquired decided habits of celibacy; some are too gave and too profligate: others too busy and too selfish: others so broken down by early dissipation and diseased by the contagious position of low vice that they are totally... unit to marry; while there are many others whose occupations (such as soldiers and sailors) most commonly prevent marriage."—*The History and Philosophy of Marriage.*

The picture is complete. Every girl to find out her own husband an overstocked market: wearisome search: debasing self humiliation: worry and anxiety: delay in motherhood: and finally failure for many women even after these trials and ordeals. Thus does gallant Europe treat her "educated" ladies on the threshold of life! But the end is not yet. A double inquiry here presents itself. What becomes of those who cannot marry and how do the married ones fare in their domestic life?

As regards the first question, the unmarried women are always on the look-out for a new chance. Better late than never. In the meantime, they work as best they can to eke out a living as clerks, teachers, typists, dressmakers, music-teachers and in other similar capacities. This sad phenomenon is one of the gravest indictments that I bring against the chivalrous men of the West. So many post-office clerks are women, that one begins to think of the post-office as a particularly feminine institution.

There these frail middle-class girls stand for hours together at counters, while they ought to have been mistresses of a home and mothers of healthy children. They take lodgers, and cook and sew for strangers. A lady once said to me:—"I work like a horse, and earn my livelihood."And her life was really one continual drudgery of cooking, sweeping the rooms, making the beds and even cleaning the boots for strangers who boarded with her. This lady came of respectable middle-class family. She had been educated at a high school, and had refined manners. But she had no husband. And the Europeans, who honour woman so much, leave their sisters and nieces and even their daughters to slave for black strangers rather than support them on account of the claims of family love. Often as I have seen these over-driven waifs and strays of this cruel society, have I asked myself with indignation:—"Have these women no brothers, uncles, or even brothers-in-law with whom they could live? Must all the womanhood be crushed out of them in this sordid commercial world, where men meet only to rob or to be robbed?"

And the roses on their cheeks were fading. Their hearts were empty as dark catacombs. Their hearts were empty as dark catacombs. Their eyes had never lit up at an infant's smile, or watched the home-coming of the beloved husband from the door-steps in the evening. The joys of maternal sacrifice were not theirs. They were mere machines, grinding their daily bread out of their bones. Their work was the work of the galley slave. For a woman, deprived of her right of motherhood, is only a slave of society, not a citizen. Their sad wistful looks, that seemed to search for something that was lost,their desire of conversation with young men, their lack of the grace and charm that motherhood alone can confer on woman, all proclaimed more loudly than words their plaint against society, which can be thus rendered:—"O men, who come to buy stamps from us, or learn music from us, or send your children to our classes, we are the wrecks of your marriage-market. We are those wretched creatures for whom your chivalrous society makes no economic provision because no man has wanted us. And our relatives drive us a way from them, for we are burdensome to them, even though we are all alone.

So we work like hired hacks, and save you so much money for your other pleasures and necessities, for are we not cheaper than men in the post offices and the educational department, as music-teachers and librarians? So learn what our fate should teach you. Hasten to find husbands for your own daughters as soon as possible. Do not leave them to the tender mercies of chance. May they never be reduced to our plight! But go and do it before it is too late."

A few women, who are left behind in the race, find a home through that efficacious lubricant of the wheels of the world—money. Marriages by purchase are common in Europe. So the missionaries need not expend all their indignation in Bengal. A large part of it is wanted for consumption at home.

Here are the words of Monsicur Ch. Letourneau, an eminent sociologist, who was General Secretary to the Anthropological Society of Paris and Professor in the School of Anthropology:—

> "The fear of marriage and the family is the particular feature of French matrimoniality.... At Paris, where the struggle for existence is more severe, and where the care for money is more predominant, late marriages abound.... Whether these facts proceed from the growing difficulties of existence, or from a fear, always augmenting also, of trouble and care, or from these two causes combined and mutually strengthening each other, the consequence is the same: marriages are becoming more and more simple commercial transactions, from whence arises the worst and most shameful of selections—selections by money. It is surely to the love of the dowry rather than to `the beautiful eyes of the casket,' that we must attribute a whole list of true marriages by purchase, much more common in our own country that elsewhere. Sometimes it is old men who conjugally purchase young girls, and sometimes old woman who buy young husbands. As regards these marriages by purchase, France is unworthily distinguished beyond other nations."

Thus are women bartered in a country, where male gallantry is supposed to have reached its perfection! All this bowing and scraping in presence of ladies is only mechanical gymnastics. It is not a homage of the heart at all. To an onlooker it appears like a cruel joke. A gentleman once said:—"I don't think a woman can reason at all." And this same gentleman was a perfect model of chivalry in social manners, and paid the utmost deference to ladies in the details of social etiquette. I was reminded of the priests who bow before their idols and offer flowers and incense, while they know that they worship only wooden figures, which they really despise in their hearts. And both the gentlemen and the priests ar entirely unconscious of the humour of the situation.

So true it is that, as Bacon says, spectators sometimes see more of the game than players. The increasing competition of educated women in the marriage-market has led to their admission to the liberal professions of law and medicine. This change is hailed by many public men of Europe as a step in advance, that establishes woman's equality with man. As a matter of fact, it is not a sign of progress at all: it is a confession of social failure.

No woman naturally wishes to practise law or medicine. *Even men adopt a trade or a profession in order to make money, and not from any idea of social service or intellectual development.* The happily-married woman does not desire to work for her living. Women have entered the liberal professions of law, medicine and journalism *because of the pressure of economic necessity,* and not from any nascent appreciation of woman's intellectual worth by the legislators of Europe.

There are already so many briefless male barristers everywhere, and the medical profession is also overcrowded with men who have nothing to do! But the number of women who fail to get married in so large that all wise parents educate their daughters for some useful profession, for no one knows what the future has in store for them. Thus women too are thrown into that selfish senseless struggle for money, from which the marriage-system at least shields them. They have been turned out of the marriage-market, and so enter the commercial or professional arena. Out of the frying pan into the fair.

If the economic system were founded on just and humane principles, woman would only benefit society and ennoble herself by doing any work for which she was fit. But in the present individualistic regime of production and distribution, every man's hand is against his neighbour, and one can hardly feed oneself without taking the bread out of some one's mouth. One man's loss is another man's gain.

Trickery and chicane are the life of business. Competition for wealth is an education in all the un-social qualities of greed, cunning and envy, and woman must thus lose many valuable traits of character, which her very dependence on man has fostered, as she has been kept out of the hideous shambles, called the "business world." She has therefore preserved her native simplicity, gentleness, sweetness, naivete and idealism.

If she has been treated like a child, she has also enjoyed that blissful ignorance of the dark and crooked ways of the world, which is a privilege of childhood. But this advancing civilisation must drag her in the mire of modern commercialism, she must also learn to lie and cheat, to haggle and calculate, to buy in the cheapest and sell in the dearest market. This is what this boasted emancipation of woman in the professions really means. In an unnatural and perverse economic system, even good turns to evil, as even bread injures a sick man, and water is fatal to one stricken with cholera. This "emancipation" is really an insulted added to an injury—the burden of fighting for bread being laid on weak woman after the denial of the rights of motherhood.

So much for the honour in which the gentlemen of Europe hold their ladies. The whole tragedy at once leaps to the surface in those "breach-of-promise" cases, which come before the courts from time to time. These cases are like volcanoes, which show how much igneous activity is going on in the bowels of the earth. So when a helpless, bewildered and wronged woman's despair breaks through the thick crust of silence and conventionality that society has laid on all such affairs, there is a "breach-of-promise" case. Pecuniary compensation is awarded by the judges. Thus even society, in its repentant moods, confesses that marriage is business, and not all romance. Truth will out, though a judicial decision be the form that that she prefers to assume in this hypocritical age.

Turning to the question of married life we find that women of the upper and middle classes are rendered miserable on account of the conjugal infidelity of their husbands. Of course, it is impossible to obtain facts and figures on such a subject, but the concurrent testimony of European writers, who are born and bred up in that society, leaves no doubt as to the very lax standard of morality recognised by Western gentlemen.

The importance attached to purity among men is a sure criterion of the position of woman in a country. Mr. August Debel, the German publicist, says:—

> "By far the greater number of married men could not support a second wife.... As a rule, they have already two and more wives. One is legitimate, and the others illegitimate."

Mr. C. Letourneau, a French author says:

> "The white race has no divine investiture. Like all the others, it has sprung form animality; like all the others, it has been polygamous and *we have only to open our eyes* to perceive that, in the present day, in countries reputed to be the most civilised, and even in the classes reputed to be the most distinguished, the *majority of individuals* have polygamic instincts which they find it difficult to resist." (Emphasis added).

We need not dwell further on this unsavoury subject.

The testimony of other competent witnesses establishes the culpability of the gallant men of Europe. This is a conclusive proof of the low position of woman in Europe.

The life of the middle and upper classes is artificial in the extreme. Women attach too much importance to the conservation of their beauty and youth. They also fear a very large family. Constant excitement also renders them unfit for motherhood. *The result is the wide prevalence of nervous disorders among women, and an increasing degree of artificial sterility. Marriage is regarded more as a means of garatification than as an institution for multiplying and replenishing the earth. The custom of the late marriage induces incurable nervous derangements among women in the prime of life.*

Another cause of the failing birth-rate of Europe and of the native Saxon stock in America is thus hinted at by Mr. Max Montesole in an article on France:—

> "It is the relaxation during several generations of the laws of conventional morality, and the diversion of natural instincts into by-paths of erotic ecstasy, which not only prevents the birth of children, but fashions men, and in a lesser degree, women incapable of becoming parents."

Surely there must be something rotten in the social system which is thus running to suicide. Over-population is not desirable, but the degeneracy of women as physical types is a very serious evil. There is something wrong somewhere, either in the ethical or the economic condition of such a society, for natural instincts can never be warped and perverted except under the influence of radically vicious surroundings. Man can defeat nature, but he must become terribly wicked and foolish or miserably unfortunate before he can succeed. Thus an individual commits suicide, when he is insane, or frightfully wretched.

A similar rule applies to social phenomena of the kind that we have been considering. As regards the education of the women of the middle and upper classes, it is meagre and superficial. Even those who go to the university learn little that makes them serious and thoughtful. *Conversation* is a very satisfactory test of the intellectual development of a nation.

Now the women of Europe like women all over the world, talk unmitigated twaddle. Their society is intolerable boredom. Gossip is their forte. If they read anything at home, they read *novels.* Circulating libraries patronised by ladies sometimes consist only of works of fiction. This fact gives us a measure of their mental stature. They are like children in their tastes. Another proof of their extremely low intellectual condition is the prevalence of strange forms of *superstition* in all Western countries. And the ladies of the cultured classes are the strongest champions of superstition. Thus every charlatan finds a happy hunting-ground among them. America is the land of science, but it is also the land of superstition. A palmist and a clairvoyant have become as necessary in almost every town of ordinary dimensions as the barber and the baker.

The sale of love-philtres is a thriving trade, and several persons have bene indicted for it in New York. In France, the women are the greatest obstacles in the way of progress. No wonder that the French cannot think very highly of their women. In Utah, the women were the most ardent advocates of polygamy. In every State of America, they are the first victims of "spiritual healers," "divine prophets," and other miracle-mongers of this restless age.

It is the women of the socialist party with whom a person can carry on a decent conversation, but they are very few. As a rule, the women of the educated classes are hopelessly superstitious and incapable of serious thought on intelligent conversation. In this respect, they are neither better nor worse than women in other lands.

But there are no traces of the immense superiority over the Turkish women, that some people ascribe to the educated ladies of the West. They are all alike *as yet.* They all have the

> "Wild hearts and feeble wings,
> That every sophister can lime."

They all chatter trifles. They are all credulous and shallow-brained. There is no great difference between the East and the West, or even between Africa and Europe in this respect. Men in Europe have gone forward, but the women have been left behind. It is the same old story.

We will now take up the working-classes, and the question of the position of woman can be best decided by studying their physical, mental and moral condition, for, after all, the well-dressed, well-fed, educated classes form an infinitesimal minority of the population. They are only the froth and foam on the surface of the real society. The nation does not live in the palace or the cottage, but in the slums. If you wish to find the real West, go to the slums. The working classes constitute the nation. And the position of woman among them is one of such terrible hardship and misery that no one who has seen them, can hear the sickening cant of missionaries and others about the "higher position" of woman in Europe without uttering that appropriate injunction first employed for protection against shameless and extravagant mendacity in Grimm's fairly tales:—"Open the widow that these lies may escape."

The life of the women of the working-classes is worse than that of helots. Girls of tender age are overworked in factories like beasts of burden. Mothers have to work in the factories, and the children are left in nurseries, or allowed to play about the streets. The generous insurance laws of Germany allow these women six weeks of rest after childbirth a provision which is considered a triumph of humane legislation, but which really carries with it a horrible reminiscence of negro-slavery days.

At Charlottenburg in Germany, nurseries are now attached to factories, so that the women may suckle their children in the intervals of toil! The excessive infant-mortality of Germany is largely due to the fact that the infants are not suckled; so 400,000 out of 2,000,000 children that are born every year, die within the first twelve months of their life! This is civilised Europe, where women cannot suckle their children, and where yet all men are horrified at Herod's atrocities! The working-woman has to work at night at home till one or two in the morning, washing clothes, and sewing and mending garments, for she returns from the factor in the evening. The young women employed at the big stores, where the middle-classes come to buy silk and satin, perfumes and ribbons, are paid less than the American equivalent of 1½ *annas* for a day of 12 or 14 hours. They have to remain standing all the time, and thus irreparable injury is done to their constitution.

And the smirking gentlemen of Europe who honour woman so much, never think of the martyrdom of these sisters, who are like flowers "wasting their sweetness on the desert air" Then the plaints and groans of these our tender sisters will resound n the ears of our grandchildren, not as wails of woe, but as poeans of triumph, for who will dare think of grief in that happy time? Then all sorrow will become sacred, because it has been the rice of the victory. Then these heroic women will stand foremost on the pedestals of our statues.

Tyranny may last so long as it torments men, for they can endure it: but it sounds its own death-knell when it touches women and children, for then it kindles the spark of heroism even in the flinty bosoms of the selfish and the indifferent. That stage has been reached in the West. It is darkest before dawn, and poverty has now reached that point, which marks the beginning of its end for all time. As a consequence of this terrible condition of things, many men desert their wives, and the "Boston Transcript" ascribes the growing frequency of this evil to economic circumstances. The recent investigations of the Royal Commission on Divorce in England revealed the fact that many young women did not wish to have children at all? What a scathing condemnation of civilisation" is implied in this unnatural phenomenon!

This is civilised Europe which kills out the maternal instinct by the poor! This stage marks the last gasp of the woman's despair, *for a woman who renounces the right of motherhood is like a man who commits suicide.* A man lives for the sake of living but a woman lives for her children. But everything is topsy-turvy in this society, where woman has been reduced to a condition of wretchedness, compared with which the harem and the kraal are heaven itself.

The "social evil," a euphemism employed by refined persons in talking of the degradation of thousands of women through poverty and the exigencies of the present marriage-system, is the product of these institutions, on which Europe plumes herself. Congresses meet to discuss the "white slave traffic," which is an organised trade now as it was in the days of Haroun-al-rashid or the Mahdi. Modern Europe is not a whit better in this respect than Morocco or old Turkestan. The "maiden Tribute" is exacted by the rich and the profligate from the working classes today as it was in antiquity. Thus Europe honours its women! Those who wish to know more about the human side of this tragedy may read the reports of special commissions and Bernard Shaw's play "Mrs. Warren's Profession." *These armies of "abandoned" women are the nemesis of society in the West.* Their existence is due not to human depravity, but to economic conditions and the marriage-customs of the people.

11

Women in Vietnam

> "When the grass looks greener on the other side of the fence, it may be that they take better care of it over there."

The people and women of Vietnam are elated at the great achievements recorded by the people and women of elsewhere over the recent years in building and defending their country, thus contributing to the growing strength of the non-aligned countries of the forces that stand for Peace, National Independence, Democracy and Progress.

Having been colonised by the French and the British the people and women of the Asian countries have been actively and heroically struggling for Independence, Freedom and have overcome the heavy consequences of colonialism.

The victory of each country has exerted positive influence on and has provided support to the others and vice-versa in the defence of national independence and nation building. We highly appreciate your experiences and hope to learn from each other.

Like the people of other Asian countries, the people and women of Vietnam through thousands of years of history in national defence and building have been continuously fighting against foreign aggressors and natural calamities and are endowed with traditions of creativeness in labour and the ardent patriotism. Our women have shown their capacity in agriculture, handicraft and small trade which were the main economic activities in the old Vietnam. They have maintained the traditional national culture. By means of lullabies, folk-songs, stories they have injected in their children the sense of patriotism, the love for labour, the respect for the national heroes and heroines. Women have played an important role in ensuring a happy and constructive family life. Further whenever the enemy comes, women have also fought against then or replace husbands and sons in the rear.

However, in the days preceding the August Revolution 1945, the capacity of women was underestimated and their social role played down.

Under the colonial rule what we had was poverty, ignorance, a backward and poor economy, a reactionary and depraved culture. There were more prisons than schools with many gambling houses, brothels, alcohol and opium dens which poisoned our people and played havoc with many families. Our people and women were heavily exploited. The climax of the French colonialists and Japanese fascists was reached when two millions Vietnamese died of starvation as the result of the French and Japanese policy of hoarding rice for war purposes.

In collusion with the feudalists and colonialists maintained feudal customs and the predominance of men over women. The women were deprived of all women had to toil for 12-13 hours but received very low wages equivalent to two third of men's wages. They were not entitled to any kind of social insurance in case of sickness, old age etc. Even more, they were subjected to various ill treatment and outrage their dignity. With their tradition of undauntedness, the

Vietnamese people have fought against the colonialists even they first set foot on our soil. Especially since 1930 when the Part of Vietnamese working class come into being the struggle has spread into the labouring masses. Educated by the Party the Vietnamese woman realised that only by fighting side by side with the whole people for national salvation and for the liberation of the working people can women be emancipated have to happy family and happy future for their children. That's why for several decades now our women have stood side by side with their husbands and sons in the fight against the French and Japanese and then the US imperialists and Beijing hegemonists and expansionists. They have made great contributions to the great victories of our people over the aggressors and now are ready to ccpe with the new aggressive acts and schemes of the enemy.

Women of Vietnam constitute an abundant force of labour. During war time they have replaced men in production have ensured stable living conditions for the people in the rear and took care of the food supplied for the front. After the liberation of the country, they have been working hard to do away with economic backwardness and poverty with the vestiges and consequences of thousands of years of colonialists rule and decades of the fiercest of war imposed on us by the USA.

Making up 60% of the labour force in agriculture, women peasants have been actively applying new techniques in transplating, selection of seeds, wiping out insects, stock-breeding. Almost the peasant households in North Vietnam have joined the co-ops and half of the peasant households in the South have joined the production groups. A contingent of female technicians has been trained from the middle level upto post-graduate level. Women technicians account for 40% of the staff of agricultural institutes and experimental farms. Thousands of women assume leading positions in the Agricultural co-ops.

After the liberation of the North in 1954, women make up only 50% of the civil servants and workers. The rate now is 43.8% with most of then having finished 10 years of general education, and 30% having required technical education upto the level of university graduates. In the emulation movements many women have initiated technical innovations, raised the productivity and economised materials thus benefiting for the country in terms of millions of Dong. Hundreds of women have become Directors and Vice-Directors of factories, 27 women have been awarded the title of heroines of Labour.

At present women make up 65% of the workforce in the light industry, 85% in handicraft, 63% in Home Trade, 61% in Public Health 60% in Education.

Women have actively participated in the eradication of illiteracy in the North and in the 1978 in the South. After the liberation of the South have helped to liquidate all kinds of reactionary and depraved publications left over by the enemy and to spread a healthy and progressive culture. We have helped to rehabilitate the victims of neo-colonialism like prostitutes and drug addicts by curing then from diseases giving them education and jobs in the fields of their native villages or in the co-ops handicraft.

Women also help the security forces and the administration in detecting and arresting robbers and hooligans.

The concern and care given by the people and the state are instrumental in helping to score these achievement.

Right after the success of the Revolution our first Constitution (January 1946) stipulated the equality in right between men and women in all fields in the family and in the society.

Female and male citizens of Vietnam enjoy the same rights in terms of voting at the age of 18 and standing for election at 21. There was only 2% of women deputies in the National Assembly at its first legislature but this percentage has rison to 21. 77% in the seventh legislature which comprises 108 women deputies representing all strata of women: workers, peasants, artists, intellectuals, ethnic minorities, different religions communities. 17 women are promoted ministers, vice ministers or occupy equivalent position. The president of the Vietnam Women's Union Mrs. Nguyen thi Ding is also a member of the council states.

The State guarantees the right to work for male and female citizens, gives them equal right in labour, the principle of equal pay for equal work. In our country women retire at the age of 55 and men at 60. They enjoy the same social and labour insurance. As mothers, women are entitled to health examinations during the period of pregnancy fully paid maternity leave, allowances for new born diapers and for delivery. They are also entitled to days off to look after their sick children, to sucking hours and allowances in case the mothers have not milk. The State develop the network of health children care and collective kitchen with the aimd to protect the health of women and lighten the burden of housework. At present 26% of children go to creches, 32% to infant classes c.e. 46. 644 creches with F. 226. 866 children and 57. 500 infant class with 1.587.000 children. Almost 100% of children at the school age are now attending the schools of general education, where tuition is free, textbooks are provided on a lending basis. Before the Revolution Vietnam has only 407.000 pupils of whom 17% are girls. We now have 14 million pupils of in general education of whom 50% are girls. In the vocational schools girls make up 49% and in the University 26%. Many laws and decrees on family and marriage, specially the law enacted in 1959 defend the equality between wife and husband in every fields. It was based on the four following principles: free choice and progressive marriage, monogamy, equality between men and women, protection of women' and children rights.

The articles 12 stipulated that either the wife and the husband should be free to choose an occupation, to take part in political, cultural and social activities. The wife and the husband enjoys equal rights to the ownership, utilisation and enjoyment of properties existing prior to or during the marriage. They are also equals in terms of duty relating to the above.

Wife the husband have the duty to love, respect and take care of each other, help each other to make progress, to take part in production and to built up a happy family.

In fact in present Vietnamese society all women take part in production and therefore are dependent economically. The family being built on the basis of free choice and true love, the relations in the vast majority of Vietnam families are characterised by equality, democracy and genuine love, husband and wife helping each other and joining hands in looking after the family affairs and the education of the children. It's the duty of the State to cater for the family life, to organise welfare amenities (canteens, creches, nurseries and kindergarten to ensure the provision of food, clothing, housing, medical service and education). The State sees to it that women can fulfill their twin function as labourers in the society and as mothers and wives in the family. Together in the State the Vietnamese women's Union take an active part in the development of these enterprises in order to take better care of the health of mothers and children. At present the Vietnamese women are actively, participating in the 'New women build and defend the Homeland' launched by the VNWU. This movement aimed at motivating and bring into full play the role and capacity of women in the building of the country. At the same time it is aimed at fostering their cultural and technical standards, their collective spirit and helping them to organise well their family.

Having gone through 30 consecutive years of war, the people and women of Vietnam have only one desire: to concentrate all their efforts in rebuilding their war torn country, bringing consolation to the widow and orphans and the war wounded and improving the conditions of life of all our people. But now a days while enjoying peace our country still has to cope with a type of man faces destructive war of Chinese expansionists and hegemonists working hands in glove with the US imperialists. At the same time our people have to face acute difficulties of a country with a poor and backward economy and freshly emerging from a long drawn war.

Together without people we try our best to attain 4 objectives from now.

(a) To meet the most urgent requirements of the people's life, gradually stabilise it and take a step in improving it.

(b) To continue to build the material and technological basis of socialism, focussing on boosting agricultural production and the production of consumer and export goods.

(c) To carry through the socialist transformation of the economy in the South, perfect the socialist relations of production in the North and consolidate them in the whole country.

(d) To strengthen national defect and firmly maintain social security and order.

Therefore let us hope to be able to develop relations with the women in all countries and together with then preserve peace and cooperation between peoples. We specially hope to develop relations of good neighbourhood with the people and women of SEA and together with them exchange the experiences, preserve peace and security in the region and safeguard independence, sovereignty and territorial integrity of each country.

Appendix

WOMEN'S GUIDANCE

The history of women's guidance goes back to 1943 when teachers of Bakht el Ruda ran the experiment of adult education in Um Jar town in white Nile area. Their target for this experiment was to give education or the father and the mother so as to upgrade their standard socially. The school alone could nor be the instrument for the development of the rural areas.

The idea, from the start was to cater to men as well as women. Dar El Galal Mohamed from the Ministry of Health along with the teachers of Bakht El Ruda participated in the experiment. She made good efforts towards women's guidance in rural areas so as to help women assume full responsibilities towards the house and the children.

The experiment of women's guidances started in Um Jar village aimed at imparting culture to woman so as to attain certain standard of social life. The women guidance is to guide the woman in the field of nutrition, hygiene and social care, then reading and writing and handicrafts such as needle work, dress making, and making of designs out of the wool materials.

The guiding team started the campaign with the help of some British women. The tenant consisted of Dar El Galal Mohamed from the Ministry of health and Um El Hassan Mohammed Ahmed from the Ministry of Education.

They started their work in Bakht el Ruda village under the supervision of Sudanese and British teachers in Ruda Institute. The experiment proved a success and was then transferred to the Gazira area.

Both the Ministry of Education and the Gazira scheme administration collaborated to start the experiment in Southern Gazira and opened the first centre for women's guidance in 1949 in El Rimaitab village. In 1950, the scheme was nationalized and the women's guidance attracted great attention; the social service section was also established within the scheme's administration which shared the duty with the Ministry of Education. But it was not as widely spread out as required. The supervision of women's guidance was in the hands of British women so, it was deemed necessary to train Sudanese women to take over. The Ministry of Education sent Mrs. Fatima Talib and Mrs. Haram El Suni to Sirs el Lyian in the United Arab Republic in 1958 to obtain a Diploma in Basic Education. Mrs Talib came back and continued work in academic education, but Mrs. El Suni came back in 1959 and assumed the responsibility of Assistant Supervision for Women's Guidance in Gazira in 1960. Later in 1951 the became the supervisor.

The Sudanese men and women who took over from the British, did very well and the work began to grow and develop. In 1950, the number of centres for women's guidance rose to Six in Gazira; in 1970 when the Managil extension was completed this number reached sixteen. The centers were distributed in the following villages; Elrityab in 1950; Direia, British, Masaad, UM Odam, El Miailik, El Siraha, Elfada, Thawia, El Meheiriba, Abu Gota, Elmahadi, Maatoug, Elmatouri, Guzel Rihaid and El Gamosa in 1970.

During the Military Government's rule between 1958 and 1964, Adult Education was shaken a bit, Just as were the other social and political organisations. These organisations, specially Women's Trade Unions were directly connected with Adult Education. They ran evening classes, seminars and so on, but under military rule the whole burden came on the Ministry of Education, in 1960. The Government decided that the Local Government must share the burden with the Ministry of Education in the field of adult education, through the municipal and rural councils. These councils indeed helped greatly in solving the financial and administrative problems but they could not replace the women's organisations which had been active in the field In 1961, the rural councils started to give assistances for woman's guidance programme and the women's Guidance Section in the Social Service Department in the Gazira Scheme, looked after technical supervision.

A Community Centre for National Development was established in 1960 in Shendi Town with the assistance of UNESCO. Women's guidance was part of its activity. This centre helped in training women teachers in the field of Adult Education and women guidance and thus made available a trained cadre.

At the beginning of the sixties, the correlation between adult education movement and women's guidance became clear, so that centres for adult education had women's guidance programmes as well.

After October 1964, Adult Education and women's guidance work made good progress because of the efforts made by the Department of Adult Education, Ministry of Education, the Social Services Department in the Gazira Scheme, the Community Development Centre in Shendi and the Nutrition Section which was established as an experimental project to spread out cultural nutrition.

The Nutrition Section also trained women responsible for evening classes for literacy and women's guidance through lectures, practical lesson and training cycles which extend to six months. Up till 1970, 8,695 students, had been trained. The project was successful and in 1970 it became one of the units of the Ministry of Education.

Women's organisations resumed their activities in the field of Adult Education after the 1964 revolution and gave it another push in 1970, the Women's Union held an International Seminar entitled "Illiteracy among women." It was a good opportunity for women to gain experience from other countries specially Arabs and Africans. The seminar was very fruitful and fulfilled the expectations and needs of the Women's Union and other institutions active in this field. It inspired the uneducated women to catch up and review their position in regard to coping with the new advances in civilisation.

This activity had been extended to eastern Sudan and those responsible for adult education felt it was necessary to make use of the Koranic school in Bija area (which were directed by pioneer women) for adult education and eradication of illiteracy. Religious guidance was the beginning after which other subjects were introduced such as reading and writing, needlework and home economics. This initiative gave a strong push to out adult education movement among women which helped in opening so many evending classes in Elgash and Aroma area.

There are many reasons why adult education progressed. Adult education among women had become a Sudanese tradition with the Fung and continued in one integrated way or another. Secondly the separation of adult women education from that of men made it suitable for the tradition bound society. Being conducted in the evening it did not interfere with the household responsibilities of women. Above all is the inherent intelligence of the Sudanese woman and her interest in education. Also there was another important factor which pushed forward then adult education movement; it was the approval by the community and the attention paid by the Ministry of Education after 1956 which was reflected in the training of supervisors.

Attention was also given to producing books specifically for women which could be used for follow up purposes. Centres also organised leisure evenings in which films on various aspects of Sudanese life were shown; lectures, plays and songs were also arranged.

Annual exhibitions organised by the women's guidance classes also played an important role. Visitors found their production worthy of pride. They extended moral and financial support by sending their wives and female family members to those centres. One of them wrote his comments on one such exhibition saying "those who speak about the outdoor activity of Sudanese women as idle or wasteful, without knowing how to benefit from it, should visit these exhibitions and see for themselves how the Sudanese women benefitted from her leisure time." "Those who speaks also about employment of women teachers, should know well that they do a very good job towards their sisters," said another.

In 1969, adult education and women's guidance resumed one of their activities, that is religious literacy. Government established Islamic Centres for women in Shumbat, Khartoum North, and Khartoum. Women from the Ministry of Endowment and Religious Affairs worked in these centres.

At the beginning of 1970, the Sudan was chosen as a

centre for Functional Literacy and the women considerably gained from this work one of the difficulties faced in the development of adult education among women and women's guidance was the preralent opinion that education was a step towards liberation and freedom from household responsibilities. At the beginning there was strong resistance in the Gezira because it was a conservative district very much tried for Islamic religion and traditions and the idea of education was associated with the missionary home visits. Restriction of women to her house and the number of children she bore hindered her activity. The syllabus of adult education among women was generally speaking not so interesting. The shortage of working women in the field of adult education was another reason; the incentive was poor and meagre. Adult education was initial:, started on voluntary basis, the system of incentives was introduced later but was not very encouraging.

In spite of these difficulties, the woman benefitted much from the adult education, system. Starting with alphabet literacy introduced by UNESCO in 1946 aimed at teaching of reading and writing it went on to civilizational literacy aiming at a social change through the participation of individuals in development. The women guidance made great contribution to help women attain their rightful position in society and improve their role inside the house. Women played good role in agricultural field, grazing and handiwork and production was improved. All this happened through evening classes for women.

Women and Koranic Schools (Khalwa)

Women's Koranic schools are meant only to impart religious instruction. Therein women learned the Koran by heart and also learnt about Islamic legislation. They began to learn reading and writing so that they could study the

Koran and Sunna. The method followed by teachers in these schools was to give lessons closely connected with women's life. So the Khalwa was regarded as a tributary to adult education among women. The women had a distinguished position in the history of Khalwa. She was a learner and later became its director. The exclusively female Koranic schools were not allowed during the course of history until social discrimination appeared at the end of the 19th Century.

The Khalwa, as a sort of national system of education was neglected and faced difficulties from the British side. The British administrators did not encourage it and did not give even aid to it. On the other hand they encouraged the missionaries to compete with the Khalwa.

In 1938 when the Graduates' Conference was held, it emphasised the importance of the Khalwa, they revived the inspiration for the Koran and rebuilt he Khalwas. The women Khalwas found good appreciation in the circumstances.

There were a large number of women Khalwas in eastern Sudan thanks to the big religious families like Elmirghani family headed by Sayed Mohamed Osman Elmirghani. They were very much interested in religious education for women. They opened many Khalwas in 1890. Many of them are still extant in eastern Sudan. In 1945 a number of women established Khalwas which are still active. For example, zeinab Mohamed Ahmed, Khadiga Omer Kashwa and Haniya Ibrahim in Tokar and Port Sudan respectively.

In 1950 some groups from Hadandaw tribes in Aroma area became active and opened Khalwas for women. Sheikh Ali Bilau from Hadandaw tribe was the first to undertake this task. He was a religious man and spent most of his time and money in opening Khalwas for both men and women. He paid more attention to women because he believed that a man needs a true Muslim woman who has learned the Koran so as to be his partner and the women as well needs a religious man. So he gave the woman the same chance for education as to the man. Whether we agree with Shaikh Bilau or not, the woman benefited greatly from these Khalwas.

These Khalwas for women were situated east and north of Khassala town. This area is parallel to the boundaries with Ethiopia and, to the west is bounded by Gash river. They were called "Hamshkoraib" Khalwas.

An inspector of the Religious Affairs Department said, I have been visiting those villages and I was really surprised to see all men, women and children--both sexes--sit together round the fire learning the Koran. Women had separate places.

Western Sudan comes in the second place regarding the number of women's Khalwas specially Kordofan Province. Although Darfur was in a position to be in contact with the Islamic world and with learned people, the big number of tribes in Kordofan and its site near Sinnar Kingdom, made the disseminating of Islamic science easier as compared with Darfur. After 1943 when the Government stopped the subventions and opened the sub-grade schools, the number of Khalwas decreased.

In 1960, when Sheikh Micheal Nobaii came to Niyala town and found ignorance of Islamic culture in both El Ginana and Nyala towns the thought of establishing a big Khalwa for women called "Women Believers House" in a village called Tayba near El Obeid. Two hundred women joined to learn the Koran under the supervision of Sheikh Micheal. Thereafter mixed Khalwas were opened in Darfur and Kordofan. They were not regular because the students would be occupied with agriculture and grazing. Sometimes the Khalwa would move to another place due to the movement of the tribe with their herds. Men and women came together in Khalwa for learning in those mixed schools; that society did not know sex segregation and it was natural for women to be by the side of men. In work and other responsibilities. The number of mixed Khalwas in Northern Darfur were 19; those exclusively for boys did not exceed four in number.

In the South, education was under the control of missionaries up till 1946, which came in the way of spreading Islamic culture. As a result the Khalwa appeared very late in the South, some time between 1950-1970. It was mixed Khalwa because there were no barriers between man and woman. There are many Khalwas in Bahr Elgazal because it is near Darfur. Their number was 18 and many citizens from the North helped in their establishment. Eight Khalwas were founded in Upper Nile Province and only three in Equatoria.

After 1964, when the conditions were encouraging, more attention was given to Khalwas. In other parts of the Sudan, like Khartoum and Gezira, there were no special Khalwas for women, they were mixed and open to both boys and girls. The concern for religious education for women, was widespread. So many specialized schools and institutes were opened for them when the mixed Khalwa failed to attract women specially in Khartoum. Gezirar and Northern Province, El Boluk Institute of Religion was founded in Omdurman in 1964. At the beginning it was efficiently ran, bur later, its programmes could not help the Sudanese

Ahlia Schools for Girls School Year 1969-1970*

	Ahlia	*Catholic Mission*	*Anglo Mission*	*American Mission*	*Egyptian Mission*	*Egyptian Private*	*Govern-ment*	*Total*
Primary or Village Schools	—	306	271	8	13	—	209	794
Primary	306	12-7 mixed	4-1 mixed	4-2 mixed	13 mixed	7 mixed	821	31, 145 mixed.
Intermediate	434	8-1 mixed	3 mixed	5	4, 8, mixed	4 mixed	101	116+434 stream + 13 mixed
Secondary	51	2	1	1	3,3 MIXED	—	18	23+51 streams +3 mixed.
Post Secondary Technical	1	—	—	—	—	—	1	2
University	1	—	—	—	—	—	1	2

* Meeting with Mr. Piter-Metropolitan of Bishopric Church-Omdurman 1976, Director of Information Office for Catholic Church, Father Jovany, Khartoum, 1976. Director Holy Book Society Offices, Khartoum, 1976 and, Educational Statistic Reports-part 3—p. 19 part 5 p/7 1969-1970.

girl to continue farther, education. So it was converted into an academic secondary school in 1969.

The activities of all these educational institutions, we talked about in this part, sowed the seeds of the women's movement, pushing forward the wheel of development. Woman became an active member in the community and assumed a distinct role in the contemporary history of the Sudan.

Occupations: Agriculture, Grazing, Trade and Industry

The Sudan being an agricultural country, its economy depends entirely on agriculture and cattle grazing. More than 35 per cent of manpower is engaged in this occupation. Agriculture in the Sudan is not well advanced, most of the rural areas follows the old system of production and primitive relations prevail. Yet during the Turkish rule agriculture registered notable success as a result the renewal in agriculture and improvement of transport, that success could be regarded as a sort of development when it was not affected by the enormous slave trade process. The Slave trade had adverse effect because productivity depended upon the number of workers deployed. The relations between land owners and workers were based on different kinds of exploitation up till the condominium (Aaglo-Egyptian Rule).

At that time there was some sort of concentration on agriculture for commercial purposes in certain areas and agricultural projects were undertaken. Cotton was, and still continues to be, the cash crop which accounts for 55 per cent of the total value of exports. Other crops such as gum, groundnuts and sisame also became important as cash crops.

The Sudanese woman has been involved in agricultural

activity since the dawn of history. She participated in different processes either by herself or under the supervision of some other person. Sometimes she also acted as supervisor and manager for the whole process of hoeing watering, cleaning, ploughing, sowing, gathering and marketing. The woman could be the owner, a partner or a worker herself.

People in Western Sudan used to employ in agricultural work more women than men; so the first thing that drew the attention was the large number of women employed in agricultural production in planting, gathering, cattle, breeding.

This was beside other leisure time occupations such as handicrafts which are regarded as a source of income for the family in Western Sudan. These handicraft articles include, woolen Togas used as tents and nets for carrying things. All of these are made of camel wool which is available in plenty. They also make colourful and attractive mats, palm leaf covers. The palm leaf manufacture needs great patience and settlement. The woman in Western Sudan is efficient in leather works as well. It is very skilfully done and the leather articles are decorated with coroorpet seeds.

Participation of women in the economic life in Western Sudan had impact on its social life as well. Some tribes gave her equal right of inheritance with man other tribes gave her even priority in inheritance. Others gave her the leadership of the tribe, so the woman in Western Sudan has a prominant position and is highly respected.

In Nuba mountains, the cultivator woman got the right of election as member in the Nuba Mountain Farmers' Union for. The first time as a recognition of her role in agriculture. In Dar Far, the woman, beside her work in agriculture, grazing and handicraft, undertakes other tough jobs such as well-digging, house building, transportation and trades.

On the other hand, this situation had created a very serious social problem, that is the multiplication of wives. In Western Sudan, some tribesmen marry four wives so as to exploit their position and labour in agriculture, grazing and marketing.

Some cultured men attributed this phenomenon, the phenomenon of the success of woman in Western and Northen Sudan, to the fact that, she found herself assuming the responsibility of the family, due to the increased emigration of men to towns for extra income, she had to rely on herself and prove her efficiency.

The following rabies show the increased number of women in comparison to men in some districts in the west and North:

Man in Western and Northern Sudan relies entirely on the labour of woman, not only in agriculture, but also in other fields. She looks after the animals roaming from one place to another across the hills and wide plains, almost running after grass and water, on foot or riding on ox. During this tour, the woman makes milk products in primitive ways. Western Sudan is famous for differents sorts of butter and cheese. In Northern Sudan the woman is concerned with dates, planting, gathering and marketing. She works hard day and night and is sometimes helped by young boys because strong men in Northern Province emigrate either to Egypt or Knartoum in order to earn their living. Woman remain alone taking all the responsibilities.

In Southern Sudan the woman shares all economic activities of man, that is, agriculture and grazing. Ninetynine per cent of the Azand women work on agriculture and cattle breeding. Generally the work in the Azand area is very cough because the fields are covered with thick weeds which hinder digging, ploughing and planting processes.

The Azand tribe is like other Sudanese tribes in the South, West and middle of the country. Collective work is the distinctive feature of their life. Once a tribe started to cultivate a piece of land for the first time, they call upon other tribes to help them. Here the woman playe a major role and often takes the front rank.

These features of the Azand tribe and common to other tribes also. For example, 60 per cent of the women in Mangia tribe work on agriculture beside house management. The percentage of women in Dinkar Nuer, and Shulk tribes, working in agriculture, is more than 50 per cent out of the total number of women. This ratio is higher among Dinka women because the Dinka women and fur women are more involved in work and participate fully in the local economy and family life; they have stronger physiques than other Sudanese women.

The effective participation of the woman in the economic-life of the district, in agriculture, animal husbandry, commerce and other occupations influenced selection of a wife: it depended on her ability for work and production, the results of a survey in Bulanda tribe showed that 30 per cent of the marriages were directly affected by this factor.

Among some Southern tribes, marriage has a direct impact on local economy because the dowry is paid in the form of cattle. This custom prevails among Dinka. Nuer and Shulk tribes. This tradition yields a healthy social practice, that is, the lower rate of divorce because divorce is connected with the return of the dowry the cattle. These tribes, therefore, prefer to have girls more than boys because girls support the family economy by cattle.

Woman in the south starts her practical life after marriage which is usually accomplished around the age of ten. Besides her work in agriculture, animal husbandry wood cutting, building and construction, grazing and hunting, she is good in handicrafts. She has fertile imagination in choosing and mixing of colours. She is very clever in palm leaf work, leather and wood works. All of these materials are available in the South. In most cases she occupies herself with sort of work after the sowing season.

Beside this, she has to work very hard. As an example the Nuer men are lazy and they depend on their women. As a result, woman in some of the southern tribes is mentally independent. She does not easily follow the instructions of her husband unless she is contented. So, some of the Southern women became leaders of their tribes.

The woman in the east also participates equally well but as a part of family life. She works on agriculture, animal husbandry only to help her husband, and not as her basic occupation. Women in Eastern Sudan, in so many circumstances assume the responsibility of the whole family, so she is a bit different from those of south and west, and her contribution towards production is secondary. Generally speaking the woman in Eastern Sudan is attached to her house and husband.

Some of the woman in Eastern Sudan work on animal husbandary and milk production. Women in the Bija tribe of Eastern Sudan, for example, have to take care of the camels and cattle. It is particularly so because the invaders and highway robbers do not attack the herds driven, by women. The woman also has top do handicraft work like those in other districts. The young girl does not work outside the house before marriage but stays indoors engaged in normal household work besides palm-leaf work such as making mats, baskets and tray covers. She weaves carpets out of hair which are used as tents and covers.

Availability of raw materials and time on hand determine the kind of activity in which women are engaged. As there has been no change in the agricultural and related processes the tradition prisists since the old Sudanese kingdoms of the sixteens century. Only in the middle of the Sudan has agriculture undergone change.

The first half of this century witnessed a considerable increase in production from land due to improvement in transport, dams construction and renewal of immigration system and the concentration on limited schemes. Of these the Gezira scheme is the most important. Its area was 207,440 Fedans in 1950, which increased to 1,288,000 Fedan in 1970 Cotton is the chief product of this Scheme as welt as in other schemes such as Managil Extension, Khasbm El Girba, Blue and White Nile private schemes, and mechanized agricultural schemes. Then ccmes other products such as sesame, wheat, millet and ground nuts etc. The woman participates in all stages of production of these commodities. She owns the land, sows it and gather the product. Some times her part in the work is seasonal because these schemes are sometimes exposed to a crisis due to shortage in manpower especially in the gathering season.

The available statistics at hand shows that *9* per cent

of the women in the Gazira Scheme own Hawashat (Tenancy of 10 Feddan)—out of the total number of the owners-1963. It was realised that the percentage decreased to 70 per cent in 1968 due to the fact that the woman, after the sixties started to work in sectors other than cultivation such as industry and office work (in both general and private sectors) which gives steady and stable income. This is due in the difficult conditions of life, instability of incomes from cultivation.

As a matter of fact, the work of man and woman in the rural areas is complementary to each other. Each depends on the other, and this is deemed necessary to develop the productivity of both man and woman Any neglect of the woman is regarded as a neglect of the productivity of half the work force in this field.

All these activities of the woman, in the economic life in rural areas, helped in making her more prominent in the rural society than in the urban society.

Commercial Work

The work of the woman with commerce is as old as that with cultivation, because the marketing process could not be separated from agriculture except in new sectors of cultivation. Both the farmer and the hardsman, man or women, takes the production to the local markets for sale and in turn, boys the necessities. The market place could be far away from the production centres, so the woman was obliged to walk on foot or ride on the back of an animal. Since the Fung days the markets are full of women because women are used to display their products specially the handicrafts, the leather products and agricultural products which meet favourable demands in the local market. These local markets which are situated in towns and big villages attract large numbers of merchants as well as other citizens. Work in commerce requires wide movement and contacts with others. This makes the woman considerably free, to move out of the narrow surrounding of home into a wider world based on commercial relations. Generally, commerce is a more advanced economic sector than agriculture. The woman was very successful in dealing with selling and buying whether in town or a village. Big shops or small ones; she managed to run them by herself.

The woman initiated the idea of mobile sale (taking goods from one place to another within the houses). This practice had started during, Turkish rule in the Sudan, at the end of the ninteenth century, when the woman was strictly prohibited from going outside the house. It was the attitude imposed on woman in Turkey and the Middle East during the 18th and 19th century. At that time, the woman bad to stay inside and was served by her slaves and maids. She relied on middle women to buy her needs. These women were either liberated slaves or villagers who were not affected by strictness of towns.

These middle women, made profits from the process of buying and selling these, mediator women are called coquetry because they started selling the beauty needs for women. During the Mahadia rule, this practice continued and supported by the Mahadia who liberated more slave-women and they followed this track.

The coquerties form a majority group of the contemporary society in the Sudan. Their role is getting very important because they sell things by instalments for other women specially working women to suit their small incomes. So the coquetries increased in number and became well-off, and made it possible to buy for the housewife everything however expensive.

This sort of work depends upon the trus testablished among people. It could not work out except in a traditional community. The main features of this traditional community are closely relations among the members, who came to know every bit of each other, community in which all the barriers are abolished and have no effect on the individual attitude.

During the fifties and sixties, the movement of coquetries became wider reflecting the liberty and freedom enjoyed by woman in the community, they interact freely and with great efficiency with big merchants and their customers (both men and women). Coquetries also dealt with men but in a limited scale.

The coquetries gained a distinguished role in society. They participated in all social and cooperative work. They form an important group in the women's organisation and political organisations as well. The political parties after the October Revolution, made use of women attracting others towards the political fronts, the thing that made her gain more political rights and to improve her status.

Work in Industry

Old industries or folk industries in which the women participated as a basic factor data back to ancient times in the Sudan. Their purpose was to make the local community self sufficient for requirement of clothing lodging and food. They run were in a primitive way and on a vary limited scale not exceeding the tribe or group of tribes living in the same place.

Industry in its new form, is something new to the economy in Sudan, because the Sudanese economy depended up till now on imports. Some industries had been established during the Second World War to fulfil the needs of the allied troops in the nearby battlefields and inside the Sudan.

Most of the factories are centralized in the capital town although the first one was constructed in 1946 in the south. It was a textile factory attached to the Zandi Scheme in which cotton is planted. Another oil factory and soap factory have been constructed to use cotton seeds for oil and soap making. The woman served as a worker there doing some work which do not need skill such as cleaning, sorting out etc.

After independence, a distilling and a data packing factory have been built in the Northern Province. Women were not involved in work because the people there are conservative and traditionalist. On the other hand the nature of the production was not encouraging; in such traditional society it was not proper that the woman should work in factories producting mainly wines.

In the early sixties, three factories for fruit and vegetable canning were constructed at Karima Town in Northern Province, Wan Town, in Bahr El Ghazal Province and the third one in Babanosa in Western Sudan mainly for milk production. Large number of women have been employed in Wau and Babanosa factories. They work done by them does not need any technical skill. They do the cleaning, sorting and prepartory work only, because the women are illiterate and are not technically trained for such work.

Womens's interest for work increased as the industry sector expanded at the end of the fifties. The Government and private sector capitals and directed to this field inspite of that, the woman did not penetrate the field of industry freely but on a very small scale. The Textile Factory, which started production in 1962 (its output was eight million yards in 1970) could not absorb all women. But a few, only 21, joined the factory in 1963 and at the end of 1964 they were dismissed because their output in production was very low compared to that of men. Women do not do night shifts. They were taken back on work in this factory in 1972.

There is a clerical section in this factory which started with, ten women; their number reached 45 in 1970. There was one specialized woman in sciences. She works in the laboratory attached to the factory. Industry in the Sudan is mainly consumer industry mainly to supply the local needs. The most important are food stuff, drinks, then comes textiles, dress and perfume industries.

In order to make the woman contribute effectively in the industrial process and to gain a better situation, all hindrances must be removed. This could be done through training cycles inside the factory or education institutions outside so as to increase her qualification and productivity. So in this manner, the woman could enter the industrial field if she found a suitable income as well as social security for her and her family. All this could be achieve through expansion of educational and training opportunities internally and abroad through the revision of labour laws to suit the circumstances of woman and enable her to perform well in the house and the factory. The application of these laws should be looked after in both the general and private sectors. The majority of women are employed in the private sector, specially in the three town Capital where all the industries are concentrated. This is due to the facilities available and marketing. The population in the three towns is 600,000 which constitutes one third of the total number in Sudan towns.

Teaching: Medical Occupations and Office Work

In the rural areas, away from the towns the woman had to work for economic reasons. Women shared work with men and under difficult circumstances, sometimes naked or half dressed and sometimes with just a national shirt or "Toub." The rural community, therefore, never felt that women broke traditions, customs or religious tenets when she worked outdoors. Her contribution varied according to the demands of work. She proved to be very efficient ana trustworthy.

The employment of women in the town started a bit late because employment was connected with education which started only at the beginning of this century and that, too, at a very slow pace. There were serious lacuna, both in quality and quantity till the second half of the century and the situation is not very different event today. The urban community still clings to the idea of the household women; she is meant only for producing children and running the household. On account of such attitude men are reluctant to let her work which would involve maxing with other men or moving among them. There is no religious sanction behind this restriction on women although it is widely sought to be justified on that score. Very few actually use religions as a tool to stop Women from Working. The Sudan had come under so many regimes, religious or colonial eras which deepened the roots of backwardness and widened the gap between man and women. As a result the woman became inward looking and withdraw into her shell.

The word is changing rapidly, so she has to develop herself, with the help of the limited educational opportunities available. She managed to be outward looking breaking the chains of illusion. She forced her way in different fields of employments. She started as a nurse, a school mistress then as an office employee, supported by women's organisations and some of the educated men. She performed so many functions and proved all success. Now the community could understand the problem of the woman as she was participating in all fields in hospitals, schools, offices, courts, commercial institutions—a natural and healthy sign.

Teaching Profession

Mother is a great teacher by nature, so teaching profession is the first to be taken up by woman since the Fung days. The number of jurisprudent women was enormous and they had vast impact and influence on the community, something that draws the attention of researchers. During the Turkih rule, women, continued to work in the teaching field although, their performance was affected by the prevailing social conditions, particularly education. Sudanese missionary woman and others became active in the field. During the Mahdia rule, the woman worked on a very small scale in the "Khalwas" nor formal primary schools for religion in comparison to the Fung days.

At the beginning of the 29th century, appeared the first pioneer women such as Sit Abuha Mustafa who worked with Sheikh Babikar Badri in his school in Rufaa and Fatima El Dinkawia, who opened a missionary school in Madani upon which Priest Joheny depends, and Zagraa' Bit El Gabani who was trained in the British school in Khartoum All of them worked in the new schools established the missionary people and by Sheikh Bablkar Badri in Rufaa. After the establishment of the Girls Teacher Training College in Omdurman, the first batch of trained schoolmistress six in number graduated in 1923. The society opposed education of Girls because it was opposed to their taking up jobs believing that education would spoil the girls and makes them more free and turn them away from the path of tradition and custom. Woman going to work and mixing with men was considered a wrong attitude and totally opposed by the town community which thinks that the veil is a thick wall, vision and sound proof.

But luckily women proved the contrary. Supported by influential men who believed that development could not be achieved without the contribution of women, she went out for work in full dress covering all her body except the eyes. Sometimes she was accompanied by chaperons during her journey to and from the school. The expenses of the chaperon were met by the state so as to maintain the traditions and customs as the British administrators repeated at that time.

The practice of being chaperond continued till the 50s when the school-mistress began to be transferred from one place to another.

Teaching profession for women kept pace with the development of education. The woman became a teacher in higher levels and took part in special education when fully trained. The job opportunity opened before her since there were openings in education and training and new educational projects.

The community was satisfied and felt the need to let the women work in teaching. So the school mistress became trustworthy because she showed great concern for her sex and helped them in her leisure time by giving them evening lessons. She progressed further and became a lecture in the University. The number of school mistresses in 60s in Primary Schools was 3035, in General Secondary (intermediate) 516, in Higher Secondary 165.

School mistresses played a prominent role in the national movement in general and particularly in the women's movement so as to improve their status, to increase the opportunities in education for both young and adult women. So during the British rule, we find that the British administration started to harass those having any social or political activities. They used different methods of punishment. Sometimes by transfer to remote places, sometimes stopping their promotions and annual increments and at others, dismissal from service. Inspite of all that the school-mistress continued to work in the social and political fields. This gave women greater influence and distinction in contemporary history.

Medical Occupation

At the end of Turkish rule, coinciding roughly with the end of the 19th century, the liberation movement of slaves became active. At that time women took to the nursing profession. They got rid of the house work and tried to gainfully use their leisure time by nursing. Success in this field came because of the Sudanese woman's great ability, perfection and keenness. She did not start with nursing right away, because nursing needs some sort of training but started as a midwife. The process of child delivery is related to preservation of mankind and after all it was done as humanitarian work in a voluntary manner and without any training. In fact this job was done fay very old women who had no idea about child care or mother's health. These old women became proficient by practice only and this was the start of nursing profession. Both nursing and delivery went side by side uptil now. Midwife must beanurse having good knowledge of nursing.

During the Mahdia and on the battle field between the Mahadia fighters and the Turkish army, the women were found behind the ranks of fighters to provide necessary treatment for the wounded soldiers. Women like khadiga Bint Sorkati, Fatima Bint Um El Hassan and Soada Bint El Hag, daughter of El Amir Mohamoud Wad Ahmed, who was killed in Toshki, became prominent in history. Another famous women was Halima Mohamed Issa, sister of El Amir Osman Azrag.

In 1927, the first batch of nurses graduated from the nursing college of Omdurman, such as Gindia Salih and Aish a El Nikhaily, who were untrained midwives. The second batch comprised Usra Masoud and El Shol Abdalla. The third batch consisted of Batool Mohamed Issa and El Donn Zakaria. This group is the pioneer of nursing and maternity. The women worked in a very stormy atmosphere at that time because they were regarded as spoilt ones, kind of moral out-laws. Some thought that the nature of woman was to be a mother and look after her house and children only. Others believed that going out for work and increasing the income implied negligence on the part of the father towards his family.

Through the spread of consciousness and briefing of people about the role of midwife, accepted the idea of letting the woman to work as midwife and nurse, then as health inspector visiting the house and advising the family about the proper hygienic ways. The first woman to do this job, in December 1948, was Zeinab Abdel Gadir, who was appointed as health inspector for houses within the limits of Omdurman municipality.

At the end of the nineteen-forties and the beginning of the fifties, there was a hot debate in newspapers about the working woman whether, a school mistress, a nurse or a midwife. Some had an astonishing outlook and in spite of that, the woman forced her wayin different fields of health occupations: midwife, nurse, inspector or health visitors. Hawaa' Sonousi was the first health visitor. The number of nurses and midwives increased. Then came the first batch from abroad, who were sent for higher education such as Awatif Ahmed Osman, now Principal of Narsing College, Fayza Yousif Zomrawi, Khadiga Mohamed Salih, Swar El Dahab and Fawzia Abdel Halim. Then the community became more sympathetic and women's enthusiasm increased. For Women, it was a great opportunity to liberate themselves from idleness and to change their status.

Those working in the health field were members of women organisations dealing mostly with politics. Mrs. Pifgha Bahta, was a good example of a woman well-known for her political activity. Nurses gained a special status on account of their concern with public issues and their collaboration with their colleagues in the field of education. This helped the Sudanese woman to obtain her natural position in society as a positive partner and not a negative follower.

The beginning of the second half of this century witnessed the first batch of Sudanese women doctors such as Khalid, Zahir Zarous Sir Kisyan. Both were good examples of women who work efficiently and at the same time played a prominent role in political movement in a period mostly characterised by the rising opposition of people to the colonial rule in the Sudan.

The number of Sudanese women doctors increased very slowly because of the limited opportunity in Khartoum University. But as soon as Sudanese girls went abroad, after independence in the middle of the fifties, the number of graduates in school of Medicinets, at Khartoum University, Egyptian Universities and Socialist countries increased.

Office Employment

In February 1949, the daily *El Sudan El Gadid* in its issue no. 704 published the following news:

> "For the first time, Sudanese girls applied for vacant posts announced by the Department of Economy and Commerce in the field of using the new calculates machines. Applicants belonged to the following nationalities: English, Egyptian, African and Sudanese. All dressed in modern European clothes, only the Sudanese was in her national dress-Toub-all covered."

In March 1949, there was a debate in the legislative assembly about the employment of Sudanese girls in clerical work and calculating machines in place of foreign women. Some were of the opinion that the foreign women be replaced by Sudanese men; a small group led by Mr. Binjamin Lockay supported the employment of Sudanese girls. Mr. Lockay said, "Since we are able to train nurses, it is easy to train clerks and I hope that the government arranges for training girls because they are the complacent of the society."

Although the woman in town became a nurse, and a school mistress (and their number is continuously increasing) and although some of them started office work back in 1920, her employment in office work was not permanent until the middle of the nineteen-forties when the first Sudanese woman joined the Department of Economics and Commerce.

The Sudanese women faced great difficulties in their work because it was for the first occasion to mix with men. Some people disapproved of this office work and considered it against the traditions and customs and began to fight against it in different ways. Some of her colleagues in office who are so fanatic, averred that they would not work with a woman at the same place. In spite of these difficulties their number increased in the Economic and Commerce. Department and became nine. Most of them are secondary graduates in addition to those working in Telephone Department.

The quick growth of economy between the sixties and seventies was clearly seen in industrialization, the establishment of a number of development schemes, the development of agricultural sector, improvement of services sector, tendency towards decentralisation, towards the diversification of education and broadening its base. All this helped to deepen the importance of the participation of woman. The women's movement for employment increased. The woman succeed in so many professions which were not within her reach. Now the door was wide open before her. This led the women to organise the woman's Union and other women's organisations. The women's Union played an important part especially in solving the problems of women concerning employment both at the people's and official levels, by trying to improve the conditions of service. The women's Union was the only organisation that adopted the law of "equal wage for equal work" in its work plan and followed it up till it was realised in 1968.

The press also played a good role. As an example, El Sarah, a bi-weekly newspaper, was the first to encourage the woman in office work and explain the importance of her role in this field as well as other areas, through its permanent columns. A special column was devoted to the subject of women and work which continued as from 1952 to 1957. In this column all the problem of women ware discussed logically and it had a very salutary effect on society. The Sudanese broadcasting organisation as well supported the woman and her contribution through talks, symposia and plays.

All those efforts helped greatly to lead the woman to contribute in all government offices according to her qualifications. This passage also helped in new openings in education. The diversification and specialization in girls' education increased her chances to work and naturally lead to a better status. This is the new understanding of employment in the developing countries. The good direction of manpower (men and women) towards employment definitely leads to the development needed by the people in the field of economic, social and political life.

The Government is a large employer of women. It absorbs all the graduates in universities and higher institutes. Data concerning the employment of woman shows that the Ministry of Education is the first government unit that employs women, then comes the Ministry of Health and thirdly the Ministry of Communication.

Other Occupations

The Sudanese woman took part in two media areas, the press and broadcasting. Since 1940 women have been working as editors in newspapers, writing short and long articles, commenting upon subjects concerning women such as marriage, divorce, circumcision, and education. It was a new practice which was opposed by many; therefore, women used to write under a pseudonym. Real names of women in newspapers were regarded as scandal and something contrary to the tradition and custom.

In 1947 appeared the first woman's magazine called *Bint El Wadi* (Giri of the Valley), edited by Takwi Sir Kisian, a Sudanese girl of Syrian origin. The appearance of this magazine-created a great furore. It was a new school for Sudanese woman. Although it was for women, it was edited all by men except a few articles by women.

The magazine was widely distributed in schools as well as houses. It succeeded in uncovering important sides of women's problems. Women became more active in writing articles, comments in newspapers urging the women to take up education and work and demanding the government to open more schools for girls. Other newspapers like *El Sudan El Gadid* (new Sudan), *El Rai Elaam* (Central Opinion), *Sout El Sudan* (Sudan Voice); *El Nil* (The Nile) *El Sarahu, Elayam El Akhbar* and *El Sahafa,* gave more opportunities to women writers).

The middle of the nineteen-fifties witnessed the publication of a purely woman's magazine called *Sawt El Maras,* (Voice of Woman) edited and issued by Fatima Ahmed Ibrahim in 1955, It was financed and edited with the collaboration of some women's union members. The magazine fought for the problems of women, ana in this respect faced many difficulties from the authority. The general trend of the magazine is leftist which was clearly manifested in the sixities.

A year later, another magazine came into being; it was called *Cultural Caravan* and was issued by Hagga Kashif in 1956 who edited it in collaboration with other cultured men. It was concerned with the problem of women within the framework of cultural and political issues.

In 1956 *El Manor* Magazine issued by Soad El Fatih, came out, but it did not last long and disappeared in the same year. Ten years later, in 1964 it was reissued by Thoria Umbabi with the help of other women, the trend of this magazine is Moslem and it reflects the opinion of Moslem Brothers Group. In March 1969, Elayam Company for Printing and Publishing, issued another magazine called *Hawaa Elgadida* (New Hawaa). It was the first magazine issued by men, but had a considerable output regarding women's problem connected with education and employment. In general, the women's journals helped the woman greatly to be more associated with and aware of her problems.

The women made great effort through broadcasting from the beginning of 1947. This effort was directed towards women's affairs, education, general knowledge and fruitful work for the country. It was also directed towards informing, the woman about her duties and rights in the community and how to be more associated with her organisations. The first to work in broadcasting were Fatima Talib and Soad Abdel Rahman. In 1947 they started presenting the women's programme and children's programme. In 1942 Mrs. Umaima Mohamed Abdel Ghani *El* Tahawi started to take part in children's plays and talks, and in 1951 started a programme called Talks of Grandmother Fatima, transmitted in the spoken local language dealing with the evils in woman's life and to find solutions for their eradication. This programme was prepared by one of the staff of the Radio and presented by Mrs. Safeia Mohamoud El Faki regularly every week.

After the formation of women's organisations, the Radio gave their leaders the chance to address the women. A programme for the women's Union was directed and presented by Aziza Mekki and Nafisa Ahmed El Amin. The involvement of women increased in this area and the programme was extended to include general knowledge, politics, economics and social affairs. Television was another media in which the women functioned by reading the news, presenting talks, debetes and plays. Mrs. Mahasin Osman was the first woman who officially became a broadcaster in 1947.

Other occupations of women are in the field of arts.

She was a singer musician, dancer sculptor, painter etc. Usha Musa (El Falatia) was the first singer introduced through Omdurman Radio in 1942. Her songs were for the entertainment of Sudanese soldiers during the Second World War fighting alongside the allied troops near the Sudanese borbers. She had a sweet voice. Her sister Hadawia Musa was a guitar player in 1945.

There are so many other fields in which the women has displayed her skill other than in which management. All those have not been described here. But it is certain that independent occupation and employment improved her status.

Some Laws of Employment Concerning Woman

The woman is now in the field of employment fortified with knowledge, and common sense, putting and end to the myth "woman must, not go out to work." She gained a distinguished position in the community but at the same time there some difficulties that she has to encounter. She could not make the necessary balance between her job as an employee and her job as housewife. She did not find the necessary support or appreciation for what she did or rather she felt the discrimination and inequality with her fellow-mate in work although she was equally qualified, and trained. So we find the situation of the working women (whether she is a labourer or an office employee) a bit difficult. The employer, whether in private or public sector, looks upon her as inferior to man in so many ways-chances for work, terms of appointment; training facilities, promotion and retirement benefits. The Government is the chief employer for woman, so her opportunities for work were limited in education and nursing only. In comprison to man, the woman is put in a lower scale at the time of appointment, while the man is posted in a permanent services, the woman is posted in temporary service. At the end of her service she is deprived of pension. Pensionable service is only for permanent posts.

Table Showing Number of Employed Women in Different Government Units

Ministry/Dept.	*No of Women*	*Remarks*
Education	4646	Except those working in the Field of Illiteracy Irradication, Nutrition
Health, Transport	10160	Number of employees in Southern Region is less.
Local Government	782	
Agriculture	290	
Finance	219	
Banks	268	
Information	231	Women in this field are numbered in Southern Region.
Public Service and Administrative Reform	191	
Public Works	70	
Commerce and Industry	50	
Irrigation	34	
Foreign Affairs	26	
Attorney General	23	In the South, no woman in working in the field of Law.

Source: Labour, Department-Statistic. Reports Manpower Kharteum

Even those who are highly qualified are not considered for permanent service. The procedure was that when she got married, her service was terminated and she has to sign a new contract for the same post on a monthly basis. The salary of a working women is four-fifths that of the man doing the same job and having the same qualification. Generally speaking the rules of service for the woman have been drawn without making any consideration for her social or natural situation. She needs special care in special circumstances such as pregnancy and maternity, absence of husband in duty whether internally or abroad and in case of his death also. In the light of these laws, the working woman could not obtain her full rights regarding the pension or reward at the end of her service and even the exchange process of pension. All these laws and acts are not adapted to suit local conditions; they are just copied from the British laws. So the Sudan since the beginning of self-rule, and up till the middle of the sixties, followed these rules and regulations. But efforts of the national movement continued to repudiate the colonial rules and regulations which were adopted without consideration of local conditions.

The demand for revising these laws was made before independence; the trade union organisations and the Woman's Union played a good role in changing the service conditions for women. A strong campaign was carried on by the Women's Union through seminars, lectures, press pages and other media on the laws, rules and regulations of service for women. The Union made efforts in this respect which yeilded good results. After the October Revolution of 1964, the women were given opportunity to take part in different fields or civil service. She was appointed as a diplomat and administrator and got equal salary as a man with the same qualification. After the May Revolution 1969 more opportunities were given to women: She has been employed for the first time in the Armed Forces, Security Section Accounts and Clerical Jobs. She has been posted also as telephone operator, typist and secretary. New avenues opened before the woman; she became a member of Administrative Boards, of some Commercial Banks and Industrial Corporations. A woman reached the top to become a Deputy Minister. The first in this area, was Mrs. Nafisa Ahmed El Amin, who was appointed Deputy

Minister for Youth and Sports. After the May Revolution, the law about temporary appointment for married women was cancelled. She has a right to continue in service after marriage.

The Council of Ministers took a decision to amend the Leave Regulations so that the married woman could be granted leave without pay for not more than four years, to accompany her husband in case of hiss posting abroad for study, secondment or transfers. Pensionable terms of service were also made applicable to the women.

In general the women benefited greatly from the new terms of services after the October and May Revolutions. Maternity leave has been increased to eight weeks, four before and four after so as to completely recover before resuming her work. As the laws of service for the woman improve, she would be more liberated in her understanding and mentality and her duties inside the house or in work Also she would be able to understand her role better as a factor for development.

It is evident from the preceding discussion that women have traversed a long journey of development and progress. We have yet to go miles ahead in the direction of achieving equal status for women in real terms Let us be optimistic for.

Bibliography

Ahmad, Taherunnessa, 1996, *Palli anganader jemon dekhecki* [Rural women as I saw them]. Comilla: PARD.

Akin Rabibhadana, *The Organisation of Thai Society in the Early Bangkok Period, 1782-1873,* Data Paper no. 74, Southeast Asian Studies Programme (Ithaca: Cornell, 1969), p. 101.

Anna Leonowens, *The Romance of the Harem* (Charlottesville: University of Virginia, first published, 1872, reprinted, 1991).

Astige, Shanta B. 2006. *Role and Status of Working Women,* Anmol, New Delhi.

Bangladesh Bureau of Statistics, 1970-1971, *Statistical digest of Bangladesh.*

Barik, Vandana, 2009, *Women's Education, Gender Equity and Fertility,* Rajat, New Delhi.

Benitez, Fernando, 1972, *Los Indios de Mexico.* Editorial Era.

Berdyaev, N., *The Meaning of the Creative Act* (translated by D.A. Laurie), (New York, 1954).

Binay Ghosh, *Vidya Sagar O Bengali Samaj* (Calcutta, 1958), Vols. I-III; Indra Mitra, *Karuna Sagar Vidyasagar* (Calcutta, 1969).

Bureau of Justice Statistics (table 2, page 15), *Criminal Victimization in the United States, 2006 Statistical Tables.*

Bureau of Justice Statistics (table 4, page 17) *Criminal Victimization in the United States, 2006 Statistical Tables* (PDF).

Bureau of Justice Statistics, *Intimate Homicide Victims by Gender.*

Bureau of Justice Statistics, *Intimate Partner Violence in the U.S.: Victims.*

Chandra, P., 2005. *Political Dynamics of Women,* Akansha, New Delhi.

Damrong Rajanubhab, *Ruang Chaloem Phrayot Chaonai* (In honour of the establishment of royal titles), (Bangkok, 1929), cited in Akin Rabibhadana, *The Organisation of Thai Society,* p. 99.

De La Colina, Jose, 1973, "Aventuras y tribulaciones del cine mexicano." *Revista de Revistas,* July 25, Mexico.

Diaz Guarrero, Rogelio, 1970, *Estudios de psicologia del mexicano* (reprinted edition). Editorial Trillas.

East Pakistan Bureau of Statistics, 1961. The master survey of agriculture in East Pakistan. *Sixth Round,* Table 2.4 (A), p. 18.

Eiji Murashima, 1988, *Journal of Southeast Asian Studies,* vol. XIX no. 1 (March), p. 88.

Elu De Lenero, Ma. Del Carmen, 1969, *Hacia donde va la mujer mexicana.* Instituto Mexicano de Estudios Sociales.

Erik Erikson "Race and the Wider Identity," in *Identity, Youth and Crisis,* (New York, 1968), pp. 295-320.

Erik H. Erikson, "Inner and Outer Space: Reflections on Womanhood." *Daedalus,* 1964 (93), pp. 582-606.

Estudio socio-religioso de Ntra. Sra. de Lourdes 1970, Unpublished private study, Monterrey, Nuevo Leon,

Mexico. *Estudio Socio-religioso de Paso del Rio* 1971, Unpublished private study. Colima, Mexico.

Family Violence Prevention Fund, *The Facts on Children and Domestic Violence.*

Frank Baron, "The Psychology of Cereativity," in Frank Barrown et al, *new Frontiers in Psychology* II, (New York, 1965), (40);

Friederich Engels, *The Origin of the Family, Private Property, and the State* (New York, 1942).

Gore, M.S., *Urbanisation and Family Change,* (Bombay, 1968).

Government of Pakistan, 1947-1967, Twenty years of Pakistan in statistics. *Ministry of Economic Affairs, Central Statistical Office.*

Gupta, Shakuntla, 2005. *Women Development in India,* Anmol, New Delhi.

Heinrich Zimmer, *Philosophies of India* (New York, 1956).

Hellbom, Anna Britta, 1967, *La participacion cultural de las mujeres indias y mestizas en el Mexico precortesiano y postrevolucionario.* Stockolm: The Ethnolographical Museum.

Henry Alabaster, *The Wheel of the Law: Buddhism Illustrated from Siamaese Sources* (Farnborough: Gregg International, 1871, reprint edition 1971), p. 65).

Hussain, Rokeya Sakhawat, 1905, *Sultana's dream.*

Instituto Mexicano De Estudios Sociales, 1969, "Extudio sociografico de la colonia Cailos, Cd. Mexico." Unpublished mimeograph.

Karl Menninger, 1942, *Love Against Hate,* New York.

King Mongkut, *Prachumprakat Ratchakan thi si* (Collected

Decrees of the Fourth Reign), (Bangkok: Khurusapha, 1961), Decree no. 255, p. 235.

Kirk Patrick, F.A., 1958, *Los conquistadores espanoles* (sixth edition). Espasa Calpe, Argentina.

L. DeMause, *The Evolution of Childhood* (New York, 1975).

Leon Salzman, "Feminine Psychology Revisited, Circa 1970," *American Journal of Psychoanalysis,* 1971 (31) pp. 123-133.

Lewis Mumford, 1961, *The City in History*, London.

Leyzaola, Margarita, 1973, "Valentina, Valentina...." *Revista de Revistas.* July 18, Mexico.

Mackinnon, D.W. , 1970, "The Personality Correlates of Creativity: A Study of American Architects," in P.E. Vernon (ed.), *Creativity,* Penguin, pp. 289-311,

Masculine and Feminine, Some Biological and Cultural Aspects," *Psychiatry,* 1944 (7), pp. 257-296.

Momratchawong Khukrit Pramoj, *Siphaendin* (our Reigns), (Bangkok, Kaona, 8th printing 1975, first published 1953).

Morris Carstairs, G., *The Twice Born,* Bloomington.

Philip Spratt, 1966, *Hindu Culture and Personality*, Bombay.

National Archives of Thailand, Yuthitham 13/8 Ruang momchao pen that laemi phuaphrai (The case of a momchao who is a slave and has a commoner for a husband) 17 April-29 August 1983)

National Coalition Against Domestic Violence (NCADV), *Domestic Violence Facts.*

National Coalition of Anti-Violence Programs (NCAVP), *Lesbian, Gay, Bisexual, and Transgender Domestic Violence In the United States in 2007.*

National Institute of Justice (pages 6-7), *Sexual Assault on Campus: What Colleges an Universitie Are Doing About It.*

Navarrete, Ifigenia, 1969, *La mujer y los derechos sociales.* Mexico: Ediciones Oasis.

NCADV, *Comparison of VAWA 1994, VAWA 2000 and VAWA 2005 Reauthorization Bill.*

NCAVP, *Lesbian, Gay, Bisexual, and Transgender Domestic Violence In the United States in 2007.*

NOW, *The Violence Against Women Act: Celebrating 10 Years of Prevention.*

Papanek, Hanna, 1971, Purdah in Pakistan: seclusion and modern occupations for women. *Journal of Marriage and the Family.* (August): 517-530.

Paz, Octavio, 1961, *The Labyrinth of Solitude.* New York: Grove Press.

Qadir, S.A., 1968, *Modernisation of an Agrarian Society.* Rural sociology research Report 1, Mymensingh: Agricultural University.

Ramos, Samuel, 1962, *Profile of Man and Culture in Mexico.* University of Texas Press.

Rojas Avendane, Mario, 1973, "Los mercados de sirvientas en la region de los Tuxtlas, Ver." July 22, Mexico: Excelsior.

Setty, E.D. 2004, *Clinical Approach to Promotion of Entrepreneurship among Women,* New Delhi, Anmol.

Sudhir Kakar, "Aggression in Indian Society: An analysis of Folk Tales," *Indian Journal of Psychology,* 1974, (49), pp. 119-126.

Sumanlata, 2005, *Women and the Rule of Law,* Akansha, New Delhi.

Index